INFORMATION SECURITY AND CCP SCHEME

Edited by

Waqas Ahmed

TAP

Toronto Academic Press

Information Security and CCP Scheme

Waqas Ahmed

Toronto Academic Press
224 Shoreacres Road
Burlington, ON L7L 2H2
Canada
www.tap-books.com
Email: orders@arclereducation.com

ISBN: 978-1-77469-785-6

Toronto Academic Press publishes wide variety of books and eBooks. For more information about Toronto Academic Press and its products, visit our website at www.tap-books.com.

ABOUT THE EDITOR

Waqas Ahmed completed his Ph.D in Cyber security from East London University in 2022. He was awarded for academic excellence in his Master's degree. He qualified data scientist in January 2020. He has more than 5 years of teaching and research experience at different universities. Waqas Ahmed published 5 research papers, 3 conference papers, and 1 book chapter in well-established journals. He works in the area of computer networks, system security, and programming. He loves to read and share interesting aspects of computer science in books. In his free time, he loves to travel and explore and give talks on spirituality, ancient customs, and traditions.

Contents

4 Stakeholders in IT Project Management 139

5 Change Management in IT Project 159

6 Methods and Tools in IT Project Management 177

7 Challenges in IT Project Management 197

8 Prospects in IT Project Management 211

INDEX 227

List of Figures

List of Tables

List of Abbreviations

AIS	Accounting Information Systems
AC	Actual Cost
ARPA	Advanced Research Project Agency
COA	Chart of Accounts Structure
CIO	Chief Information Officer
COTS	Commercially Off-the-Shelf
CNSS	Committee on National Security Systems
CPI	Cost Performance Index
CV	Cost Variance
EV	Earned Value
EVM	Earned Value Management
EDI	Electronic Data Interchange
EI	Emotional Intelligence
EAI	Enterprise Application Integration
ERP	Enterprise Requirements Planning
GE	General Electric
GPS	Global Positioning System
IS	Information System
IT	Information Technology
IaaS	Infrastructure as a Service
JAD	Joint Application Development team

LAN	Local Area Network
MULTICS	Multiplexed Information and Computing Service
OS	Operating System
PV	Planned Value
PaaS	Processing Platform as a Service
RP	Rate of Performance
RAM	Responsibilities Assignment Matrix
SPI	Schedule Performance Index
SV	Schedule Variance
SecSDLC	Security Framework Life Cycle for Development
SLA	Service Level Agreement
SaaS	Software as a Service
UDP	User Information Protocol
WBS	Work Breakdown Structure

PREFACE

Information security is a critical aspect of modern society, where information is an asset that must be protected. The rapid growth of technology and the internet has created new opportunities for information sharing, but it has also led to increased risks of cyber threats and attacks. The importance of information security has been recognized globally, and many organizations have established various security frameworks and schemes to ensure the confidentiality, integrity, and availability of their information.

One of the most widely recognized information security schemes is the Common Criteria for Information Technology Security Evaluation (CC). The CC scheme is an international standard (ISO/IEC 15408) that provides a framework for evaluating the security of IT products and systems. The CC scheme has been adopted by governments, military organizations, and private companies worldwide to ensure that their IT products and systems meet stringent security requirements.

This book, "Information Security and CCP Scheme," aims to provide a comprehensive overview of the CC scheme and its application in information security. The book covers the basic concepts of information security, the CC scheme's history and development, the CC evaluation process, and the practical application of the CC scheme in different domains. The book also includes case studies and real-world examples to help readers understand the practical implications of the CC scheme.

This book is intended for students, researchers, and practitioners who want to understand the CC scheme and its application in information security. The book is also suitable for professionals who are involved in IT product development and security evaluation. We hope that this book will provide readers with valuable insights into the CC scheme and its role in ensuring the security of IT products and systems.

CHAPTER 1

INTRODUCTION TO INFORMATION SECURITY

UNIT INTRODUCTION

Cybersecurity, usually referred to as information security, is a major concern for people, companies, and governments all around the globe. Sensitive information systems, including networks, are safeguarded against unlawful access, disruption, usage, disclosure, alteration, and destruction. The environment of threat for information security has grown more complicated and sophisticated due to our growing reliance on technology as well as the internet. Cybercriminals and other hostile actors are continuously developing novel methods to exploit holes and access important data (Soomro et al., 2016).

A multi-layered strategy that incorporates technology and management, including physical controls, is necessary for the adequate security of information. Technical measures restrict unauthorized users' utilization of sensitive information by using tools including antivirus programs, antivirus software, systems for detecting and preventing intrusions, encryption, and access restrictions. Rules, processes, and instructions are examples of managerial controls that are used to ensure that staff members are aware of the value of information security and know how to apply best practices to safeguard important information. Physical security measures are safeguards against unwanted physical access to networks and devices, including access cards, locks, including biometric verification (Vroom & Von Solms, 2004). The internal threat, known as the danger, provided by workers or additional insiders that have lawful access to private data but abuse or leak it for personal benefit or other motives, is one of the major challenges regarding data security. Threats made by insiders can be deliberate or accidental, which can be brought on by several things such as avarice, vengeance, carelessness, or ignorance. Organizations should put in place the necessary safeguards, including checks on history, access limits, and monitoring, including training, to lessen the likelihood of insider threats (Von Solms, 1999).

Cybercrime, which is defined as illegal action carried out through the internet and other forms of digital technology, is a significant danger to data security. Cybercrime encompasses a variety of behaviors including hacking, ransomware, spyware, and identity theft, and even can have serious financial, a matter of reputation, and legal repercussions. Organizations must have robust safety protocols in place to prevent cybercrime, including encryption, secure passwords, and frequent security upgrades. They must also instruct their clients and employees about how to spot and avoid typical cyber threats (Tsohou et al., 2015).

Governments are very concerned about information security, especially regarding public defense and safety. Numerous prominent cyberattacks on important infrastructure and government institutions have occurred recently, underscoring the necessity of solid information security procedures to guard against these dangers. To ensure that their security measures and processes are compliant with democratic ideals and the rights of individuals, governments must find a balance between their desire for security for the need for transparency and responsibility (Siponen & Oinas, 2007).

Learning Objectives

At the end of this chapter, readers will be able to:

- Explain the interconnections between business processes and Accounting Information Systems (AIS).
- Classify various types of AIS.
- Describe client-server computing in the context of AIS.
- Describe cloud computing and its relevance to AIS.
- Analyze the different segments of the accounting software market.
- Analyze the various input methods used in business processes.
- Explain the process of accounting data processing in an AIS.
- Summarize the outputs generated from the AIS that are relevant to business processes.
- Discuss the importance of documenting processes and systems in an AIS.
- Evaluate ethical considerations in the design and use of AIS.

Key Terms

1. Accounting information system
2. Attribute
3. Bar code
4. Batch processing
5. Business process
6. Client-server computing
7. Cloud computing
8. Data flow diagram
9. Database as a Service (DaaS)
10. Document flowchart
11. Electronic Data Interchange (EDI)
12. Enterprise Application Integration (EAI)
13. Entity relationship diagram
14. General Journal
15. General ledger
16. Infrastructure as a Service (IaaS)
17. Legacy system
18. Online Processing Platform as a Service (PaaS)
19. Point of sale system
20. Process map
21. Real-time processing
22. Screen scraper
23. Service Level Agreement (SLA)
24. Software as a Service (SaaS)
25. Subsidiary ledger
26. System flowchart
27. Turnaround document

1.1. HISTORY OF INFORMATION SECURITY

Computer security is where the past security of information starts. The earliest mainframes, created to assist calculations in communicating code breaking (see Figure 1.1), was used during World War II, which led to the necessity for computer security—that is, the requirement to safeguard actual locations, software, and hardware against threats. The accuracy of the data stored on these mainframes was maintained by the implementation of many security layers. For instance, security guards used badges, keys in order, and face recognition to identify authorized persons while granting access to critical military facilities. Computer security measures gradually became increasingly intricate and technologically advanced as a result of the rising necessity to protect national security (Gritzalis et al., 2014).

Earlier versions of the German code machine Enigma were first broken by the Poles in the 1930s. The British and Americans managed to break later, more complex versions during World War II. The increasingly complex versions of the Enigma, especially the submarine or *Unterseeboot* version of the Enigma, caused considerable anguish to Allied forces before finally being cracked. The information gained from decrypted transmissions was used to anticipate the actions of German armed forces. "Some ask why, if we were reading the Enigma, we did not win the war earlier. One might ask, instead, when, if ever, we would have won the war if we hadn't read it."

Figure 1.1. Illustration of the enigma (Source: National Security Agency, Creative Commons License).

In the beginning, data protection was a basic procedure made up mostly of physical safety and uncomplicated document classification algorithms. Theft of physical devices, espionage of the systems' outputs, and sabotage constituted the main security risks. Early in the 1960s, while the system administrator had been working on a MOTD (message of the day) file and an additional administrator was altering the password file, a few of the earliest known security issues that didn't fit into these categories happened. Due to a software error, each output file contained a printout of the whole password file (Hong et al., 2006).

1.1.1. The 1960s

Numerous additional mainframes were put online throughout the Cold War to carry out increasingly complicated jobs. It became imperative to give these mainframes a less time-consuming method of communication than sending tapes with magnets between computer centers (Donohue, 2001). To assist the military's exchange of data, the Department of Defense's Advanced Research Project Agency (ARPA) started looking into the viability of a redundant, interconnected communications system. The project, which was first known as ARPANET, was created by Larry Roberts, widely regarded as the inventor of the Internet. The ARPANET was the forerunner of the Internet (a portion of the ARPANET Program Plan is shown in Figure 1.2) (van Biene, 2007).

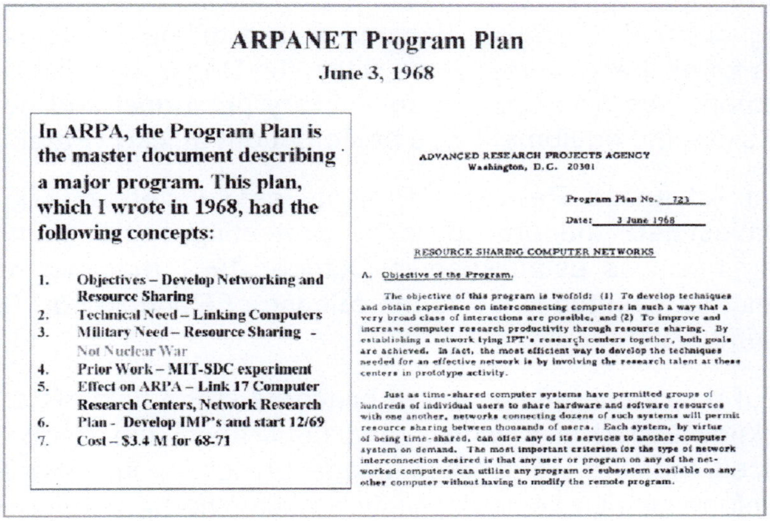

ARPANET Program Plan

June 3, 1968

In ARPA, the Program Plan is the master document describing a major program. This plan, which I wrote in 1968, had the following concepts:

1. Objectives – Develop Networking and Resource Sharing
2. Technical Need – Linking Computers
3. Military Need – Resource Sharing - Not Nuclear War
4. Prior Work – MIT-SDC experiment
5. Effect on ARPA – Link 17 Computer Research Centers, Network Research
6. Plan - Develop IMP's and start 12/69
7. Cost – $3.4 M for 68-71

ADVANCED RESEARCH PROJECTS AGENCY
Washington, D.C. 20301

Program Plan No. 723

Date: 3 June 1968

RESOURCE SHARING COMPUTER NETWORKS

A. Objective of the Program.

The objective of this program is twofold: (1) To develop techniques and obtain experience on interconnecting computers in such a way that a very broad class of interactions are possible, and (2) To improve and increase computer research productivity through resource sharing. By establishing a network tying IPT's research centers together, both goals are achieved. In fact, the most efficient way to develop the techniques needed for an effective network is by involving the research talent at these centers in prototype activity.

Just as time-shared computer systems have permitted groups of hundreds of individual users to share hardware and software resources with one another, networks connecting dozens of such systems will permit resource sharing between thousands of users. Each system, by virtue of being time-shared, can offer any of its services to another computer system on demand. The most important criterion for the type of network interconnection desired is that any user or program on any of the networked computers can utilize any program or subsystem available on any other computer without having to modify the remote program.

Figure 1.2. Development of the ARPANET Program Plan (Source: Dr. Lawrence Roberts, Creative Commons License).

1.1.2. The 1970s and 80s

The potential for abuse of ARPANET increased over the following ten years as it gained popularity and usage. Robert M. was born in December 1973. "Bob" Metcalfe saw critical issues with ARPANET security and is credited with creating Ethernet, becoming one of the world's most well-liked networking technologies. The controls and measures at individual distant locations were insufficient to safeguard data from illegal remote users. Other issues included the weakness of password structures and forms, the lack of dial-up connections safety measures, and the absence of identification for users and permission to the system (Gibbs & Mei, 1970).

Cellphone booth walls prominently displayed contact information, making it simple for hackers to get to the ARPANET. Network security is often referred to as system insecurity due to the wide range and rate of privacy and security violations as well as the explosive growth in the number of hosts as well as users on ARPANET. Well-known research titled "Protection Analysis: Final Report" was released in 1978. It concentrated on an ARPA initiative to identify the security of operating systems' weaknesses. See Table 1.1 for a chronology that covers this along with other important computer security research (Urban, 2011).

The Rand Report R-609, a single report funded by the Department of Defense that sought to outline the many controls and processes required for the safety of a multilayer computer system, catalyzed the shift towards security which went beyond the physical safety of sites. The document, which was kept under wraps for over 10 years, is today recognized as the one that launched the field of computer security research (Blau & Goodstein, 2010). During the summer and spring of 1967, scientists became aware of the safety—or lack thereof—of systems for exchanging resources within the Department of Defense. Security at the moment was a top priority for military personnel and defense-related businesses since the equipment was being bought quickly (Patel, 2000).

The Agency for Advanced Research Projects established a task group in June 1967 to investigate the procedure for protecting secret information systems. This task force was established in October 1967 that met often to develop suggestions that eventually led to the release of Rand Report R-609's conclusions (Marklund, 2015).

The relevance of policy and management concerns in the field of computer safety was first acknowledged in a widely read publication, the Rand Report R-609. It was noticed that the widespread usage of networking elements in military systems of information presented security concerns that were unavoidable given the standard procedures then in place to keep these systems safe. This chapter marked a turning point in the history of computer security, as the field's focus considerably widened to cover not just the protection of physical infrastructure but also the following (Easter, 2021):

- Locking up the data
- Limiting illegal, sporadic access to such data
- Including employees at various organizational levels in data security-related issues (Eriksson & Giacomello, 2006).

1.1.2.1. Multics

Multiplexed Information and Computing Service (MULTICS) was the focal point of a lot of the initial studies on the security of computers. MULTICS is notable because it was the initial operating system to include security in its fundamental operations, even though it is now out of date. Midway through the 1960s, a group led by General Electric (GE), Bell Laboratories, with the Massachusetts Institute of Technology (MIT) created a mainframe, or time-sharing operating system (OS) (Corbató & Vyssotsky, 1965).

A fresh operating system named UNIX was developed in the middle of 1969, shortly when the MULTICS project was reorganized by Dennis Ritchie, Ken Thompson, Rudd Canaday, with Doug McIlro. The UNIX technology did not use several levels of safety or passwords, but the MULTICS system did. Textual processing, which was its main purpose, didn't need as much protection as its predecessor's system did. In reality, the password function, the most basic security feature, was not included in UNIX until the beginning of the 1970s (Karger & Schell, 2002).

The microprocessor gave rise to the personal computer as well as a new era of technology in the latter part of the 1970s. The PC took the place of a data center as the mainstay of contemporary computing. The decentralization of information processing systems throughout the 1980s gave the development of networking, or the linking of mainframe and individual computers, which allowed the whole computing industry to make the most of all of its capabilities (Neumann, 1978).

1.1.3. The 1990s

Computer networks proliferated during the end of the 20th century and with them the requirement to link them together. The World Wide Web, the first worldwide collection of networks, was created as a result. In the 1990s, internet access became accessible to members of the public after previously only being used by the government, academic institutions, and devoted businesspeople. Almost any computer that could connect to a phone line or an Internet-connected local area network (LAN) now has access to the Internet. Following the Internet's commercialization, the technology spread quickly, touching practically every country on the planet and having a wide range of applications (Lopez, 1985).

The worldwide web has expanded from being a means for exchanging defense-related information to connecting millions of systems. Since there were no formal requirements for the connectivity of systems at that moment, these links first relied on de facto norms (Autor & Duggan, 2006). Although some level of security was added as a result of these antecedent technologies being extensively used and becoming industry standards, such de facto standards offered little to guarantee the security of data. However, security wasn't given much attention throughout the initial Internet rollout. In reality, this initial lack of protection is the cause of many of the issues that affect e-mail around the Internet today (Kvist, 2003). At that point, mailing server authentication, as well as email encryption, did not appear essential because everyone on the Internet was a (supposedly reliable) computer scientist. Earlier computing methods depended on the protection that was incorporated into the actual data center environment where the machines were located. The capacity to physically safeguard a computer connected to the internet was lost when networking became the predominant computing method, therefore the information stored there was increasingly vulnerable to security risks (Murai, 2004).

1.1.4. 2000 to Present

Millions of unprotected computer networks are now constantly in contact with one another thanks to the Internet. presently, the security of the data held on each computer depends on the protection of each additional machine to which it is linked. In the past few years, there has been an increase in recognition of the requirement for security-related improvement and the significance of information safety to the defense of the nation. Governments as well as companies are now more conscious than ever before of the need to protect the computerized infrastructure that controls utilities and other key services from cyberattacks. Additionally, there is rising worry over nation-states participating in data warfare and the risk that if left undefended, commercial as well as private information systems might suffer fatalities (Diekman & Eagly, 2000).

1.2. WHAT IS SECURITY?

Security is typically defined as "the characteristic or condition that makes one secure—to being without danger." In simple terms, the goal is to defend yourself against enemies—from those that would hurt you, either purposefully or accidentally. For instance, national defense is a multilayered structure that safeguards a state's sovereignty as well as its properties, assets, and citizens. A complex system is necessary to ensure that an organization has the right degree of security (Ullman, 1983).

The following many levels of protection should be in place at a successful business to safeguard its operations:

- Physical protection, preventing illegal access to and exploitation of physical resources
- Personnel security safeguards the person as well as a group of people with the authorization to access the company and its activities.
- Operational security is the safeguarding of the specifics of an action or set of actions.
- Protection of communication medium, technology, as well as material through the security of communications

- To safeguard networking elements, links, and contents, implement security measures for networks (Cable, 1995).
- The safety of data is the safeguarding of data assets' accessibility, privacy, and integrity throughout the process of creation, storage, and transfer. It is accomplished through putting legislation, knowledge, instruction, and awareness to use, together with technology (Baldwin, 1997).

Information security, according to the Committee on National Security Systems (CNSS), is the safeguarding of data and all of its essential components, such as the technology and software used to utilize, store, and transfer it. Data security encompasses the broad categories of safety for information management, computers and data protection, and security of networks, as shown in Figure 1.3. The C.I.A. triangle, a concept created by the computing security sector, served as the foundation for the CNSS framework for information security (Bueger, 2015). Since the advent of the mainframe, the C.I.A. triangle has served as the official industry norm for computer security. It is predicated on the three qualities of information—confidentiality, integrity, and availability—that provide value to enterprises. Although the protection of these three aspects of information is still crucial today, the C.I.A. triangular model no longer fully accounts for the environment's continual change. Information security risks now include a wide range of incidents, such as theft, unintentional or unauthorized alteration, accidental or purposeful harm, destruction, and additional misuse from both human as well as nonhuman threats (Zedner, 2003).

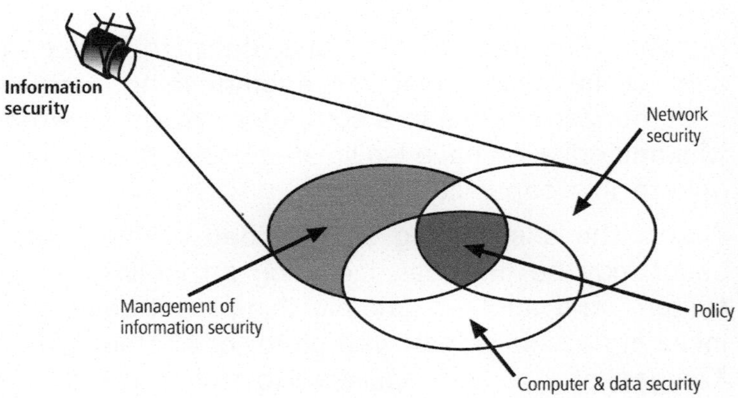

Figure 1.3. Components of Information Security (Source: Technology/Cengage Learning, Creative Commons License).

The creation of a stronger framework that takes into account the intricacies of the contemporary information security ecosystem has been spurred by this novel setting of numerous continuously shifting threats. A list of crucial aspects of information is included in the enlarged model; they are discussed in more detail in the coming section. Due to the volume of material, it depends on, this chapter uses C.I.A. triangle nomenclature (Pfleeger & Cunningham, 2010).

1.3. KEY INFORMATION SECURITY CONCEPTS

Many words and ideas that are fundamental for any discussion of the security of information are used in this book. A number of these concepts are shown in Figure 1.4, but all of them are explained in more detail in later chapters (Siponen & Oinas, 2007).

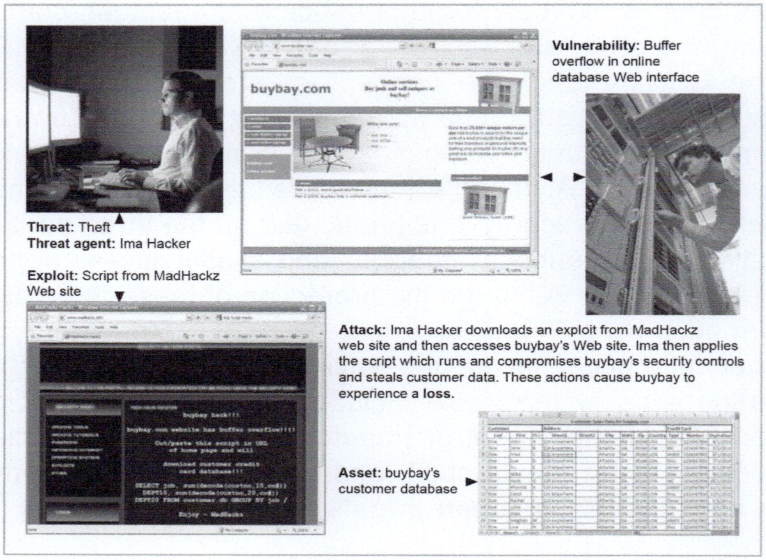

Figure 1.4. Information Security Terms (Source: Technology/Cengage Learning, Creative Commons License).

- Access: The capacity of one thing to utilize, control, alter, or have an impact on another thing. Hackers have unauthorized access to a computer system, whereas those with authorization have legitimate access. Access restrictions govern this capability.
- Asset: The asset being safeguarded by the company. An asset may be physical, including an individual, computer system, and another tangible thing, or it could be logical, including an individual, web page, or another type of data. The goal of security initiatives is to protect assets, especially information assets, which is the main objective of these efforts (Van Niekerk et al., 2010).
- Attack: A deliberate or accidental act that endangers data as well as the systems which sustain it by causing harm or in some other way interfering with it. Attacks may be

either indirect or direct, aggressive, or passive, and purposeful or accidental. Passive aggression occurs when someone casually reads sensitive material that wasn't intended for them. A deliberate attack occurs when a hacker tries to get access to a system of information. An inadvertent attack occurs when lightning strikes sets a structure on fire. A hacker utilizing a personal computer to access a system is known as a direct assault. A hacker compromising one system and then employing it to attack another system, for instance, as a component of a botnet (slang meaning robot network), is known as an indirect assault. These hacked machines can function independently or beneath the attacker's direct supervision to harm systems, steal data from users, or launch distributed denial-of-service assaults while running the attacker's choice of malicious software. The danger itself is the source of direct assaults. Indirect assaults come from an asset or system that has been hacked and is malfunctioning or acting in the direction of danger (Cavalli et al., 2004).

- Control, protect, or preventative measure: precautions, policies, or practices that effectively thwart attacks, lower risks, address vulnerabilities, and generally enhance security inside an organization. In the parts of the book that follow, the different levels and kinds of controls are covered in more detail (Hassanzadeh et al., 2014).
- Exploit: A method for compromising a system. This phrase may be used as a noun or a verb. Threat actors may try to use a network or another data asset unlawfully for their advantage to exploit it. A documented method for taking advantage of a flaw or exposure, typically in programs, which is either built into the program itself or was deliberately produced by the attacker is known as an "exploit." Exploits make advantage of already-built software tools or specially-created software parts (Zheng et al., 2021).
- Exposure: A situation or a state of exposure. Exposure to information security occurs when a flaw that an attacker is aware of is present.
- Loss: A single occurrence in which the data asset is harmed, altered without authorization, or disclosed. An organization experiences a loss when its data is taken (Singh & Karaulia, 2011).
- Protection profile or security posture: The whole system of protections and controls which the business employs (or fails to employ) to safeguard its assets, involving technology, knowledge, instruction, and knowledge. Although the phrase security program frequently includes administrative components of security, such as planning, people, and subsidiary programs, both phrases are occasionally used interchangeably (Vorobiev & Bekmamedova, 2010).
- Risk: The likelihood that something undesirable may occur. To meet

their risk appetite—the amount and kind of risk the company is ready to accept—organizations must reduce risk.

- Subjects and objects: According to Figure 1.5, a computer may be the intended target of an attack (the agent entity employed to carry out the assault) or the subject of such attack (the agent entity being attacked). If a computer, for instance, is attacked (the object), hacked, and then utilized for attacking additional systems (the subject), it might be both the target and the object of an assault.
- Threat: A group of things, people, or other things that endanger an asset. Threats are constantly there and might be intentional or random. Hackers, for instance, purposely put unsecured information systems in danger, whilst extreme weather also puts structures and their data in danger.
- Threat agent: The occurrence or a part of a threat. For instance, while all hackers offer a global threat, Kevin Mitnick, who was found guilty of breaking into telecommunication systems, is a particular threat agent. The hazard posed by severe storms also includes agents such as lightning, hail, and tornadoes (Eloff & von Solms, 2000).
- Vulnerability: A weakness or defect in a system or defense mechanism which makes it vulnerable to assault or harm. Vulnerabilities include things like holes in software packages, exposed system ports, and open doors. Others are still latent (or unknown), despite certain popular vulnerabilities having been researched, recorded, and published (Tarafdar & Zhang, 2005).

1.4. CRITICAL CHARACTERISTICS OF INFORMATION

Information's worth derives from the qualities it contains. Information's value usually grows or, more frequently, falls when a feature is altered. Information's value to consumers is influenced by a variety of factors, some more so than others. It depends on the situation since the information that is supplied too late loses a great deal of its value. As an example, the timing of information might be crucial (Hamel et al., 2000). The qualities of information are understood by both information security experts and end users, yet conflicts can still occur when the requirement to protect the data from threats competes with the final users' desire for unrestricted access to that information. For example, a tenth-of-a-second delay during the calculation of data may be seen by consumers as an unnecessary irritation. However, information security experts can view which tenth of a second is simply a small delay that permits a crucial activity, such as data encryption. Within the sections below, we define every C.I.A. triangle's important element of data (Raymon et al., 2013).

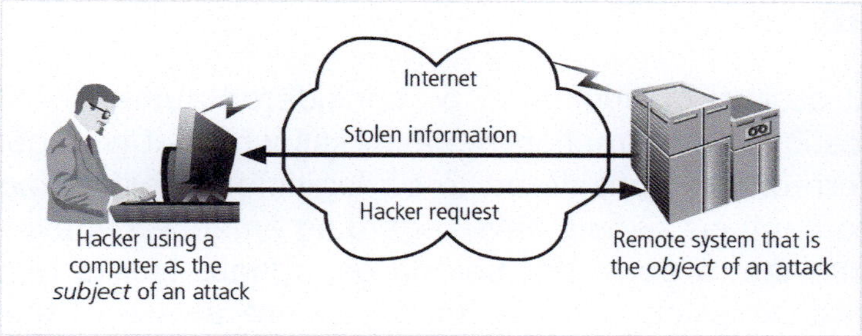

Figure 1.5. Computer as the Subject and Object of an Attack (Source: Technology/ Cengage Learning, Creative Commons License).

1.4.1. Availability

The information must be available for authorized users—whether people or computer technologies—to access it freely and get it in the proper format. Think of research libraries in general, for instance, where entry requires identification (Bhagwan et al., 2003).

The library's materials are safeguarded by librarians to ensure that only authorized users may access them (Andrefsky, 1994). Before being granted free use of the book stacks of data, a customer must have their identity accepted by the librarian. Registered users expect the data they require to be available in a usable format as well as in a language they are acquainted with once they gain access to the data of the stacks, and that in this context usually means that it is bound into a book and composed in English (Tversky & Kahneman, 1973).

1.4.2. Accuracy

When data is error-free and meets the end user's expectations, it is said to be accurate. Information that has been altered, whether consciously or unconsciously, no longer remains accurate. Think of a bank account, for instance. You depend on the data in your bank account to be a true reflection of your financial situation (Swets, 1988). Your checking account may include inaccurate information as a consequence of either external or internal faults. The knowledge's value is altered, for example, if a bank teller accidentally adds or subtracts excessively from your account. Alternatively, you can unintentionally put the wrong amount in the account for your registration. In any case, having an incorrect bank balance might lead to blunders like bouncing checks (Diebold & Mariano, 2002).

1.4.3. Authenticity

The information must be real or original to be considered authentic—it cannot be a copy or a fabrication. If information remains still where it was generated, put, saved, or transferred, it is considered to be legitimate. Take a moment to think about some presumptions people have regarding email. Whenever you get an email, you presume that a particular person or organization is responsible for its creation and transmission—you assume you are aware of the email's source. The opposite is not always true. Since the changed field frequently contains the sender's address, email spoofing—the act of delivering an email message using a modified field—is a concern for many individuals today. Email recipients can be tricked into believing that messages are genuine traffic by forging the sender's address, which encourages them to open emails that they normally might not have received. User information protocol (UDP) packet spoofing is one example of how spoofing may change data being transported over a network and provide an attacker access to information stored on computer systems (Lehman et al., 2019).

Phishing is a version of spoofing in which an attacker uses deceptive tactics to try and get financial or personal data, frequently by pretending to be someone else or a legitimate company. When done by law enforcement officers or private investigators, professing to be somebody you are not is referred to as pretexting. E-mail spoofing sends victims to a Web site that is not affiliated with the company it pretends to be in a phishing attack to acquire their personal information, including account numbers as well as passwords (Van Leeuwen, 2001). The most typical variations involve pretending to be an online retailer, bank or brokerage, or Internet service provider. Pretexting may not always result in a satisfying result, even when it is permitted. Patricia Dunn, the CEO of Hewlett-Packard Corporation, permitted contract investigators to "smoke out" a corporate director who was allegedly leaking sensitive information in 2006. Ms. Dunn eventually left the firm as a result of the ensuing negative media storm (Erickson, 1995).

1.4.4. Confidentiality

Information is considered confidential whenever it is shielded from exposure and disclosure to unapproved people or systems. Only those having the proper authorization and credentials for obtaining data are permitted to do so thanks to confidentiality. Confidential is violated when unapproved people or systems have access to data. You can take a variety of steps to safeguard the confidentiality of data, such as the ones listed below (Siegler, 1982):

- Information classification
- Secure document storage

- Application of general security policies
- Education of information custodians and end users

Like the majority of informational qualities, confidentiality depends on additional features and is closest to the privacy feature (Duncan et al., 2011).

When it comes to the private data of clients, patients, or clients' workers, confidentiality is extremely important. Whether an entity is a corporation or a federal agency like the Internal Revenue Service, people who trade with it anticipate that their data will be kept private. When businesses provide sensitive information, issues develop. Confidential information may be accidentally disclosed, such as when it is unintentionally emailed to a third party rather than an internal recipient. Occasionally this disclosure is purposeful, but it also occurs sometimes. Offline: Unintentional Disclosures describe several privacy violations.

Other instances of confidentiality breaches include when a worker disposes of a document that included sensitive information lacking shredding it or when a hacker successfully gains access to a company's internal database as well as steals client data like addresses, names, as well as debit or credit card numbers (Singer et al., 1995).

As a customer, you nearly always trade some of your data for convenience as well as value. You reveal a few of your expenditure patterns when you use a grocery shop "members only" card. You trade bits of your personal information for internet access while you respond to an online survey. The data that you divulge in small amounts is duplicated, sold, repeated, circulated, and finally combines to construct profiles and even whole dossiers about you as well as your life. Salami theft is a type of criminal activity that employs a similar method. Although deli employee is aware that they cannot steal a whole salami, they may steal a few pieces here and there and take them home secretly. Finally, the deli employee has taken one entire salami. Salami theft in the context of the security of information occurs when a worker steals bits and pieces of information while aware that stealing more might draw attention; ultimately, however, the employee obtains something comprehensive or useful (Fischel, 1998).

1.4.5. Integrity

Whenever information is full, complete, and unaltered, it has integrity. Whenever information is subjected to disruption, damage, destruction, or any other alteration of its true condition, its integrity is put in jeopardy. While knowledge is being sent or stored, corruption might happen. Most computer worms and viruses are created specifically to damage data. Because of this, one of the most important ways to identify a virus or worm is by checking for modifications to the integrity of the file as indicated by the file's size (Taylor & Gaita, 1981). Files hashing, which involves reading a file via a particular algorithm that utilizes the value of each of the bits within the file to get a single big number termed a hash value, is another important technique for guaranteeing data integrity. Every set of bits has a distinct hash value. The integrity of the data is destroyed whenever a computer system applies the same hashing technique to a file and receives a result that differs from the value of the hash which was stored for that file. Because information is useless if consumers cannot confirm its accuracy, data integrity is the foundation of all information systems (Clark & Fujimoto, 1990).

File corruption may not always be a result of outside factors, like hackers. Data loss due to noise within the transmission medium, for example, is another possibility. Data can be altered and corrupted when it is transmitted through a circuit with low voltage. Threats regarding the integrity of the data can come from both within and outside, however redundant bits with check bits can counteract this. The integrity that the data is guaranteed throughout each transmission using algorithms, and hashing values, including error-correcting coding. Retransmission of data whose integrity was seriously damaged (Stewart & Feder, 1987).

1.4.6. Utility

Information is useful when it serves some goal or is useful in some way. When knowledge serves a purpose, it is valuable. Information that is accessible but not presented in a way that the end user can understand is useless (Samuelson, 1937). For instance, to a private individual, While Census information from the United States can quickly grow overwhelming and challenging to analyze, for a politician, it provides details on the district's people, like their age, gender, and race. The next campaign plan for a politician may be influenced by this knowledge (Farquhar, 1984).

1.4.7. Possession

Information management refers to ownership or control of a subject. Independent of its format and other features, information is considered to be within one's possession once it is obtained. A breach of control may not necessarily lead to a violation of confidentiality, but a breach of confidence always leads to a breach of possession. For illustration, let's say a business uses a file encryption system to keep its important client data (Boddy, 1994). An ex-employee decides to grab a copy from the backup tapes to sell the client's information to the rival company. Removing the cassettes from their safe location is a violation of possession. However, due to the encryption of the information, neither the staff member nor another person can decode it; as a result, there has been no confidentiality violation. People who are found selling trade secrets now risk jail time and increasingly harsh fines. Additionally, businesses are becoming less and less willing to recruit people who have a history of dishonesty (Baldi & Nuti, 2010).

1.5. CNSS SECURITY MODEL

The National Training Standard for Information Systems Security Professionals NSTISSI No. 4011 from the CNSS served as a foundation for some of the terms of information safety in this work. The NSTISSC was renamed the Committee on National Security Systems (CNSS) after this document was published; the library of papers is being renamed as the texts are being revised.) Commonly used assessment standards for assessing the safety of information systems, this paper gives a complete information security paradigm (Cherdantseva & Hilton, 2013). The model, commonly referred to as the McCumber Cube, was developed by John McCumber in 1991 and offers a graphical depiction of the architectural strategy frequently employed in computers and data security. In Figure 1.6, the McCumber Cube displays three dimensions.

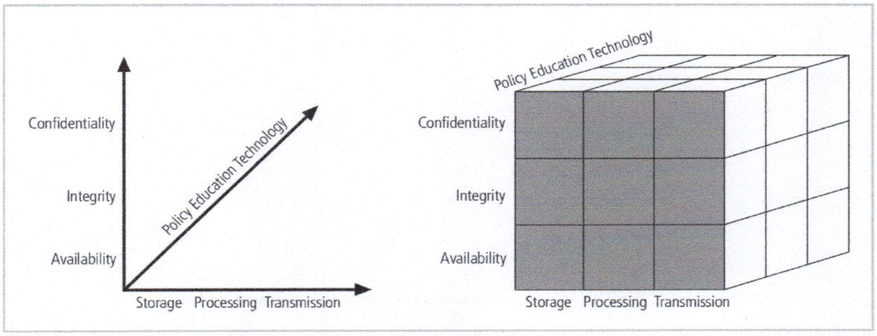

Figure 1.6. The McCumber Cube (Source: National Security Agency, Creative Commons License).

A system to identify host intrusion which safeguards information integrity by warning managers of security of anticipated changes to a crucial file is one example of this type of control. The requirement for rules and regulations that give guidance for the usage and application of technology is frequently overlooked in such models.

The 27 cells that make up the 3 ×3 ×3 cube that results from extrapolating the three degrees of every axis symbolize the many issues that should be resolved to safeguard today's information networks (Iskhakov et al., 2017). Every one of the 27 categories has to be adequately addressed throughout the safety procedure to guarantee system security. For instance, control and safeguarding which satisfies the requirement to employ technology to maintain the integrity of data during storage are needed at the point of intersection of technological devices, integrity, with storage.

1.6. COMPONENTS OF AN INFORMATION SYSTEM

An information system (IS), as seen in Figure 1.7, consists of the full combination of hardware, software, staff, processes, and networks that enable the company to exploit its information capabilities. These six essential elements make it possible to enter, process, output, and store data. Every of these IS elements has distinct qualities and applications, as well as distinct strengths and limitations. Additionally, every information system element has unique security needs (Clayton et al., 2003).

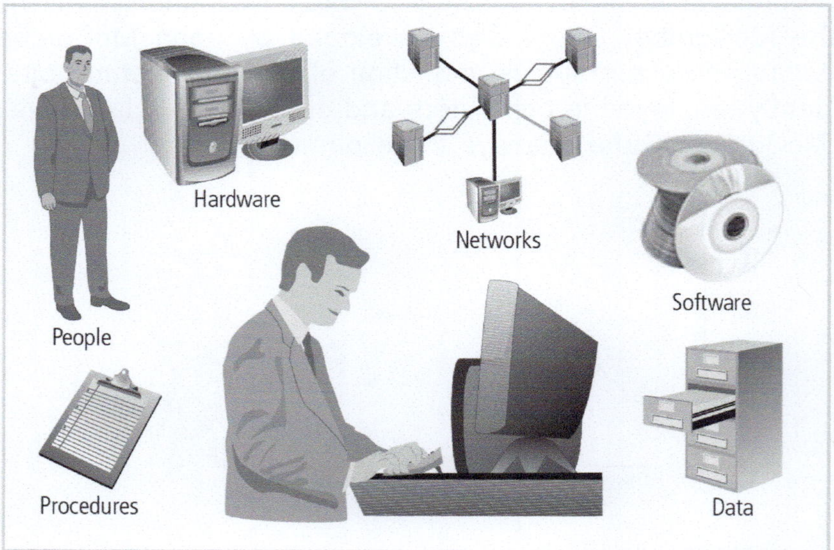

Figure 1.7. Components of an Information System (Source: Technology/ Cengage Learning, Creative Commons License).

1.6.1. Software

The IS's software consists of many command tools, and systems of operation, including applications. The hardest IS element to secure is probably the software. A large fraction of assaults on information is the result of the exploitation of coding faults in software (Gonze, 2005). There are numerous reports of software flaws, bugs, vulnerabilities, and other basic issues in the digital technology sector. In truth, faulty software has an impact on many aspects of everyday life, including crashes to defective vehicle control systems that cause recalls (Hindle et al., 2016).

The data that is the lifeblood that flows through a company is technology. Unfortunately, management of project restrictions that place limits on time, money, and labor are frequently used to construct software applications. All too frequently, information security is introduced as an afterthought instead of as an inherent part from the start. Software programs can constitute a convenient target for unintentional or deliberate assaults (Osterweil, 2011).

1.6.2. Hardware

The actual technology known as hardware is what contains and runs the software, saves and transfers data, and has interfaces for adding and removing information within the system's memory. Hardware is a physical asset, as well as physical assets need to be protected from damage and theft according to physical security rules. The use of locks and keys, as well as other conventional physical security measures, limits access as well as communication with a data system's hardware elements. Because a compromise in physical security may result in the loss of data, it is crucial to secure both the actual positioning of computing devices and the computers themselves. Unfortunately, the majority of information systems are constructed on hardware systems which, if unfettered access to such hardware is allowed, cannot provide any type of security for information (Zhang et al., 2004).

Before September 11, 2001, airport laptop thefts were rather prevalent. As the holder of the computer moved it across the conveyor scanners, two individuals attempted to take it. The initial offender swiftly passed past the protective area before the unwitting target. When the victim put the computer they were using through the baggage scanning device, the second offender waited behind them. The second police officer fell behind the victim as well as walked into a metal detector using a sizable collection of keys, money, as well as similar items, decreasing the process of detection and permitting the first offender to grab the device and flee in a crowded path as the computer systems were being sped through (Zhang et al., 2013).

Hardware may continue to be stolen inside airports as well as other public areas, even though the security reaction to September 11, 2001, did strengthen the security procedure at airports. Even while laptop business notebook computers cost a few thousand dollars or more, the data that they hold may be far more valuable to businesses and people (Gupta & De Micheli, 1993).

1.6.3. Data

A computer system's ability to save, analyze, and transfer data needs to be secure. Data is sometimes the most important asset that a company possesses, and it also is the major target of malicious assaults. Management database solutions are probably used by systems created recently. When done correctly, this ought to increase the safety of the program including the data (Witten et al., 2005). Unfortunately, the security features of database management platforms are not always fully utilized in system design projects, as well as in some circumstances, databases are designed using techniques that render them less secure than conventional file systems (Shorten & Khoshgoftaar, 2019).

1.6.4. People

People have long posed a hazard to information protection while being frequently disregarded in computer safety concerns. According to legend, a large army endangered the stability and quiet of the Chinese dynasty circa 200 B.C. The Hun invasions were so fierce that the Chinese emperor ordered the building of a massive wall to protect against them (Schneider, 1987). Kublai Khan eventually succeeded in achieving what the Huns had been attempting for countless years around the year 1275 A.D. The Khan's troops initially made an effort to scale, tunnel under, and breach the wall. The Khan just bought off the official in the end, and the remainder is history. Regardless of whether this incident truly happened, the lesson here is that humans may be a company's weakest link when it comes to data security (Diener & Diener, 1996). They will continue to be the weakest link until appropriate use is made of policy, training and education, knowledge, and technology to stop individuals from inadvertently or purposefully harming or destroying information. Human mistake is commonplace, and social engineering may take advantage of these factors. It may be employed to influence people's behavior to get access to computerized information (Unger, 1979).

1.6.5. Procedures

Procedures are an additional aspect of an IS that is usually disregarded. Procedures are detailed instructions for carrying out a certain activity. An organization's methods are at risk of being obtained by an outsider, which jeopardizes the accuracy of the data. For instance, utilizing the easily accessible processes of the computer center, an advisor to a bank learned how to wire cash (Gebala & Eppinger, 1991). This bank advisor directed several million dollars to be automatically sent to his account by exploiting a security flaw (lack of verification). About ten million dollars were lost as a result of lax security measures before the problem was fixed. The majority of businesses send processes to their authorized staff members so they may access the data system, however, a lot of these businesses frequently neglect to adequately educate their workers on how to secure the processes. As crucial as physically protecting the information infrastructure is educating staff about safety protocols.

Following all, procedures themselves are information. As a result, individuals in the business should only share vital information with those who need to know about processes (Sugarbaker, 2003).

1.6.6. Networks

Networking is a key element of IS that contributed significantly to the demand for greater computer as well as data security. New security issues arise quickly when data systems are linked together to create local area networks (LANs), as well as when these LANs are linked to other networks, like the Internet. Each level of business can use the actual technology which renders network activities possible (Gulati et al., 2000). It's still vital to use keys and locks and other classic physical security measures to prevent access to and communication with a data system's hardware elements, but as systems for computing become more networked, these measures are insufficient. It is crucial to take action to ensure network security and to develop alarm and incursion systems to notify system administrators of continuing intrusions (Dorogovtsev & Mendes, 2002).

1.7. BALANCING INFORMATION SECURITY AND ACCESS

Information security cannot be achieved perfectly, even with the finest planning and execution. Remember James Anderson's opening comment in this chapter, which emphasized the need to strike a balance between security and access? Security of information is a method and not a finished product, hence it can't be considered absolute. anybody, anyplace, at any time, within any method, can have access to a system. That open access, though, puts the information's security in jeopardy. On the reverse side, no one would be able to access an entirely protected information system. For example, Microsoft had to take off all networking components and run the computer using just a console in a protected room to pass the challenge to obtain a TCSEC C-2 level security certification for their operating system, Windows (Lane & Schur, 2010).

The degree of safety should allow appropriate access while protecting against risks to achieve balance, which is to manage a system of data that pleases both the user as well as the security expert. While balancing the security of data and access, many conflicting voices have to be taken into account. This is illustrated in Figure 1.8 (Thiarai et al., 2019).

The information system and information-processing department might get overly enmeshed in the administration and safety of systems due to the safety issues and challenges of today. Whenever the end user's demands are compromised due to an excessive emphasis on managing and safeguarding the information systems, there might be an imbalance (Nosworthy, 2000). To guarantee that the data will be accessible while and as information is required, with the fewest possible delays or impediments, both information security specialists, as well as users, need to understand because both groups support the same organizational overall goals. In a perfect world, even when issues with damage, loss, intercepting, or destruction are all taken care of, this degree of availability can still be achieved (Baskerville et al., 2014).

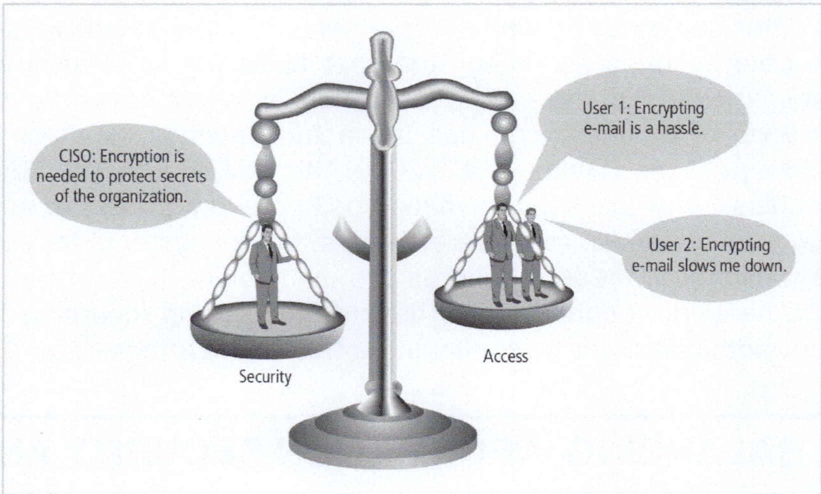

Figure 1.8. Balancing Information Security and Access (Source: Technology/Cengage Learning, Creative Commons License).

1.8. APPROACHES TO INFORMATION SECURITY IMPLEMENTATION

Security of information cannot be implemented quickly in an organization; it has to start sometime. In reality, protecting data assets is a gradual process that needs planning, patience, as well as time. Security of information can start as a grassroots initiative where administrators of systems work to make their systems' security better. This is frequently described as a bottom-up strategy. The technical proficiency of those who are managers is the top benefit of the bottom-up strategy. These administrators have in-depth expertise that may significantly improve the creation of a security system for information since they often work with computer systems. They are aware of the dangers posed by their networks and are aware of the defenses required to properly defend them. Unfortunately, this strategy seldom succeeds since it is lacking some essential components, namely participant engagement and organizational endurance (Al-Awadi & Renaud, 2007).

The top-down strategy, whereby the work is started by higher-level executives who establish rules, and regulations, then processes, mandate the objectives and projected outcomes, and set accountability for every necessary activity, has a greater success rate. This strategy can change corporate culture, strong riser-management support, a committed advocate, often dedicated financing, and a defined planning and execution procedure. The top-down methodology that is most effective also incorporates a formal development process known as a systems growth cycle.

Each organization-wide initiative must have the full backing of management to be successful. It is impossible to overestimate the part the champion performed in this endeavor. This champion usually takes the shape of a senior executive, including the Chief Information Officer (CIO) or Vice President of Information Technology (VP-IT), who drives the project ahead, makes sure it is handled effectively, and promotes acceptability throughout the company (Kadam, 2007). Most mid-level managers struggle to find the time to complete the project or consider it to be of poor priority lacking this high-level assistance. The support and involvement of the final users are also essential to ensuring the success of this kind of initiative. These people should be incorporated into the information security procedure because they will be most immediately impacted by the project's methodology and results. A joint application development team (JAD) should be given responsibility for key end users. The JAD needs to be resilient if it is to prosper (Ponka et al., 2020). It should be resilient to staff changes and shouldn't be subject to shifts in personnel within the team designing the data security system. This means that the corporate culture should be integrated and the procedures and processes should be documented. The upper levels of the organization should accept and promote them. Figure 1.9 depicts the organizational structure as well as bottom-up versus top-down strategies (Stambul et al., 2011).

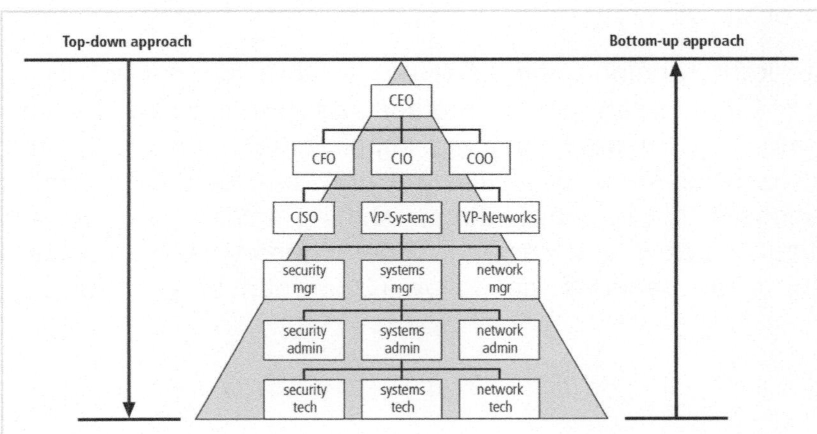

Figure 1.9. Approaches to Information Security Implementation (Source: Technology/ Cengage Learning, Creative Commons License).

1.9. THE SYSTEMS DEVELOPMENT LIFE CYCLE

Like each other big system set up by a business, data safety should be controlled. Implementing the Security Framework Life Cycle for Development (SecSDLC), a version of the Systems Development Life Cycle (SDLC), is one method for building a system to protect the information in a company with no or little official security in place. You have to first understand the fundamentals of the methodology it is founded on to grasp the safety system's development lifecycle (Sabale & Dani, 2012).

1.9.1. Methodology and Phases

An information system may be designed and implemented using an approach called the SDLC. A methodology is a systematic approach to problem-solving that uses an organized series of steps (Bauschke et al., 2003). Utilizing a methodology guarantees a disciplined procedure with a distinct objective and raises the likelihood of success. Once a technique has been chosen, the major checkpoints are determined, a team of people is chosen, and they are given responsibility for achieving the project objectives (Chen, 2008).

There are six standard phases in the conventional SDLC. You could have seen a model with a variable number of stages if you took a course in systems analysis and design. The three to twelve stages can be found in SDLC models, all of that has been translated into the six described below. Figure 1.10's waterfall diagram shows how each step starts with the findings and knowledge from the one before it (Sims & Heather, 2018).

An organized analysis or reality assessment is conducted after every phase, throughout which the entire group decides whether the project may be continued, abandoned, outsourced, delayed, or moved back to an initial phase based on whether it is progressing as anticipated and whether more expertise, knowledge of the organization, as well as additional assets, are required (Ellwood et al., 2012).

The system is kept running (and updated) for the balance of its period of operation when it has been put into place. As the process is repeated throughout time, any kind of data systems implementation could go through several iterations. Every system, particularly a program for data security, can live up to expectations within the continuously shifting environment upon which it is put via continual review and renewal. Every phase of the conventional SDLC is described in the sections that follow (Goodman et al., 1995).

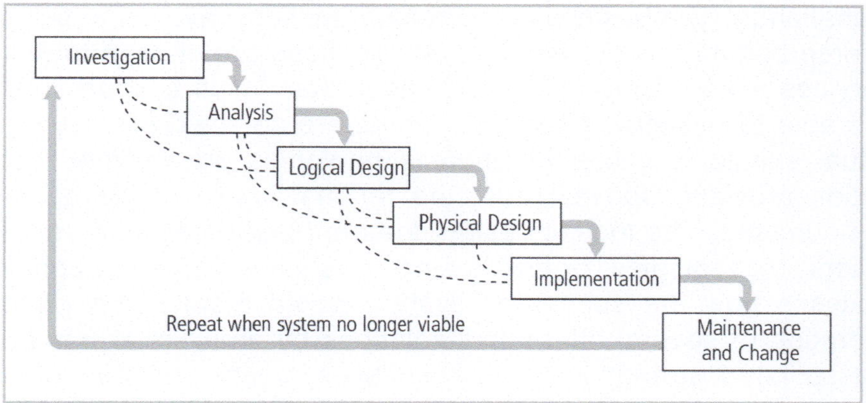

Figure 1.10. SDLC Waterfall Methodology (Source: Technology/Cengage Learning, Creative Commons License).

1.9.2. Investigation

The most crucial stage is the first one, research. What issue is the mechanism being created to address? Examining the action or plan that starts the process marks the beginning of the research phase. The goals, limitations, and project scope are laid out during the inquiry phase (Fullard & Reiling, 1976). The alleged advantages and the acceptable cost levels supporting those benefits are assessed in a preliminary cost-benefit analysis. A feasibility study determines the process's economic, scientific, and behavioral viability at the end of this phase along with each succeeding step to make sure its implementation is worthwhile for the business's time and energy (Shanahan et al., 1992).

1.9.3. Analysis

The information gathered during the research phase serves as the foundation for the analysis phase. Analyses of the business, its present systems, and its capacity to support the suggested systems make up the majority of this phase (Yong & Pearce, 2013). The first thing analysts must do is figure out what the fresh system is supposed to achieve and the way it will work with current systems. The documenting of the results and revisions to the feasibility assessment marks the conclusion of this stage (Jombart & Ahmed, 2011).

1.9.4. Logical Design

The data gathered from the data analysis process is utilized in the logical planning step to start developing the response of a system for a business challenge. The business requirement must always come first and be the driving force behind any IT solutions. Applications are chosen to deliver the required services according to business needs, after which support for data and frameworks able to deliver the required inputs are selected (Teorey et al., 1986). The actual solution's implementation technologies are outlined based on the information provided above. Thus, the rational layout is the blueprint for the intended outcome. The logical design does not make any references to particular suppliers, technologies, or goods since it is implementation agnostic. Instead, it discusses how the suggested system would resolve the issue at hand. The generation of several alternative solutions by analysts at this point, every having associated strengths and weaknesses, costs and advantages, enables a broad assessment of the possibilities available. Additional feasibility evaluation is conducted at this stage (Meng et al., 2019).

1.9.5. Physical Design

Particular technologies are chosen through the physical design stage to facilitate the alternatives found and assessed during the logical design. Following a make-or-buy choice (create the components internally or acquire them from an external vendor), the chosen components are assessed. Various elements and technology are integrated into finished designs. The full solution is given to the management team for approval following an additional feasibility investigation (Bruno & Chaudhuri, 2007).

1.9.6. Implementation

Any necessary software is developed during the setting up phase. Ordered, obtained, and checked materials are used (Love, 2004). Users are then taught, and accompanying documentation is produced. After each component has undergone separate testing, the entire system as a whole is installed as well as tested. Once more, an assessment of feasibility is created, and sponsors are subsequently shown the system for an evaluation of its usability and acceptability testing (Stonebraker et al., 1990).

1.9.7. Maintenance and Change

The method's biggest and most costly step is the routine care and modification phase. All duties required to maintain and improve the structure for the balance of the system's useful life cycle are included in this stage. The life cycle of a project continues even if official development could be finished at this point unless it is decided that the procedure should start over from the inquiry phase (Holiman & Schilit, 1991). The system is periodically checked for compliance, while the viability of continuation vs termination is assessed. Updates, fixes, and modifications are controlled. The systems which help the organization must evolve as the demands of the organization develop. The efficiency of the processes in connection with the outside world of the company must be constantly monitored by the people who administer and support systems. The project is canceled and a new one is started when an existing system could no longer fulfill the organization's developing mission (Loveland, 2003).

1.9.8. Securing the SDLC

The safekeeping of the network that is being constructed and the data it utilizes should be taken into account throughout each phase of the SDLC. The implementing company oversees making sure the system is utilized safely, regardless of whether it was created from scratch, bought and then modified, or was commercially off-the-shelf (COTS) (Sugiantoro et al., 2020). This indicates that every system deployment is safe and does not put the business's data assets' privacy, honesty, or accessibility in danger. A summary of the security issues for each stage of the SDLC is provided in the part that follows, which is an adaptation of NIST Special Publication 800–64, rev.1.

A minimal set of security actions is included in any of the sample SDLC phases [described previously] to successfully integrate security for a system throughout development (Karim et al., 2016).

A company will either employ the standard SDLC outlined [before] or will have created a customized SDLC to suit its unique requirements. In either event, NIST advises businesses to integrate these broad SDLC processes for IT security into their growth process (Kang & Kim, 2020).

1.9.8.1. Investigation/Analysis Phases

Any breach of security that results in an absence of privacy, reliability, or accessibility is classified as having a low, moderately difficult, or high potential effect on businesses or people. Guidelines for security classification help businesses choose the right security measures for their computer systems (Carrier & Spafford, 2006).

A preliminary assessment of risks yields a starting point for the system's fundamental security requirements. The danger environment in which the system will function should be defined by a preliminary risk analysis (Filardi, 2020).

1.9.8.2. Logical/Physical Design Phases

Risk analysis is an investigation that, through a rigorous assessment of risks method, pinpoints the system's protective needs. This study is going to be more thorough and focused than the first risk assessment carried out at the Starting phase (Bolchini et al., 2003).

Assessment of functional needs for security which may contain the following elements:

- Environment for system security (i.e., corporate security of information policy and corporate security architecture); and
- Functional needs for security (Scholtz et al., 2013).

Analysis regarding safety assurance needs, including efforts to develop and assuring evidence, is necessary to provide an acceptable level of trust that data security will function properly and efficiently. The assessment will be utilized as the foundation for deciding how much and which types of assurance are necessary, depending on legal as well as functioning security needs (Lockett & Lawson, 2020).

The amount of development cost that may be assigned to data safety throughout the system's lifetime is determined by cost considerations including assessment. Software, hardware, manpower, and training are all included in these expenses (Mejía et al., 2017).

Planning for security—ensures that all security measures, whether they are in existence or being considered, are thoroughly recorded. The security strategy also includes a comprehensive description or explanation of the data system and relates to important documents that provide backing for the organization's information safety program (such as the configuration management schedule, contingency plan, incident handling schedule, security education, and instruction plan, guidelines for conduct, risk analysis, protection test and evaluation outcomes, system connections contracts, security approvals/accreditations, etc.) and a list of all the information systems that are included.

Development of security controls: This process makes certain that the security measures outlined in the corresponding security plans are created, developed, and put into action. The security strategies for information systems that are presently in use may need the creation of new security measures to augment those which are already implemented or a change of a few measures that are thought to be insufficient.

A freshly implemented information system's security measures are tested and evaluated during the development process to make sure they are reliable and effective (Bushroe et al., 1997).

Certain security measures (mostly non-technical controls), which are often management as well as operational control measures, are unable to be tested and assessed until the data system is implemented. Other planning elements—ensures that when integrating security under the life cycle, all essential elements of the development procedure are considered. These elements include choosing the proper contract type, having the required organizational functional units participate, having the certification body and accreditor participate, and developing and implementing the required contracting strategies and processes (Nilsson et al., 1982).

1.9.8.3. Implementation Phase

- *Inspections and approval*—ensures that the company checks and confirms that the products delivered involve the features outlined in the requirement.

  Integrating the system with the operating site wherever the data is going to be put for use assures that the technology is functioning properly. According to vendor specifications and any security implementation guidelines available, safety control configurations and switching are turned on (Verweij, 2015).
- *Security certification*—gives organization executives confidence that the proper protections and countermeasures are in place to secure the information system of the business by ensuring that the controls are properly applied through specified verification methodologies and processes. Additionally, security certification identifies and characterizes the knowledge system's known weaknesses (Verweij & Gerrits, 2015).
- *Security accreditation*—gives a system of data the appropriate security permission for it to handle, save, or send information. This approval is given by a senior organizational official and is predicated on the recognized residual danger to agency resources or activities and the efficacy of security procedures having been confirmed to a certain level of certainty (Lee et al., 2015).

1.9.8.4. Maintenance and Change Phase

- *Configuration management and control*—guarantees that the possible security effects of modifications to a database or its surroundings are taken into proper consideration. Developing a starting foundation of software, and hardware, including firmware elements for the data system, and thereafter regulating and keeping a precise record of any modifications to the system depending on configuration management as well as control methods (Podlesnik et al., 2017).
- *Continuous monitoring*—conducting regular testing and evaluation, guarantees that controls remain efficient in use. A thorough information security program must include security control observing, which involves confirming the controls' ongoing efficacy throughout time, as well as reporting on the safety condition of the data system to all necessary agency personnel (Grivas et al., 2014).

- *Information preservation*—guarantees that data is kept on file as long as needed to comply with the law as it stands and to account for any future technological advancements that might make the retrieval technique outdated (Khoshgoftaar & Lanning, 1995).
- *Media sanitization*—guarantees that information is removed, wiped clean, and appropriately overwritten (Renner et al., 2012).
- *Hardware and software disposal*—makes certain that both software and hardware can be disposed of by the data system security officer's instructions (Gupta & Sharma, 2015).

Modified from Security Issues in the Life Cycle of Information Systems.

Security of information must be built into an organization from the beginning rather than incorporated afterward or while implementation. To reduce danger to the networks and details, systems of information that were created without security capabilities or with security features added as a final afterthought frequently need to be patched, updated, and maintained continuously. A popular proverb states that "an ounce of preventive is worth one pound of cure." Considering this, enterprises are shifting toward greater security-focused methods of development to enhance both the usability of their existing systems and customer confidence in their offerings (Fredendall et al., 1997). Beginning in 2002, Microsoft essentially stopped working on several of its products as it put its application managers, OS testers, and OS engineers through a rigorous training course on safe software development (Stubbs et al., 2011). To resolve serious security vulnerabilities, it also postponed the introduction of its flagship server Operating System (OS). Following Microsoft's recent example of integrating security into its development procedure, several other firms are doing the same (Hartmann & Robson, 1989).

1.10. THE SECURITY SYSTEMS DEVELOPMENT LIFE CYCLE

Security of information implementation for projects can be supported by adopting the identical stages used in the conventional SDLC. Although the two procedures' intentions and particular steps may be different, their general technique is the same (Kao et al., 2012). Managing information security is fundamentally about detecting certain dangers and developing measures to thwart those attacks. This process is unified by the SecSDLC, which transforms it from a collection of seemingly unrelated, random activities into a program that makes sense.

1.10.1. Investigation

Higher management issues a directive during the start of the investigation phase of the SecSDLC that specifies the project's methodology, results, and objectives along with its financial resources and other limitations. The execution of a security program inside the firm is outlined in a company information security policy (EISP), which frequently marks the beginning of this phase (tokawa et al., 2008). Challenges are examined, groups of responsible executives, staff members, and contractors are formed, and the task's scope, along with any extra restrictions not covered by the program's policy, is established. To assess if the company has the finances and dedication required to carry out an effective security study and design, an overall organizational viability analysis is conducted (Yanase et al., 1991).

1.10.2. Analysis

The findings from the inquiry phase's records are examined in the analysis stage. The team in charge of development does an initial study of the safety measures or programs which are currently in place, as well as the recorded current risks and related controls (Burland, 1999). A legal study of pertinent concerns that may have an impact on the design of the safety measure is also part of this step. Decisions about computer systems that control private data are increasingly influenced by privacy legislation. Several states have recently enacted laws making some computer-related activity unlawful. It is essential to comprehend these concerns in great depth (Sheeran et al., 2014).

1.10.3. Logical Design

Information security plans are developed during the logic-based planning process, which also studies and puts into practice important regulations that may affect decisions made later. The emergency response steps to be performed in the case of a minor or catastrophic loss are also planned at this point by the team. Planning provides solutions to the following queries (Yoeli & Rosenfeld, 1965):

- Continuity planning: How will operations carry on if there is a setback?
- Incident response: What actions are performed in the event of an attack?
- Disaster recovery: What steps must be taken right away following a terrible occurrence to restore information and crucial systems?

A feasibility study is the next step in deciding whether to move on with the project or outsource it (Wang et al., 1997).

1.10.4. Physical Design

The physical design step develops different options, examines the data security technologies required for supporting the blueprint specified in the conceptual design, and chooses the final design. Whenever the physical design is finished, the data in the security blueprint might be reviewed to maintain it in line with the modifications that are required. During this step, criteria for defining what constitutes effective solutions are additionally developed. The physical security features that will go along with the suggested technical solutions are currently included within the designs. The champions and supporters are then shown the design after a feasibility analysis establishes whether the organization is prepared to fund the proposed endeavor. When the project is put into action, all stakeholders have an opportunity to approve it at this point (Bruno & Chaudhuri, 2007).

1.10.5. Implementation

The SecSDLC's stage of implementation is comparable to the conventional SDLC. The safety measures are created (or purchased), tested, put into use, and then tested once again. The effectiveness of certain educational and training initiatives is assessed about personnel concerns. Finally, senior management is provided with the fully tested bundle for final clearance (Stonebraker et al., 1990).

1.10.6. Maintenance and Change

The final phase—maintenance and change—may be the most crucial due to the constantly shifting threat landscape today. The information safety mechanisms of today require continuous observation, testing, alterations, upgrading, and maintenance. Applications systems created using the conventional SDLC architecture are not intended to foresee a software assault that necessitates some level of application rebuilding (Holiman & Schilit, 1991). The fight for stable, dependable systems is a preventive one in terms of data safety. Restoring damage and recovering information frequently requires ongoing battles with an invisible foe. An organization's information security profiles must be updated when new threats appear and existing ones change to stop risks from accessing sensitive data. This continual watchfulness and security might be likened to the defense of a fortress, where dangers from both the outside and the inside have to be regularly watched and checked by ever-evolving, cutting-edge technologies (Kwasnicka et al., 2016).

1.11. SECURITY PROFESSIONALS AND THE ORGANIZATION

To support a diversified data safety program, a wide spectrum of experts is required. Security of information is best started from the top down, as was mentioned before in this chapter. The most important element and driving force behind the effective execution of a program to protect information is the upper management. However, administrative assistance is also necessary for creating and carrying out certain safety measures and processes, and technological know-how is required for carrying out the particulars of the data security plan. The usual security-related duties associated with different professional jobs within an organization are described in the sections that follow (Posey et al., 2014).

1.12. SENIOR MANAGEMENT

The Chief Information Officer (CIO) is normally the top technology executive, nevertheless, a vice president of data, VP of data technology, or vice president of networks may also be employed. The chief information officer's main duty is to counsel the chief executive officer, as president, or business owner on strategic choices that have an impact on the control of information inside the firm. The CIO converts the organization's overall objectives into informational strategic strategies for the company's information technology or data processor division. When this is done, CIOs collaborate with managers below them to create the division's tactical along with operational strategies as well as to make system management and planning possible (Seddon et al., 2002).

The Chief Information Security Officer (CISO) is in charge of overseeing the organization's data security strategy, administration, and evaluation. The person in charge of IT security, the safety manager, or any title like these can additionally be used to refer to the CISO. While in bigger businesses it is normal for several layers of administration to exist above the two, the CISO often reports immediately to the CIO. Yet, the CISO's suggestions to the CIO should be accorded equal, or even higher, priority compared to other ideas relating to information and technology. The location of the CISO and auxiliary security personnel in the organizational structures are now being debated throughout the sector (Albrecht & Travaglione, 2003).

1.13. INFORMATION SECURITY PROJECT TEAM

A variety of people with knowledge of one or more of the necessary technical as well as nontechnical domains should be included on the database security team for the project. Safety design requires numerous of the same abilities as managing and putting security into practice. The following duties are filled by team members on the safety project:

- *Champion:* A senior executive that supports the project and makes sure it has cooperation at the most senior levels of the business, both economically and technically.

- *Team leader:* A project director who is knowledgeable about the technological necessities for the security of data, and human management, including department management of lines.
- *Security policy developers:* People who are familiar with the corporate culture, current policies, and specifications for creating and putting into effect successful policies (Kotulic & Clark, 2004).
- *Risk assessment specialists:* Individuals who are knowledgeable about the techniques for assessing financial risk, the worth of organizational resources, and the appropriate security measures.
- *Security professionals:* Individuals who are committed, educated, and skilled in all facets of the security of data, including from a technical as well as a non-technical perspective.
- *Systems administrators:* Individuals who are in charge of running the systems that store the data employed by the company.
- *End users:* Those with disabilities will be most immediately impacted by the new system. Within an ideal scenario, the team is supported in concentrating on the development of realistic controls implemented in manners that do not interfere with the crucial business operations they wish to safeguard by selecting users from diverse departments, stages, and levels of professional competence (Scarfone et al., 2008).

1.14. DATA RESPONSIBILITIES

Below is a list of the three different forms of data ownership with their associated duties:

- *Data owners:* Those in charge of a certain collection of information's protection and utilization. They might be CIOs and are often in upper management. The degree of data categorization (described below) and any modifications to that classification necessitated by organizational shifts are typically decided by the information owners. To manage the daily handling of the data, information owners collaborate with lower-level managers (Corrall, 2012).
- *Data custodians:* Data custodians, who collaborate closely with those who own the data, are in charge of maintaining, protecting, and storing the data. This might be a separate role, like the CISO, or it could be an extra duty for a system administrator or other members of technology management, based on the size of the firm. A data custodian's responsibilities frequently involve monitoring data backup and storage, carrying out the precise processes and rules outlined in security guidelines and strategies, and providing information to the information owner (Tammaro et al., 2019).

- *Data users:* Users are those who utilize the data to carry out their given tasks and further the organization's goal. Users of data are referred to here as people having an information security responsibility since everybody in the company is accountable for the protection of data.

1.14.1. Communities of Interest

Every company establishes and upholds its own distinctive culture and principles. Several communities are relevant that grow and change within any corporate culture. According to this definition, a community that interests is a collection of people who work together in a business and who also have a shared interest in seeing the organization succeed. This book covers the three most prevalent communities of interest that hold positions and duties in the security of information, however, there may be numerous different groups of interest within an organization. Although in principle one position should support another, that's frequently not the situation in practice (Fischer, 2001).

1.14.2. Information Security Management and Professionals

The objectives and objectives of the data security communities of interest are connected with the responsibilities of those working in information security. The organization's computer networks, and stored data are protected against threats by these job duties and organizational responsibilities (Soomro et al., 2016).

ACTIVITY 1.1

How do you think technological advancements have affected the role of accounting information systems in today's business world?

1.14.3. Information Technology Management and Professionals

A lot of the goals of the data safety community are shared by a group of interest formed up of managers of IT and experts in computer design, computer programming, connections, and other relevant fields. However, the participants place more emphasis on transactional response time, convenience accessibility for users of the system, timeliness regarding system formation, and expenses associated with system construction and operation. According to the structure of the organization, there may be a conflict if the aims of the data security and IT communities may not always completely congruent (Joseph et al., 2007).

1.14.4. Organizational Management and Professionals

Other significant groups of interest include the organization's core management group as well as the remainder of its assets. To name a few, this wide category almost typically comprises subcategories of varied interests, including executive management, production management, employees, economics, and litigation. These demographics are commonly referred to as technical consumers in the information technologies industry, but safety consumers in the data protection industry. This community serves as a constant reminder that all IT systems and data security aims to assist the greater business society's goals. The best IT systems managed in the most secure manner possible are useless without their being beneficial to the firm as a whole (Hein & Riegel, 2012).

SUMMARY

This chapter provides a comprehensive overview of the fundamental concepts and principles in the field of information security. It begins by defining information security as the practice of protecting information and information systems from unauthorized access, use, disclosure, disruption, modification, or destruction. The chapter highlights the increasing importance of information security due to the widespread use of technology and the potential risks associated with cyber threats.

It explores the key goals of information security, which include ensuring the confidentiality, integrity, and availability of information. Confidentiality refers to protecting sensitive data from unauthorized disclosure, while integrity focuses on maintaining the accuracy and trustworthiness of the information. Availability ensures that authorized users have timely access to information and system resources.

Various threats and vulnerabilities to information security are discussed, ranging from malicious activities such as hacking, malware, and social engineering to non-malicious incidents like natural disasters and human errors. The chapter emphasizes the importance of risk management and the need to identify, assess, and mitigate risks by implementing security controls.

Additionally, the chapter introduces different types of attackers, including insiders, outsiders, advanced persistent threats, and their motivations and techniques. It also covers the concept of defense in depth, which involves employing multiple layers of security controls to protect information systems effectively.

REVIEW QUESTIONS

- What is the primary goal of information security and why is it important in today's digital age?
- Define the concept of a threat in the context of information security. Provide examples of different types of threats.
- What are the three fundamental principles of information security? Explain each principle and their significance.
- Describe the CIA triad and its role in ensuring information security. Provide examples of how each component can be compromised.
- What is the difference between vulnerability and risk in information security? How are they related?

MULTIPLE CHOICE QUESTIONS

1. **Which of the following is the correct definition of information security?**
   a. The protection of information from unauthorized access, use, disclosure, disruption, modification, or destruction
   b. The process of encrypting information for secure transmission
   c. The prevention of computer viruses and malware attacks
   d. The implementation of physical controls to protect information
2. **Which of the following is NOT a fundamental principle of information security?**
   a. Confidentiality
   b. Integrity
   c. Availability
   d. Efficiency
3. **Which of the following is an example of a physical control in information security?**
   a. Encryption
   b. Firewalls
   c. Biometric authentication
   d. Security cameras
4. **Which of the following is a common vulnerability in information security?**
   a. Weak passwords
   b. Regular software updates
   c. Intrusion detection systems
   d. Strong encryption algorithms
5. **What is the purpose of risk assessment in information security?**
   a. To eliminate all potential risks
   b. To identify and prioritize risks to information assets
   c. To ensure compliance with legal regulations
   d. To establish secure network connections

Answers to Multiple Choice Questions

1. (a) 2. (d) 3. (d) 4. (a) 5. (b)

REFERENCES

1. Al-Awadi, M., & Renaud, K. (2007, July). Success factors in information security implementation in organizations. In *IADIS International Conference e-Society* (pp. 169–176).
2. Albrecht, S., & Travaglione, A. (2003). Trust in public-sector senior management. *International Journal of Human Resource Management*, *14*(1), 76–92.
3. Andrefsky, W. (1994). Raw-material availability and the organization of technology. *American Antiquity*, *59*(1), 21–34.
4. Autor, D. H., & Duggan, M. G. (2006). The growth in the social security disability rolls: a fiscal crisis unfolding. *Journal of Economic Perspectives*, *20*(3), 71–96.
5. Baldi, P., & Nuti, A. (2010). Possession. In *Constituent Syntax: Quantification, Numerals, Possession, Anaphora* (Volume 3, pp. 239–388).
6. Baldwin, D. A. (1997). The concept of security. *Review of International Studies*, *23*(1), 5–26.
7. Baskerville, R., Spagnoletti, P., & Kim, J. (2014). Incident-centered information security: Managing a strategic balance between prevention and response. *Information & Management*, *51*(1), 138–151.
8. Bauschke, H. H., Combettes, P. L., & Luke, D. R. (2003). Hybrid projection–reflection method for phase retrieval. *JOSA A*, *20*(6), 1025–1034.
9. Bhagwan, R., Savage, S., & Voelker, G. M. (2003). Understanding availability. In *Peer-to-Peer Systems II: Second International Workshop, IPTPS 2003, Berkeley, CA, USA, February 21–22, 2003. Revised Papers 2* (pp. 256–267).
10. Bishop, M. (2003). What is computer security?. *IEEE Security & Privacy*, *1*(1), 67–69.
11. Blau, D. M., & Goodstein, R. M. (2010). Can social security explain trends in labor force participation of older men in the United States?. *Journal of Human Resources*, *45*(2), 328–363.
12. Boddy, J. (1994). Spirit possession revisited: Beyond instrumentality. *Annual Review of Anthropology*, *23*(1), 407–434.
13. Bolchini, C., Salice, F., Schreiber, F. A., & Tanca, L. (2003). Logical and physical design issues for smart card databases. *ACM Transactions on Information Systems (TOIS)*, *21*(3), 254–285.
14. Bruno, N., & Chaudhuri, S. (2007, April). An online approach to physical design tuning. In *2007 IEEE 23rd International Conference on Data Engineering* (pp. 826–835).
15. Bueger, C. (2015). What is maritime security?. *Marine Policy*, *53*, 159–164.
16. Burland, T. G. (1999). DNASTAR's Lasergene sequence analysis software. *Bioinformatics Methods and Protocols*, 71–91.
17. Bushroe, R. G., DasGupta, S., Dengi, A., Fisher, P., Grout, S., Ledenbach, G., ... & Steele, R. (1997, April). Chip hierarchical design system (CHDS) a foundation

for timing-driven physical design into the 21st century. In *Proceedings of the 1997 International Symposium on Physical Design* (pp. 212–217).

18. Cable, V. (1995). What is international economic security?. *International Affairs*, *71*(2), 305–324.
19. Carrier, B. D., & Spafford, E. H. (2006). Categories of digital investigation analysis techniques based on the computer history model. *Digital Investigation*, *3*, 121–130.
20. Cavalli, E., Mattasoglio, A., Pinciroli, F., & Spaggiari, P. (2004). Information security concepts and practices: the case of a provincial multi-specialty hospital. *International Journal of Medical Informatics*, *73*(3), 297–303.
21. Chen, L. Q. (2008). Phase-field method of phase transitions/domain structures in ferroelectric thin films: a review. *Journal of the American Ceramic Society*, *91*(6), 1835–1844.
22. Cherdantseva, Y., & Hilton, J. (2013, September). A reference model of information assurance & security. In *2013 International Conference on Availability, Reliability and Security* (pp. 546–555).
23. Clark, K. B., & Fujimoto, T. (1990). The power of product integrity. *Harvard Business Review*, *68*(6), 107–118.
24. Clayton, P. D., Narus, S. P., Huff, S. M., Pryor, T. A., Haug, P. J., Larkin, T., ... & Gundersen, M. L. (2003). Building a comprehensive clinical information system from components. *Methods of information in medicine*, *42*(01), 1–7.
25. Corbató, F. J., & Vyssotsky, V. A. (1965, November). Introduction and overview of the Multics system. In *Proceedings of the November 30--December 1, 1965, Fall Joint Computer Conference, Part I* (pp. 185–196).
26. Corrall, S. (2012). Roles and responsibilities: Libraries, librarians and data. *Managing Research Data*, 105–133.
27. Diebold, F. X., & Mariano, R. S. (2002). Comparing predictive accuracy. *Journal of Business & Economic Statistics*, *20*(1), 134–144.
28. Diekman, A. B., & Eagly, A. H. (2000). Stereotypes as dynamic constructs: Women and men of the past, present, and future. *Personality and Social Psychology Bulletin*, *26*(10), 1171–1188.
29. Diener, E., & Diener, C. (1996). Most people are happy. *Psychological science*, *7*(3), 181–185.
30. Donohue, L. (2001). In the name of national security: US Counterterrorist Measures, 1960–2000. *Terrorism and Political Violence*, *13*(3), 15–60.
31. Dorogovtsev, S. N., & Mendes, J. F. (2002). Evolution of networks. *Advances in Physics*, *51*(4), 1079–1187.
32. Duncan, G. T., Elliot, M., Salazar-González, J. J., Duncan, G. T., Elliot, M., & Salazar-González, J. J. (2011). *Why Statistical Confidentiality?* (pp. 1–26).
33. Easter, D. (2021). The impact of 'Tempest'on Anglo-American communications security and intelligence, 1943–1970. *Intelligence and National Security*, *36*(1), 1–16.

34. Ellwood, P., Asher, M. I., Stewart, A. W., Aït-Khaled, N., Mallol, J., Strachan, D., & ISAAC Phase III Time Trends Study Group. (2012). The challenges of replicating the methodology between Phases I and III of the ISAAC programme. *The International Journal of Tuberculosis and Lung Disease*, *16*(5), 687–693.

35. Eloff, M. M., & von Solms, S. H. (2000). Information security management: a hierarchical framework for various approaches. *Computers & Security*, *19*(3), 243–256.

36. Erickson, R. J. (1995). The importance of authenticity for self and society. *Symbolic Interaction*, *18*(2), 121–144.

37. Eriksson, J., & Giacomello, G. (2006). The information revolution, security, and international relations:(IR) relevant theory?. *International Political Science Review*, *27*(3), 221–244.

38. Farquhar, P. H. (1984). State of the art—utility assessment methods. *Management Science*, *30*(11), 1283–1300.

39. Filardi, V. (2020). Hallux valgus (HV): A multi-approach investigation analysis. *Journal of Orthopaedics*, *18*, 166–170.

40. Fischel, D. R. (1998). Lawyers and confidentiality. *The University of Chicago Law Review*, *65*(1), 1–33.

41. Fischer, G. (2001, August). Communities of interest: Learning through the interaction of multiple knowledge systems. In *Proceedings of the 24th IRIS Conference* (Vol. 1, pp. 1–13).

42. Fullard, W., & Reiling, A. M. (1976). An investigation of Lorenz's "babyness." *Child Development (Vol.1, pp. 1191-1193)*

43. Gebala, D. A., & Eppinger, S. D. (1991, September). Methods for analyzing design procedures. In *International Design Engineering Technical Conferences and Computers and Information in Engineering Conference* (Vol. 7477, pp. 227–233).

44. Gibbs, N., & Mei, P. (1970, December). A planarity algorithm based on the Kuratowski theorem. In *Managing Requirements Knowledge, International Workshop on* (Vol. 1, pp. 91–91).

45. Gonze, X. (2005). A brief introduction to the ABINIT software package. *Zeitschrift für Kristallographie-Crystalline Materials*, *220*(5–6), 558–562.

46. Goodman, S. N., Zahurak, M. L., & Piantadosi, S. (1995). Some practical improvements in the continual reassessment method for phase I studies. *Statistics in Medicine*, *14*(11), 1149–1161.

47. Gritzalis, D., Kandias, M., Stavrou, V., & Mitrou, L. (2014). History of information: the case of privacy and security in social media. In *Proc. of the History of Information Conference* (pp. 283–310).

48. Grivas, P. D., Daignault, S., Tagawa, S. T., Nanus, D. M., Stadler, W. M., Dreicer, R., ... & Hussain, M. (2014). Double-blind, randomized, phase 2 trial of maintenance sunitinib versus placebo after response to chemotherapy in patients with advanced urothelial carcinoma. *Cancer*, *120*(5), 692–701.

49. Gulati, R., Nohria, N., & Zaheer, A. (2000). Strategic networks. *Strategic Management Journal*, *21*(3), 203–215.
50. Gupta, A., & Sharma, S. (2015). Software maintenance: Challenges and issues. (1), 23–25.
51. Gupta, R. K., & De Micheli, G. (1993). Hardware-software cosynthesis for digital systems. *IEEE Design & Test of Computers*, *10*(3), 29–41.
52. Hamel, J. C., Stapert, D., Moermann, J. K., & Ford, C. W. (2000). Linezolid, critical characteristics. *Infection*, *28*, 60–64.
53. Hartmann, J., & Robson, D. J. (1989, October). Revalidation during the software maintenance phase. In *Proceedings. Conference on Software Maintenance-1989* (pp. 70–80). IEEE.
54. Hassanzadeh, M., Jahangiri, N., & Brewster, B. (2014). A conceptual framework for information security awareness, assessment, and training. In *Emerging Trends in ICT Security* (pp. 99–110). Morgan Kaufmann.
55. Hayam, A., & Oz, E. (1993). Integrating data security into the systems development life. *Journal of Systems Management*, *44*(8), 16.
56. Hein, S. G., & Riegel, C. D. (2012). Human resource and organizational management content in the hospitality curriculum: How the professionals view it. *Journal of Human Resources in Hospitality & Tourism*, *11*(2), 165–181.
57. Hindle, A., Barr, E. T., Gabel, M., Su, Z., & Devanbu, P. (2016). On the naturalness of software. *Communications of the ACM*, *59*(5), 122–131.
58. Holiman, M., & Schilit, R. (1991). Aftercare for battered women: How to encourage the maintenance of change. *Psychotherapy: Theory, Research, Practice, Training*, *28*(2), 345.
59. Hong, K. S., Chi, Y. P., Chao, L. R., & Tang, J. H. (2006). An empirical study of information security policy on information security elevation in Taiwan. *Information Management & Computer Security*, *14*(2), 104–115.
60. Iskhakov, S. Y., Shelupanov, A. A., & Meshcheryakov, R. V. (2017). Simulation modelling as a tool to diagnose the complex networks of security systems. In *Journal of Physics: Conference Series* (Vol. 803, No. 1, p. 012057).
61. Jombart, T., & Ahmed, I. (2011). adegenet 1.3–1: new tools for the analysis of genome-wide SNP data. *Bioinformatics*, *27*(21), 3070–3071.
62. Joseph, D., Ng, K. Y., Koh, C., & Ang, S. (2007). Turnover of information technology professionals: A narrative review, meta-analytic structural equation modeling, and model development. *MIS Quarterly*, 547–577.
63. Kadam, A. W. (2007). Information security policy development and implementation. *Information Systems Security*, *16*(5), 246–256.
64. Kang, S., & Kim, S. (2020). CIA-Level Driven Secure SDLC Framework for Integrating Security into SDLC Process. *Journal of the Korea Institute of Information Security & Cryptology*, *30*(5), 909–928.

65. Kao, T. C., Mao, C. H., Chang, C. Y., & Chang, K. C. (2012, June). Cloud SSDLC: Cloud security governance deployment framework in secure system development life cycle. In *2012 IEEE 11th International Conference on Trust, Security and Privacy in Computing and Communications* (pp. 1143–1148).
66. Karger, P. A., & Schell, R. R. (2002, December). Thirty years later: Lessons from the multics security evaluation. In *18th Annual Computer Security Applications Conference, 2002. Proceedings.* (pp. 119–126).
67. Karim, N. S. A., Albuolayan, A., Saba, T., & Rehman, A. (2016). The practice of secure software development in SDLC: an investigation through existing model and a case study. *Security and Communication Networks*, *9*(18), 5333–5345.
68. Khoshgoftaar, T. M., & Lanning, D. L. (1995). A neural network approach for early detection of program modules having high risk in the maintenance phase. *Journal of Systems and Software*, *29*(1), 85–91.
69. Kotulic, A. G., & Clark, J. G. (2004). Why there aren't more information security research studies. *Information & Management*, *41*(5), 597–607.
70. Kvist, J. (2003). A Danish welfare miracle? Policies and outcomes in the 1990s. *Scandinavian Journal of Public Health*, *31*(4), 241–245.
71. Kwasnicka, D., Dombrowski, S. U., White, M., & Sniehotta, F. (2016). Theoretical explanations for maintenance of behavior change: a systematic review of behavior theories. *Health Psychology Review*, *10*(3), 277–296.
72. Lane, J., & Schur, C. (2010). Balancing access to health data and privacy: a review of the issues and approaches for the future. *Health Services Research*, *45*(5p2), 1456–1467.
73. Lee, S. J., Lee, J. H., & Gershon, R. R. (2015). Musculoskeletal symptoms in nurses in the early implementation phase of California's safe patient handling legislation. *Research in Nursing & Health*, *38*(3), 183–193.
74. Lehman, D. W., O'Connor, K., Kovács, B., & Newman, G. E. (2019). Authenticity. *Academy of Management Annals*, *13*(1), 1–42.
75. Lockett, H., & Lawson, C. (2020). Using requirement-functional-logical-physical models to support early assembly process planning for complex aircraft systems integration. *Journal of Manufacturing Systems*, *54*, 242–257.
76. Lopez, G. A. (1985). A university peace studies curriculum for the 1990s. *Journal of Peace Research*, *22*(2), 117–128.
77. Love, A. (2004). Implementation evaluation. *Handbook of Practical Program Evaluation*, *2*, 63–97.
78. Loveland, M. T. (2003). Religious switching: Preference development, maintenance, and change. *Journal for the Scientific Study of Religion*, *42*(1), 147–157.
79. Marklund, C. (2015). American Mirrors and Swedish Self-Portraits: us Images of Sweden and Swedish Public Diplomacy in the USA in the 1970s and 80s. In *Histories of Public Diplomacy and Nation Branding in the Nordic and Baltic Countries* (pp. 172–194).

80. Mejía-Gutiérrez, R., & Carvajal-Arango, R. (2017). Design verification through virtual prototyping techniques based on systems engineering. *Research in Engineering Design*, *28*, 477–494. Bushroe, R. G., DasGupta, S., Dengi, A., Fisher, P., Grout, S., Ledenbach, G., ... & Steele, R. (1997, April). Chip hierarchical design system (CHDS) a foundation for timing-driven physical design into the 21st century. In *Proceedings of the 1997 International Symposium on Physical Design* (pp. 212–217).
81. Meng, Q., Hu, H., Zhou, L., Zhang, Y., Yu, B., Shen, Y., & Cong, H. (2019). Logical design and application of prodrug platforms. *Polymer Chemistry*, *10*(3), 306–324.
82. Murai, T. (2004). The foundation of the Mexican welfare state and social security reform in the 1990s. *The Developing Economies*, *42*(2), 262–287.
83. *Neumann, P. G. (1978, December). Computer system-Security evaluation. In Managing Requirements Knowledge, International Workshop on (pp. 1087-1087). IEEE Computer Society.*
84. Nilsson, M. I., Änggård, E., Holmstrand, J., & Gunne, L. M. (1982). Pharmacokinetics of methadone during maintenance treatment: adaptive changes during the induction phase. *European Journal of Clinical Pharmacology*, *22*, 343–349.
85. Nosworthy, J. D. (2000). Implementing information security in the 21st century—do you have the balancing factors?. *Computers & security*, *19*(4), 337–347.
86. Osterweil, L. (2011). Software processes are software too. *Engineering of Software: The Continuing Contributions of Leon J. Osterweil*, 323–344.
87. Patel, B. N. (2000). Legal Consequences for States of the Continued Presence of South Africa in Namibia (South West Africa) Notwithstanding Security Council Resolution 276 (1970). In *The World Court Reference Guide* (pp. 834–839).
88. Pfleeger, S., & Cunningham, R. (2010). Why measuring security is hard. *IEEE Security & Privacy*, *8*(4), 46–54
89. Podlesnik, C. A., Kelley, M. E., Jimenez-Gomez, C., & Bouton, M. E. (2017). Renewed behavior produced by context change and its implications for treatment maintenance: A review. *Journal of Applied Behavior Analysis*, *50*(3), 675–697.
90. Ponka, T. I., Ramich, M. S., & Wu, Y. (2020). Information policy and information security of PRC: Development, approaches and implementation. *Vestnik RUDN. International Relations*, *20*(2), 382–394.
91. Posey, C., Roberts, T. L., Lowry, P. B., & Hightower, R. T. (2014). Bridging the divide: A qualitative comparison of information security thought patterns between information security professionals and ordinary organizational insiders. *Information & Management*, *51*(5), 551–567.
92. Raymon, A., Pakianathan, P. S., Rajamani, M. P. E., & Karthik, R. (2013). Enhancing the critical characteristics of natural esters with antioxidants for power transformer applications. *IEEE Transactions on Dielectrics and Electrical Insulation*, *20*(3), 899–912.
93. Renner, B., Hankonen, N., Ghisletta, P., & Absetz, P. (2012). Dynamic psychological and behavioral changes in the adoption and maintenance of exercise. *Health Psychology*, *31*(3), 306.

94. Sabale, R. G., & Dani, A. R. (2012). Comparative study of prototype model for software engineering with system development life cycle. *IOSR Journal of Engineering*, *2*(7), 21–24.

95. Samuelson, P. A. (1937). A note on measurement of utility. *The Review of Economic Studies*, *4*(2), 155–161.

96. Scarfone, K., Souppaya, M., Cody, A., & Orebaugh, A. (2008). Technical guide to information security testing and assessment. *NIST Special Publication*, *800*(115), 2–25.

97. Schneider, B. (1987). The people make the place. *Personnel Psychology*, *40*(3), 437–453.

98. Scholtz, B., Cilliers, C., & Ferreira, C. (2013, November). The ATDM methodology to support the design and implementation of an enterprise data warehouse. In *Proceedings of the First International Conference on Enterprise Systems: ES 2013* (pp. 1–9).

99. Seddon, P. B., Graeser, V., & Willcocks, L. P. (2002). Measuring organizational IS effectiveness: An overview and update of senior management perspectives. *ACM SIGMIS Database: the DATABASE for Advances in Information Systems*, *33*(2), 11–28.

100. Shanahan, P., O'Sullivan, D. J., Simpson, P., Glennon, J. D., & O'Gara, F. (1992). Isolation of 2, 4-diacetylphloroglucinol from a fluorescent pseudomonad and investigation of physiological parameters influencing its production. *Applied and Environmental Microbiology*, *58*(1), 353–358.

101. Sheeran, P., Harris, P. R., & Epton, T. (2014). Does heightening risk appraisals change people's intentions and behavior? A meta-analysis of experimental studies. *Psychological Bulletin*, *140*(2), 511.

102. Shorten, C., & Khoshgoftaar, T. M. (2019). A survey on image data augmentation for deep learning. *Journal of Big Data*, *6*(1), 1–48.

103. Siegler, M. (1982). Confidentiality in medicine—a decrepit concept. *New England Journal of Medicine*, *307*(24), 1518–1521.

104. Sims, S. T., & Heather, A. K. (2018). Myths and Methodologies: Reducing scientific design ambiguity in studies comparing sexes and/or menstrual cycle phases. *Experimental Physiology*, *103*(10), 1309–1317.

105. Singer, E., Von Thurn, D. R., & Miller, E. R. (1995). Confidentiality assurances and response: A quantitative review of the experimental literature. *Public Opinion Quarterly*, *59*(1), 66–77.

106. Singh, S., & Karaulia, D. S. (2011, December). E-governance: Information security issues. In *International Conference on Computer Science and Information Technology (ICCSIT'2011) Pattaya* (pp. 120–124).

107. Siponen, M. T., & Oinas-Kukkonen, H. (2007). A review of information security issues and respective research contributions. *ACM SIGMIS Database: the DATABASE for Advances in Information Systems*, *38*(1), 60–80.

108. Soomro, Z. A., Shah, M. H., & Ahmed, J. (2016). Information security management

needs more holistic approach: A literature review. *International Journal of Information Management*, *1*, *36*(2), 215–225.

109. Stambul, M. A. M., & Razali, R. (2011, July). An assessment model of information security implementation levels. In *Proceedings of the 2011 International Conference on Electrical Engineering and Informatics* (pp. 1–6).
110. Stewart, W. W., & Feder, N. (1987). The integrity of the scientific literature. *Nature*, *325*, 207–214.
111. Stonebraker, M., Rowe, L. A., & Hirohama, M. (1990). The implementation of POSTGRES. *IEEE Transactions on Knowledge and Data Engineering*, *2*(1), 125–142.
112. Stubbs, J., Whybrow, S., Teixeira, P., Blundell, J., Lawton, C., Westenhoefer, J., ... & Raats, M. (2011). Problems in identifying predictors and correlates of weight loss and maintenance: implications for weight control therapies based on behavior change. *Obesity Reviews*, *12*(9), 688–708.
113. Subramanian, N., & Whitson, G. (2010). Implementing a CNSS 4012 Certification in an Information Systems Curriculum. In *Proceedings of the 14th Colloquium for Information Systems Security Education, Baltimore Inner Harbor, Baltimore, Maryland June 7* (Vol. 9, p. 2010).
114. Sugarbaker, P. H. (2003). Peritonectomy procedures. *Surgical Oncology Clinics*, *12*(3), 703–727.
115. Sugiantoro, B., Anshari, M., & Sudrajat, D. (2020, June). Developing Framework for Web Based e-Commerce: Secure-SDLC. In *Journal of Physics: Conference Series* (Vol. 1566, No. 1, p. 012020).
116. Swets, J. A. (1988). Measuring the accuracy of diagnostic systems. *Science*, *240*(4857), 1285–1293.
117. Tammaro, A. M., Matusiak, K. K., Sposito, F. A., & Casarosa, V. (2019). Data curator's roles and responsibilities: An international perspective. *Libri*, *69*(2), 89–104.
118. Tarafdar, M., & Zhang, J. (2005). Analysis of critical website characteristics: A cross-category study of successful websites. *Journal of Computer Information Systems*, *46*(2), 14–24.
119. Taylor, G., & Gaita, R. (1981). Integrity. *Proceedings of the Aristotelian Society, Supplementary Volumes*, *55*, 143–176.
120. Teorey, T. J., Yang, D., & Fry, J. P. (1986). A logical design methodology for relational databases using the extended entity-relationship model. *ACM Computing Surveys (CSUR)*, *18*(2), 197–222.
121. Thiarai, M., Chotvijit, S., & Jarvis, S. (2019). Balancing information governance obligations when accessing social care data for collaborative research. *Records Management Journal*, *29*(1/2), 194–209.
122. tokawa, H., Shi, Q., Akiyama, T., Morris-Natschke, S. L., & Lee, K. H. (2008). Recent advances in the investigation of curcuminoids. *Chinese Medicine*, *3*, 1–13.
123. Tsohou, A., Karyda, M., Kokolakis, S., & Kiountouzis, E. (2015). Managing the

introduction of information security awareness programmes in organizations. *European Journal of Information Systems*, *24*(1),pp. 38–58.

124. Tversky, A., & Kahneman, D. (1973). Availability: A heuristic for judging frequency and probability. *Cognitive Psychology*, *5*(2), 207–232.
125. Ullman, R. H. (1983). Redefining security. *International Security*, *8*(1), 129–153.
126. Unger, P. (1979). Why there are no people. *Midwest Studies in Philosophy*, *4*, 177–222.
127. Urban, H. B. (2011). Four. The “Cult of All Cults”? Scientology and the Cult Wars of the 1970s and 80s. In *The Church of Scientology* (pp. 118–154).
128. van Biene-Hershey, M. (2007). IT security and IT auditing between 1960 and 2000. In *The History of Information Security* (pp. 655–680).
129. Van Leeuwen, T. (2001). What is authenticity?. *Discourse Studies*, *3*(4), 392–397.
130. Van Niekerk, J. F., & Von Solms, R. (2010). Information security culture: A management perspective. *Computers & Security*, *29*(4), 476–486.
131. Verweij, S. (2015). Producing satisfactory outcomes in the implementation phase of PPP infrastructure projects: A fuzzy set qualitative comparative analysis of 27 road constructions in the Netherlands. *International Journal of Project Management*, *33*(8), 1877–1887.
132. Verweij, S., & Gerrits, L. M. (2015). How satisfaction is achieved in the implementation phase of large transportation infrastructure projects: A qualitative comparative analysis into the A2 tunnel project. *Public Works Management & Policy*, *20*(1), 5–28.
133. Von Solms, R. (1999). Information security management: why standards are important. *Information Management & Computer Security*, *7*(1), 50–58.
134. Vorobiev, A., & Bekmamedova, N. (2010). An ontology-driven approach applied to information security. *Journal of Research and Practice in Information Technology*, *42*(1), 61–76.
135. Vroom, C., & Von Solms, R. (2004). Towards information security behavioral compliance. *Computers & Security*, *23*(3), 191–198.
136. Wang, X. S., Bettini, C., Brodsky, A., & Jajodia, S. (1997). Logical design for temporal databases with multiple granularities. *ACM Transactions on Database Systems (TODS)*, *22*(2), 115–170.
137. Witten, I. H., Frank, E., Hall, M. A., Pal, C. J., & DATA, M. (2005, June). Practical machine learning tools and techniques. In *Data Mining* (Vol. 2, No. 4, pp. 11–22).
138. Yanase, T., Simpson, E. R., & Waterman, M. R. (1991). 17α-hydroxylase/17, 20-lyase deficiency: from clinical investigation to molecular definition. *Endocrine Reviews*, *12*(1), 91–108.
139. Yoeli, M., & Rosenfeld, G. (1965). Logical design of ternary switching circuits. *IEEE Transactions on Electronic Computers*, (1), 19–29.
140. Yong, A. G., & Pearce, S. (2013). A beginner’s guide to factor analysis: Focusing

on exploratory factor analysis. *Tutorials in Quantitative Methods for Psychology*, *9*(2), 79–94.

141. Zedner, L. (2003). Too much security?. *International Journal of the Sociology of Law*, *31*(3), 155–184.
142. Zhang, F., Wang, J., Sun, K., & Stavrou, A. (2013). Hypercheck: A hardware-assisted integrity monitor. *IEEE Transactions on Dependable and Secure Computing*, *11*(4), 332–344.
143. Zhang, P., Sadler, C. M., Lyon, S. A., & Martonosi, M. (2004, November). Hardware design experiences in ZebraNet. In *Proceedings of the 2nd International Conference on Embedded Networked Sensor Systems* (pp. 227–238).
144. Zheng, P., Wang, X., & Li, J. (2021). Exploration and practice of curriculum ideological and political construction reform——take “information security” course as an example. *ASP Transactions on Computers*, *1*(1), 1–5.

CHAPTER 2

THE HUMAN RESOURCES OF IT PROJECT MANAGEMENT

UNIT INTRODUCTION

People, procedures, and technology are the three main components of an IT project management strategy. While procedures offer a framework and direction for administering and completing the project, technology is merely a tool. Conversely, the many project stakeholders along with who is (or isn't) on the development team frequently impact the success of any project. A key element in designing and advancing the project's infrastructure is the expertise area known as human resource management. The PMBOK Guide states that project team organization, management, and leadership are all included in project human resource management. The individuals allocated responsibilities and tasks for the project's completion make up the project team. As the project continues, the kind and number of project crew members may change. Members of the project team might also be known as project staff. Whereas project team members' particular duties and tasks may be specified, the participation of all teammates in project decision-making and planning can be helpful. Team members' early participation and engagement contribute to their experience during the planning procedure and enhance their dedication to the project.

The related processes are (Swierczek & Shrestha, 2003):

- *Create Human Resource Plan*: Developing a staffing management strategy that defines and records the reporting linkages along with each team member's function, role, and essential abilities, is the focus.

- *Hire Project Team*: Affirms the availability of specified human resources for the project.
- *Develop Project Team*: Concentrates on the techniques to enhance the project team's skills, engagements, and overall team atmosphere.
- *Control Project Team*: Guarantees the monitoring of the performance of the project team, the provision of feedback, the resolution of interpersonal conflicts, and the management of organizational transformation.

In the following section, we will discuss organizational and project planning. The functional, initiative, and matrix organizational structures will be explained. As a project leader or member of a team, it is essential to comprehend an organization's structure, as it determines powers, roles, duties, channels of communication, and available resources.

Although the typical organizational structure will identify official positions, duties, and reporting links, there will also be informal interactions that exist outside of the formal framework. It is essential to have an understanding of both the reasons behind the existence of these informal structures and associations as well as how these structures and interactions might affect the interactions between the various project participants (Tohidi, 2011). In addition, gaining a grasp of not just the formal organizations but also the informal organizations can assist you in gaining an understanding of not only who determines particular decisions but also the reasons why particular decisions are being made.

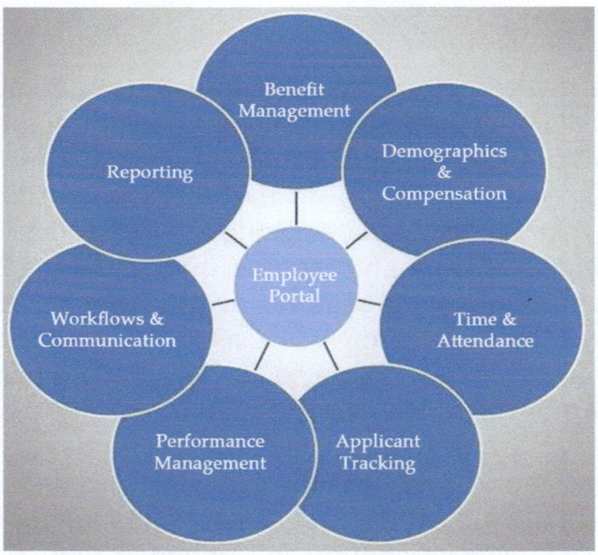

Figure 2.1. Illustration of components of human resources (Source: Loni Leedom, Creative Commons License).

The many functions of the project leader will also be emphasized. The selection and recruiting of the project team are, generally, among the project manager's most important duties. Once the team has been assembled, the project manager should ensure that everyone on the team collaborates to achieve the project's MOV. As a result, genuine team terminology and rules will be established rather than those of work groups. Assessing the characteristics of the design team will be based on these ideas (Figure 2.1).

Learning Objectives

At the end of this chapter, the reader will be able to understand:

- The human resources of IT project management
- The importance of project planning
- The significance of formal, and informal organization
- The process of functional and matrix organization
- The importance of project team
- Abilities and responsibilities of a manager
- The concepts about learning cycles and their applications

Key Terms

1 Human Resources
2 Business Strategy
3 Project Isolation
4 Networking
5 Functional Organization
6 Pseudo Team
7 Matrix Organization
8 Project Manager

2.1. ORGANIZATION AND PROJECT PLANNING

The performance of an organization or a project is influenced largely by how well its resources are organized. Structures are generally built inside an organization to control resource input, execution, and output. For instance, divisions or areas are developed based on the specific qualifications required to manage a specific resource, such as accounting and finance managing money resources, personnel managing employees, and information systems managing information resources. As an outcome, numerous firms adopt a function-based structure (Zhuge et al., 2002). Other firms might structure themselves according to the services they offer or the clients they serve. Brand management or regional divisions could be employed in these frameworks. Nevertheless, an organization's structure should fit its approach, and since organizations may follow different strategies, it makes sense that no single structure can work well for every organization. As a result, there are a variety of organizational structures and methods that may be utilized to successfully and efficiently administer not just the resources of the business but also the work and procedures that are associated. A certain structure and approach will continue to be in place so long as the corporation continues to function successfully. On the other side, when a company performs poorly, it might be necessary to make adjustments to its organizational structure or business strategy (Meares & Sargent, 1999).

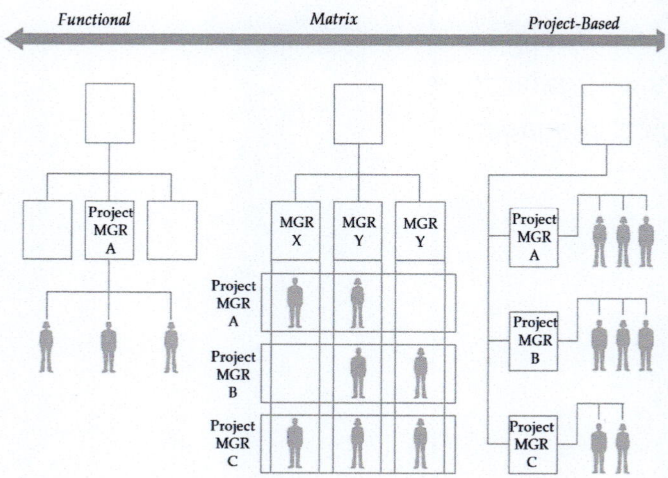

Figure 2.2. Schematic of types of organizational structure (Source: Jack T. Marchewka, Creative Commons License).

Projects are a component of a firm and can be viewed as miniature entities requiring resources, procedures, and structure. In addition, these capabilities, procedures, and structures are primarily controlled by the organizational structure of the sponsoring or parent organization and might affect or define the resources available for reporting linkages, and project tasks and responsibilities (Rouse, 2000). Thus, it is essential to comprehend how the project will interact with the host or affiliated companies and how it will be structured. This section will examine three formal structures that link projects to the organization. Every structure presents unique challenges and opportunities and selecting and adopting the organization framework can have a substantial effect on the project and the company (Figure 2.2).

2.2. THE FORMAL ORGANIZATION

The formal categorizations and specialties of operations are revealed by an organization's structure. The lines of power, channels of communication, reporting links, and duties of employees and teams within the organization are typically clarified and depicted in an organizational chart. The formal structure of an organization doesn't reveal anything about the unofficial channels of communication that exist between its parts, but it does reveal how an initiative will interact with the primary or assisting organization (Gardner et al., 2003). To put it another way, the formal organizational framework will decide how resources are distributed, who has control over those sources, and who is actually in command of the project.

The three most typical organizational structures are a functional organization, matrix organization, and project-based organization. (Demchenko, 2004). Remember that these groups are not all-inclusive; they reflect a continuum of strategies that might change over time or as an outcome of a specific circumstance. To construct a hybrid organization, like a functional matrix or project matrix, an organization might decide to mix these forms in a variety of ways.

2.2.1. The Functional Organization

It is possible to consider the organization's functional structure to be the more typical form of organizational form. The specific structure that is based on managing resources to carry out particular tasks or actions to accomplish the objectives of the organization is called a "task or activity-oriented structure." Individuals and subunits are capable of performing the same duties and are knowledgeable in the same subject areas (Dewey & Ratner, 2008). After that, project management takes place within the framework of the preexisting functional structure.

In functional departments, projects are frequently managed through traditional channels and contained inside a certain function. A project to set up a new machine, for instance, might be a self-contained project within the production process since the expertise needed for the task would be located inside the manufacturing subunit. The project leader would most probably be an executive manufacturing supervisor, and the development team would consist of engineers and production workers (Katzenbach & Smith, 1999). As an outcome, the manufacturing component would be in charge of project management as well as sourcing and organizing all project resources.

Did you Know?

At the commencement of a project, two major problems should be settled: Who is going to be in charge of the project? What resources will be offered by each subunit?

A project, though, might cross functional lines. In an IT project, the area or functional knowledge might well be located inside one of the functional subunits, whereas the knowledge and experience required to design and construct an application might be in the information systems subunit (Kolb & Yeganeh, 2012). The project team therefore may be made up of people from two or even more functional domains.

Projects supported by an organization with functional structures provide several benefits (Jurison, 2002).

2.2.1.1. Enhanced Flexibility

When necessary, the project can have additional resources, including experienced professionals, assigned to it. Furthermore, a person might be a member of the project team either totally or partially. After the completion of the project, the participants in the project are free to go back to their original functional units (Nicholas, 1990).

2.2.1.2. Depth of Knowledge and Experience

A subunit's members can provide a wealth of information, skills, and insight into the project. This expertise can be developed further as an outcome of their project experiences. As a result, the project experience might result in higher professional growth chances within the component. If the project tries to cross-functional areas, there is a chance for these employees to learn from one another to build a less specialized solution (Moran, 2005).

2.2.1.3. Less Duplication

Since specialized talents and resources are stored within a functional area, the collaboration of resources and capabilities can result in less duplication of resources across projects. Since a main basic area is accountable for and eventually assumes the responsibility of the project, it appears to be more concentrated (Guide, 2001) (Figure 2.3).

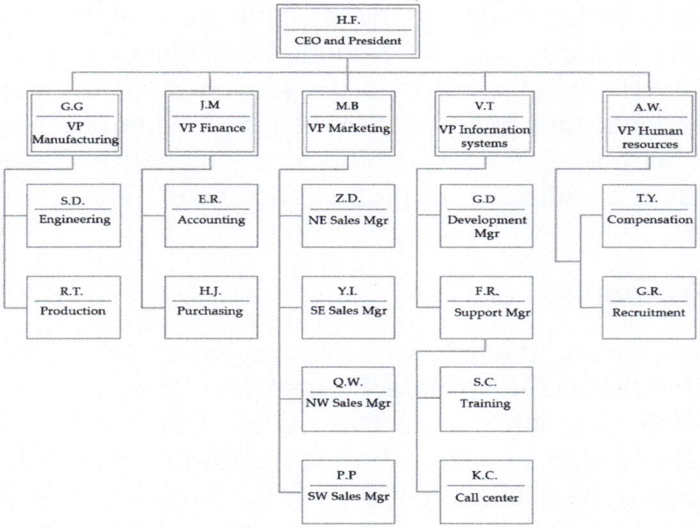

Figure 2.3. Illustration of functional organizational structure (Source: Jack T. Marchewka, Creative Commons License).

Moreover, several drawbacks are connected to the initiatives that are funded by institutions that have functional structures. These are the following (Merrow & Nandurdikar, 2018).

2.2.1.3.1. Defining Power and Responsibility

As previously said, identifying who has authority and accountability for a project should be determined from the beginning, particularly when the project encompasses more than 1 functional area. Through an IT project, for instance, will the project leader come from the IS division or the functional area? A project leader from the IS department might have experience and skill in technology but lack key business knowledge. A project leader from the functional area, on the contrary hand, might grasp the business but not the technologies. Moreover, the project manager might have had an egocentric picture of the project is, the project manager's affiliation and commitment to a single functional area might drive her or him to concentrate purely on the preferences of that functional area. The probability of this occurrence grows when the project crosses more limits. Other functional areas might start to wonder what's in it for them and might even withhold funds if their expectations and needs are not met. The project manager might not have the power to acquire and provide the necessary resources, yet he or she will be held liable for the project's collapse (Verma, 1996).

2.2.1.3.2. Poor Response Time

Who makes particular decisions is determined by the functional structure's typical lines of command and communication. If significant choices need to be reviewed by multiple tiers of leadership and across multiple functional areas, projects might take much longer (Varajão et al., 2014). Unfortunately, what's important to you may not be important to me if a particular functional unit has a dominant role or interest in a project. Problem-solving may fail due to finger-pointing or attempting to assign blame for the issue instead of concentrating on problem solutions because of the risk of parochial concerns.

2.2.1.3.3. Poor Incorporation

As a strategy to avoid several of these local concerns, the organizational culture might promote functional areas to isolate themselves from the organization as a whole. Nonetheless, this can lead to two issues. First, employees within a functional area might behave in their interests rather than adopting an organizational or global perspective on the project. Secondly, the functional area might seek to achieve self-sufficiency by gaining information, skill, and technology beyond its regular area of expertise. Even though the specialization of talents and skills can minimize the repetition of activities and operations, the functional structure might exacerbate this redundancy. As functional areas fight for resources and obscure responsibility lines, this may result in an institution of warring tribes (Slevin & Pinto, 2007).

2.2.2. The Project Organization

The project organization resides on the complete opposite end of the continuum from the functional firm (Griffith-Cooper & King, 2007). This organizational structure, which is also known as the pure project organization on occasion, includes assistance for the use of projects as the primary mode of conducting business. In most cases, a program organization will be supporting several different projects at the same time and will incorporate various tools and approaches for project management all through the business. Within the context of the organization, every project is handled as if it were a distinct and largely autonomous unit. Whereas the parent or sponsoring organization is responsible for providing fiscal and administrative controls, the full power and accountability for the program and its resources rest with the project manager. Full-time commitments are often required of the project leader as well as the members of the project team when working on a specific project (Whitty & Schulz, 2007).

There are both positives and negatives connected to initiatives that are encouraged by the project organization. The following are some major benefits (Verma, 1995; Georg Gemünden, 2014).

2.2.2.1. Enhanced Communication

A clear chain of command results in more productive and effective communication.

Furthermore, channels of communication are simplified since the project manager can circumvent the traditional channels of distribution connected with the functional organization. As an outcome of this framework, interaction is more effective and there are fewer communication difficulties (Packendorff, 1995).

2.2.2.2. High Level of Integration

Increased levels of cross-assimilation within the business may be possible as a result of improved communication inside the organization. The project team, for instance, can contain subject matter specialists with business or technological expertise. Fewer conflicts over resources arise since each project has resources dedicated solely to it.

There are several drawbacks to projects funded by project organization structures. These negative aspects include the following (Buckle & Thomas, 2003).

2.2.2.2.1. Project Isolation

There is the possibility that every project will become compartmentalized from the other projects carried out by the organization because each project might be conceived of as a self-sufficient entity. Inconsistencies in policies and project management approaches may occur across a project if every project is not supervised by a project management team or a program manager (Shenhar, 2004). Furthermore, project managers and project crews might not have many opportunities to talk to certain other project leaders and project crews about their thoughts and feelings, which would impede learning through the organization.

2.2.2.2.2. Duplication of Effort

While resource disputes are less likely to occur, different projects might necessitate resources that are duplicated on other projects. Project leaders might attempt to accumulate the most talented individuals and other assets that might be utilized by the later project. Then, every project should cover the salaries of members of the devoted project team whose skills aren't always required (Henrie & Sousa-Poza, 2005). The challenge then arises of how to deal with these individuals once the project is finished and they have not been deployed to a new project. Numerous consulting businesses, for instance, refer to individuals between assignments as being at the beach or sitting on the bench. To maximize their waiting times, advisors are frequently sent to training for seeking their next engagement.

2.2.2.2.3. Projects

This can happen when the project leader and project crew become emotionally involved in the project and with one another. As a result, these members might struggle to let go, and the project might take hold of its own with no clear conclusion in sight. To limit the probability of this occurrence, the program leader or project office should make sure that the equipment controls are implemented (Hornstein, 2015) (Figure 2.4).

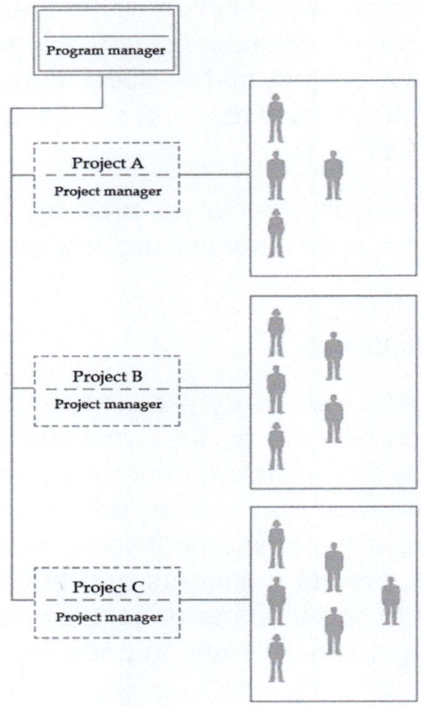

Figure 2.4. Diagram of project organization structure (Source: Jack T. Marchewka, Creative Commons License).

2.2.3. The Matrix Organization

The matrix structure is the 3rd category of organizational form. The vertical functional framework and the horizontal project framework are combined in the matrix structure (Robin et al., 2007). So, a lot of the potential and difficulties that come with functional and project companies are also present in the matrix structure.

Integrating departments and resources across a corporation is the matrix organization's key strength. Additionally, experts in the field can be brought on board the project either permanently or on a part-time approach (Thiry, 2002). Regrettably, because each member of the project will report to more than one supervisor, the oneness of command is broken, raising the likelihood of misunderstanding, irritation, disagreement, and conflicting loyalties. Whereas the project manager is in charge of organizing these capabilities, the functional manager is in charge of delivering many of the personnel and other facilities to the project. In brief, although the functional areas offer the resources to perform those duties, the project manager organizes all project work for the functional departments (dos Santos Durão et al., 2017).

The matrix organization is capable of morphing into a variety of different shapes, which can lead to the formation of a hybrid organization. The following are the most prevalent types (Betts & Lansley, 1995).

2.2.3.1 Balanced Matrix

In the format of the balanced matrix, the project coordinator is responsible for outlining all of the tasks that will be included in the project, whereas the functional managers are in charge of determining how those tasks will be performed (Huffman & Kilian, 2012).

2.2.3.2 Functional Matrix

There is a general tendency for the functional matrix organization to adopt more of the characteristics of a functional department. In this scenario, the project leader is to concentrate on coordinating the efforts associated with the project, whereas the functional managers are accountable for finishing the project that is connected to their specific area (Ziek & Anderson, 2015).

2.2.3.3 Project Matrix

Therefore, it stands to reason that a project matrix structure might start to resemble a project organization more. In this situation, the project leader has primary control over establishing and carrying out the project tasks, whereas the functional managers offer support and resources as required (Alsène, 1999) (Figure 2.5).

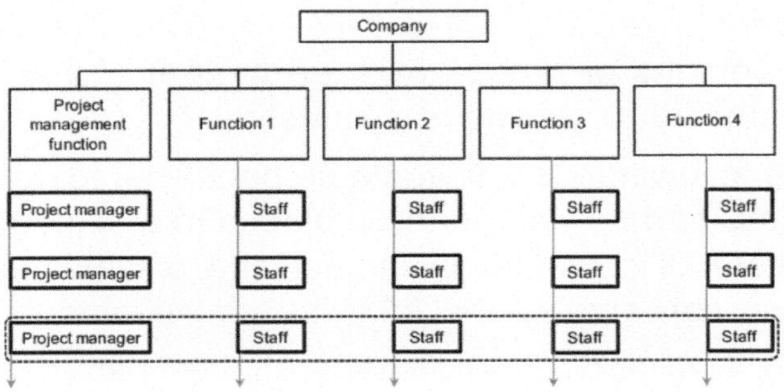

Figure 2.5. Schematic of matrix organization structure (Source: Dylon et al., Creative Commons License).

2.3. THE INFORMAL ORGANIZATION

The written structure that establishes the formal lines of power, duties, and reporting links is known as the formal organization. The formal structure of a company explains how people or groups may interact, but it does not explain how they often do. Due to the inescapable good and bad ties that develop over time in any company, the informal organization frequently escapes the official channels of power and communication. While information should be shared through established routes in formal organizations, the famous "grapevine"—a network of unofficial relationships—allows information to spread far more quickly and in any direction. Thus, one's level of power inside a company is influenced by both their position in the hierarchy and their level of informal network connectivity (Alleman, 2002). Whether data is obtained or not depends heavily on how attached an individual is to the informal organization.

Obtaining or creating a documented organizational chart is typically straightforward. Even for well-connected professionals, the informal structure could be more challenging to understand or explain. To assist the project leader and project team understand the informal organization, one might do a stakeholder assessment to figure out who needs to be attached to the project and what their responsibilities should be (Kalogeropoulos et al., 2020). To create a stakeholder assessment, one can begin with the documented organizational chart and afterward add to it as the complexity of the informal organization becomes apparent. Since the objective of the stakeholder assessment is to get an understanding of the informal organization, it might be preferable to see this as an activity instead of a publication. The following steps outline a procedure for producing an assessment of stakeholders (Hartman & Ashrafi, 2002):

1. Make a list of those who have a stake in the matter. Include people, teams, and institutions in the discussion if they are required to offer resources to the project or if they have a stake in the result of the project, whether it is effective or not.
2. Give each stakeholder a "+1" next to their name if they possess a significant interest in the project's success and a "–1" if they have a low interest in the project's success. This will help you determine every stakeholder's level of interest in the project. A score of "0" can be assigned to persons or groups that are neutral. If you are unsure, indicate to a partner that you have a question.
3. Moving on to the following step, it would be beneficial to determine how much impact every partner has on the project. On a scale ranging from zero to five, where 0 indicates no impact and 5 indicates extremely great impact, one can employ the following definitions:
4. After figuring out how much say each shareholder has in the situation, the following step is to examine whether or not there is a chance that

the various stakeholders will be in confrontation with one another. A deliberate organizational transformation is an IT project, and some of the participants in the project may behave in their self-interest. This self-interest typically competes with the self-interest of certain other participants in the situation, which can result in disagreements. For instance, a single person or a group can have the objective of elevating the system's level of functionality. This expansion in functionality will demand more money and effort, which may cause a dispute with some other groups or individuals that wish to restrict the project's expenditure or reduce the project's timetable. Increasing the functionality will require longer effort and resources.

5. In this step, every stakeholder will be assigned a role. Every initiative, for instance, must have an advocate or someone important within the firm who will publicly endorse the effort. Additionally, the project's owner must be identified. This list might comprise a person, team, or institution that will receive the project's product for transfer. Other possible positions comprise consultant, policy maker, advocate, partner, opponent, foe, and so on. Use words or analogies to convey a concise understanding of the stakeholder.
6. Once you have determined who has an involvement in the venture, what that passion is, and how much sway they might also have, it might be good to establish a goal for every stakeholder. It might involve giving specialized resources, knowledge, or direction for negotiating the political seas of the organization. In the event of possibly antagonistic stakeholders, it might necessitate obtaining their agreement or consent for specific project features.
7. Last but not least, it is essential to determine a variety of methods suited to every stakeholder. Building, sustaining, developing, and re-establishing connections may be required to implement these techniques. This list ought to give a brief explanation of the various ways in which the goal might be accomplished.

Remember

The first stage in human resource management is to hire and supply workers, and if this stage isn't completed effectively, the existence of inappropriate individuals in the project generates apparent and hidden issues.

2.4. THE PROJECT TEAM

Every one of us has a distinct definition of the word "team." These words undoubtedly have had both positive and bad connotations. Although information technology projects need a variety of resources, individuals are the most important and have the biggest impact on the project's success. A systems development project's human resources can account for as much as 80% of its costs (Besner & Hobbs, 2012). Therefore, the project leader and team members must be carefully selected. To ensure that project success isn't a coincidental occurrence, people should also make certain to help the project team.

As a result, individuals' characteristics must be given special consideration. Employing qualified personnel is critical in IT firms, which means that individuals who are self-reliant and competent are ideal for IT projects. For instance, if your temperament matches that of a specialist in information technology, you are poorer at communicating and better at decision-making. Most IT professionals are introverted and often lack communication skills (Chan, 2008; Soda & Zaheer, 2012).

2.4.1. Support Skills

Friendly and conservative demeanor, tolerance, sympathy, and assistance for those who are dissatisfied or have problems, attentiveness to people's concerns and difficulties, and focus on their interests (Gulati & Puranam, 2009).

2.4.2 Training and Assistance

Providing training and valuable guidance, as well as a context in which to encourage capacity building, entrepreneurship, and business improvement.

2.4.3. Networking

Establishing routine ties through meetings, phone calls, letters, and attendance at social gatherings as well as casual communication with those who have valuable information. The majority of top information systems experts adhere to the notion that communication makes up 80% of project management. They aren't mistaken. Any project must meet certain requirements to succeed, and poor communication frequently fails even though the program has a solid technical base (Behson, 2005). Therefore, IT managers must make the significant ability to preserve an efficient communication structure when it is being created. They must also give importance to people's personality characteristics when hiring them for projects and place them in the right roles.

2.4.4. The Abilities of the Project Manager

The selection of a project leader or manager is among the most crucial choices in project management. Typically, the project manager is appointed during the first phases of the program life cycle; however, a substitute might be brought in during the latter phases.

The project manager should serve multiple functions. The project manager should first assume a managerial position that emphasizes planning, coordinating, and supervising. For instance, the project manager is in charge of designing the project plan, coordinating the project's assets, and then supervising the plan's implementation. The project manager should also conduct a variety of administrative tasks, such as performance evaluations, project monitoring and documenting, and other regular day-to-day duties (McConkie & Boss, 1986; Molina, 2001).

Even though this work appears to be very basic and uncomplicated, even the best-laid ideas do not always turn out as expected. Consequently, the project manager has to understand when to maintain the path and when to adjust or alter the project plan by accelerating specific processes or intervening as an issue handler (Reif et al., 1973).

The project's success is dependent on not just the project team, but also on the support and engagement of all project participants. As a result, the project leader should establish and maintain connections with the various stakeholders. To accomplish so successfully, the project manager should exercise strong leadership (Petrič & Roer, 2022). While management concentrates on planning, coordinating, and supervising, leadership concentrates on motivating people and steering them in the correct direction toward a mutual goal.

Selecting a project manager is comparable to employing someone. Consider his/her background, expertise, technical skills, and general strengths and shortcomings. An effective project manager has the following characteristics (Ali, 2016; Hunter, 2016):

- *The aptitude to communicate with people*: Strong communication abilities are required for a project manager position. A project manager doesn't need to be an excellent orator, but they must be able to communicate with people, find a common goal, and encourage everybody to engage or head in the correct direction.
- *The aptitude to deal with people*: A project manager needs to be skilled at interacting with customers, their personalities, and their objectives in addition to being a competent communicator. The project manager should have good listening skills so that they can comprehend what others are saying. When people aren't being entirely honest or transparent, this competence enables the project manager to probe deeper without upsetting or rejecting them. Additionally, a project manager needs a wicked sense of humor. Project teams and supervisors frequently have to work under pressure, but by keeping a sense of humor, these

circumstances can be easier to handle. Even if a project manager doesn't have to be everybody's closest friend, they must at least come across as personable and allow for open communication. The project manager should be ready to share his or her expertise and abilities with others and to support each person in realizing their full potential (Sarlak & Salamzadeh, 2014).

- *The aptitude to create and enduring relationships*: A successful project manager should be able to construct bridges rather than walls. It might be essential to act as a mediator or negotiator between the potential customer or partner, managing directors, the project team, clients, suppliers, contractors, subcontractors, etc. Additionally, the project manager must be an effective seller. A competent project manager should consistently convince all participants of the project's value and exert impact on those over whom he/she has no direct control (Jancsics, 2015).
- *The aptitude to organize*: A project manager should be skilled at organizing—forming a project plan, procuring resources, and establishing a successful project environment. The project leader should also know and grasp both the intricacies and the large picture, which necessitates acquaintance with the project plan's contents as well as a comprehension of how uncertainties might affect the plan (Everett & Krackhardt, 2012).
- *Managerial and technical knowledge of IT managers:* Lack of technical and administrative skills on the side of the project manager is occasionally one of the leading causes of discontent with IT projects (Cao, 2011). Whereas the outcome of IT projects depends on precise technical and managerial assistance from senior managers of the company, IT projects are frequently managed by experts who lack formal education in management. In some cases, one of the issues facing the IT project staff is a lack of true interpretation of the professional responsibilities of project staff by IT project leaders.

TIPS

In recruitment, employees are recruited for the project team and then given specific roles within the team.

2.4.5. Responsibilities of IT Project Manager

The role of IT project manager comes with a variety of duties. T Some of these responsibilities are as follows (Edmondson & Nembhard, 2009).

2.4.5.1. Selection of Team and Acquisition

The process of choosing and equipping the project is another essential responsibility of a project manager.

One of the decisions that might have an impact on the final result of the project is the selection of a team that has the appropriate balance of people with technical and nontechnical talents. Even though a project leader must make every effort to recruit the most talented and capable individuals, members of the project team must be selected with the following skills in mind (Fong, 2003; Ford & Sullivan, 2004):

- *The skills of technical staff:* Expanding expenditure on information technology has a significant association with the overall increase in the usage of sophisticated knowledge and the demand for highly educated individuals. In other words, among the primary contributing factors to the success of IT initiatives is the technical expertise of the project's personnel. Also in our society, the effectiveness of IT initiatives is largely dependent on the technical talents of project workers; therefore, the primary challenge is to keep and grow personnel with strong technical skills (Ericksen & Dyer, 2004; Jones & Harrison, 1996). Depending on the type of the project, personnel with certain technological job skills will be necessary, such as programmers, system engineers, network experts, etc.
- *Business/organization abilities*: Though technology abilities are crucial for IT initiatives, having access to or having individuals with domain expertise is just as crucial. To supplement the technical skill needs, these skills encompass knowledge or experience within a particular subject along with an understanding of a specific business or industry (Tuuli et al., 2012).
- *Interpersonal abilities*: Communication with other group members and stakeholders is a crucial skill for members of the team. It is critical not only for teams to develop an understanding with one another but also for the management team to comprehend the needs of the project sponsor. Other ideal attributes must include inventiveness, a tolerance for uncertainty, tolerance of diversity, versatility in adjusting to changing jobs, and the ability to take calculated risks, given the nature of several projects (Sherstyuk et al., 2016; Pinto M. & Pinto J., 1990).

2.4.5.2. Anachronism

Professional or early anachronism is typically one of the core issues with IT workers. If IT managers were ignorant of this problem, they might rapidly lose their talented workers because of the extremely fast pace of communication and information technology (Allen et al., 1998). When a person lacks the information, abilities, and competencies required for the position, it is considered premature. According to Charlotte Veko in this scenario, all workers working on major projects in information technology will discover that their skills are quickly lagging due to the technology's fast evolution, making the need for on-the-job training inevitable (Scott-Young & Samson, 2008). IT project management initiatives must be extensive, and they must be aware that the main aim of the plan is to focus on the future. People will be efficient if they aren't only eradicated but also do not feel betrayed or fall behind. As a result, they should indeed offer project personnel reskilling chances, work, and research activities in addition to recurring and daily initiatives, and they should recognize that these activities are investments rather than costs (Zuofa & Ochieng, 2017).

The size of the project team is determined by the project's complexity or scope (He et al., 2007). Though smaller teams might work quickly and generate a product in less time, bigger teams can give a larger base of knowledge and varied views. However, larger teams have the propensity to work more slowly. Establishing subgroups to make the program more doable and to improve communication and action could be one answer to the latter difficulty (Newell et al., 2004).

Internal or external team members might be recruited by the project manager. People might be obtained from functional domains, for instance, in a functional or matrix structure. In a project-based company, a project leader might hire individuals who are halfway through projects or who'll shortly be leaving an ongoing project. The project leader might have to engage with other leaders for particular persons with particular abilities or areas of experience. A project manager might be required to employ employees from outside the firm. In any scenario, training might be needed for a certain project (White & Leifer, 1986). Thus, the timing of a people's ability to start work on the site is a critical issue that can affect the project's timetable.

2.4.5.3. Team Performance

The project's result is directly impacted by the project team's decisions and actions. As a result, the performance of the team must remain the primary focus of the project manager's attention at all times. In their 1999 book, "The Wisdom of Teams," Jon R. Katzenbach and Douglas K. Smith present a method that is both incisive and extremely applicable for comprehending the language of teams as well as the discipline they practice. They recognize the difference between different sorts of teams and work groups as part of their effort to improve the language surrounding teams.

- *Work Groups:* The workgroup is founded on the traditional method, in which one person is in charge, makes the majority of the choices, is delegated to subordinates, and keeps track of the status of the work allocated to them. As a result, the effectiveness of a work team is significantly influenced by its leader (Weiser & Morrison, 1998).

Members of a work team can also communicate with one another to exchange ideas, industry standards, and information. Workgroups might not even generally match the same performance objectives, don't generally create collaborative work products, and don't necessarily hold each other responsible, even though the participants might be engaged in each other's success (Ochieng & Price, 2010; Pinto et al., 1993).

- *Real Teams:* Teams are preferable when numerous persons should generate a shared work result. A team is "a small group of people with complementary abilities who are dedicated to a similar purpose, performance targets, and methodology for which they consider themselves mutually responsible"

Furthermore, labeling a group of individuals as a team doesn't make them one, and neither does performing together make them one. Teamwork relies on effectiveness rather than formation. As a result, various team fundamentals define a true team (Dennis & Garfield, 2003):

A small group of people: A project team should typically consist of two to twelve members. Even though a large group of people can form a team, a large group might provide logistical and communication challenges. As a result, instead of attempting to operate as a single enormous unit, a large team must be divided into subteams (Forgues & Koskela, 2009).

- *Complementary abilities*: A team must possess or develop a combination of complementary abilities to accomplish its objective. These abilities include (Jiang et al., 2003; Cheng et al., 2005):
    - Technical or functional capability
    - Problem-solving capability or decision-making abilities
    - Interpersonal abilities
- *Commitment to a mutual aim and performance objectives*: Katzenbach and Smith make a distinction between activity goals and performance targets. Similar to the idea of the MOV, a performance objective establishes the tone and ambitions of the team and lays the groundwork for establishing unified team roles and responsibilities. As an outcome, the team gains focus, energy, and dedication to its job. In addition, a shared performance objective and aim fosters pride since individuals comprehend how their collective work product will influence the company. A shared objective also provides the team with an identification that transcends the individuals engaged (Ramazani & Jergeas, 2015).

- *Commitment to a mutual approach*: Even though teams need to have a shared aim and objective, they also need to have a common strategy for how they will collaborate. Teams need to spend equal amounts of effort establishing their goals and purposes as they do devise their strategies. A method of working that is shared by all members of the team must place equal emphasis not only on issues and concerns relating to the economy and administration but as well as the social problems and problems that will determine how effectively the team collaborates (Ropponen & Lyytinen, 2000).
- *Mutual responsibility*: Members of a group must keep each other responsible for them to function as a team. It is significantly more powerful to believe that "we hold ourselves responsible" than "the boss makes me responsible." Therefore, if everyone concentrates on their responsibility, there can be no team. Every team member must make an honest commitment to both themselves as well as the other team members to be held accountable (Crawford, 2006; Thomas & Mengel, 2008). Since it goes against the individualism-centric concentration found in many cultures, this responsibility calls for both trust and dedication. In conclusion, it can be challenging for several people to entrust others with the fate of their identities and jobs. Individuals could struggle to hold one another responsible as a team unless a shared strategy and goal have been established. Katzenbach and Smith present several rational conclusions following their thorough analysis of numerous teams:
- *Teams inclined to excel on a challenging performance challenge:* A well-defined performance objective is more critical to the success of a team than engaging in activities designed to foster teamwork, launching unique projects, or recruiting members who possess excellent profiles (Pant & Baroudi, 2008).
- *The team fundamentals are habitually ignored:* The pseudo team is the poorest of all groupings because it isn't concentrated on a single performance objective (Grant & Pennypacker, 2006). If a team can't define a unified goal, it will provide unsatisfactory results. We can't just tell a bunch of individuals to work together as a team.
- *Most organizations desire individual responsibility over team responsibility:* Many job titles, compensation schemes, and career trajectories stress personal achievements, making employees uneasy about entrusting their careers to results that are contingent on the work of others (Jugdev et al., 2007; Buvik & Tvedt, 2017).

Katzenbach and Smith also make some unusual discoveries:

- *Strong performance objectives incline to spawn more real teams:* A project team can't become a true team just by being labeled as such or by being required to engage in team-building tasks or practices. Conversely, their findings imply that actual teams flourish when performance-based objectives are set (Keil et al., 2013; Olaisen & Revang, 2017).

- *High-performance teams are uncommon:* Katzenbach and Smith discovered high-performing teams in their research of teams. These are genuine teams that surpass all other groups and even their predetermined objectives. This unique form of team necessitates an exceptionally high level of dedication to other members of the team and can't be handled (Atkinson et al., 2006).
- *Real teams offer the foundation of performance:* Real teams integrate the knowledge, expertise, and opinions of the teammates to produce a harmony that can't be produced by adding up individual contributions. Teams are by far the most effective way to develop a common vision and clear direction across the company (Liebowitz & Megbolugbe, 2003; Mueller, 2015).
- *Teams naturally assimilate performance and learning:* Team members acquire the abilities necessary to attain performance objectives and shared objectives. The members of a group are more likely to share their thoughts and skills so they can learn from each other as an outcome of transparent communication and trust. Additionally, efficient teams have even more fun and have more memorable moments that reflect both the team's accomplishments and the individual members' individual growth (Thiry, 2002; Clarke, 2010).

2.4.5.4. Suitable Work Environment

IT employees frequently complain about their work environment uncomfortably and convincingly. Crowded and noisy workplaces, as a consequence of management's overzealous desire to cut expenses, have a negative impact on professional motivation and rewards (Too et al., 2014). Evaluation of the working environment, as well as safety and security rules at work, is an unquestionable necessity in the area of information technology. One aspect of project profitability is the evaluation of project personnel health (Muzio et al., 2007).

2.5. PROJECT TEAMS AND KNOWLEDGE MANAGEMENT

Real teams must have common performance objectives and a common goal as their major task. This difficulty necessitates that project teams adhering to the IT project approach define and reach a consensus on the project's MOV. It is also essential that employees learn from one another in the expertise of other project teams (Bredillet, 2008).

2.5.1. Receive Background Information at Face Value

In a nutshell, the majority of teams simply acknowledge the project objective as it is initially presented and don't question their existing notions regarding the nature of the issue or potential, as well as what they are expected to accomplish (Pheng & Chuan, 2006).

2.5.2. Approach Jobs in a Linear Manner

Projects have start and finish dates, and the project management plan details all of the procedures that must be taken to finish the project on schedule and without going over the allotted budget. Conventional teams tend to concentrate on the timeline of the project, and as a result, they measure the outcomes of the program based on whether or not it was completed on schedule and within the allotted budget (Desouza & Evaristo, 2006).

2.5.3. Offer Run-of-the-Mill Solutions

The team never fully understands the difficulty because they are focused on how it was presented to them and as a result, they offer alternatives that have little influence on the business. In other words, because the solutions remain inside the initial frame or how the problem was first communicated to them, the team might concentrate on a diagnosis and, thus, rarely focus on the actual problem or potential (Wagner & Hoegl, 2006).

Redding contrasts this by defining a radical team as one that can address the problem or difficulty at its core. Radical teams typically don't take the initial performance challenge at face value (Kolisch, 1999). Questioning and challenging the initial conceptualization of the issue or difficulty at hand is the main goal of a radical team.

2.6. LEARNING CYCLES AND LESSONS LEARNED

John Dewey introduced the learning cycle theory in 1938, and it is employed to explain how individuals learn (Kolb, 1984). The idea of learning cycles has lately been introduced to project team members and knowledge management. More precisely, learning cycles offer a method for resolving unclear circumstances by repeating a sequence of problem-solving thoughts (Hornstein, 2015) (Figure 2.6).

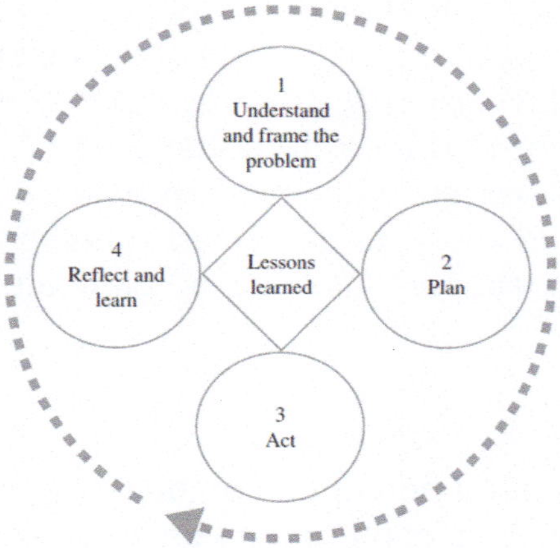

Figure 2.6. Illustration of learning cycles and lessons learned (Source: Jack T. Marchewka, Creative Commons License).

According to Redding (2000), a team learning cycle contains four stages.

2.6.1. Understanding of the Issue

A project team must not take the offered concerns and obstacles at face value. Since the issue or challenge as it is initially framed might not be the actual issue that occurs, it is necessary to expose and test preconceptions. Consequently, the project team should figure out the source of the issue. At the outset of a project, the teammates' comprehension of the assigned task m be extremely general, or they might feel as though they do not comprehend it at all (Sackmann & Friesl, 2007). Regrettably, few individuals are prepared to accept that they don't have all of the solutions or have a small understanding of the team's difficulty. On the other side, other teammates might tackle the task with a high level of predictability; that is, they might act as if they already know what the remedy is and that the team simply has to figure out the implementation details. Views are frequently taken at face value, which can lead to incorrect preconceptions that steer the program team in the wrong direction or prevent them from tackling the true issue (Wickramasinghe & Widyaratne, 2012). In addition, the team is frequently under pressure to move quickly to deliver the task on schedule and within budget. In either scenario, the team faces the danger of failing to identify the true cause of the issue and coming up with suggestions for fixes that won't change the company (Olaisen & Revang, 2017). For instance, a sponsor might inform a project team that the organization has an inventory issue. More particular, the price of storing the company's excess inventory has increased to an unaffordable level. The program team can see for themselves after taking a tour of the facility that the particular project is piled to the ceiling and occupies nearly all of the accessible floor space.

As a result, the project team should come to terms with two concepts: Preconceived ideas are likely to yield mediocre results, and thus teams must promote open humility (Navimipour & Charband, 2016). In other words, teammates should realize and accept that they don't have all of the solutions, particularly at the start of a project. As an outcome, teammates might feel more at ease acknowledging they have more unanswered questions, and the possibility of presumptions leading to subpar solutions is eliminated.

2.6.2. Planning

Teams must develop a shared perception of the issue or potential to comprehend and reinterpret the issue. This comprehension involves defining what the team's goals are and how they intend to achieve them. The team can generate ideas regarding what they know, what they believe they know, and what they do not know (Mueller, 2014). A team might have more concerns and preconceptions than facts at the beginning of a project. This is to be taken for granted by the team's potential lack of comprehension of the issue or difficulty. Thus, it is the job of each team member to distinguish between facts and assumptions (Lovell, 1993). Alternatively, if the team finds items it doesn't know, they can be categorized as queries to be addressed.

The team might make a list of the facts, presumptions, and queries to be addressed after speaking with the sponsors and viewing the facility. All the information or proof from their visit to the facility is listed in the first column. To prevent the team from tackling the incorrect issue or just a manifestation of the issue, the second column makes an effort to differentiate between the sponsor's viewpoint and the truth. One can acknowledge that no one now possesses all the solutions in the third column, but solutions can be developed. The project team can come up with a strategy once it has determined what it knows, what it believes it fully understands, and what it must learn. Team members might volunteer for or be given particular things that call for hypothesis testing or question-answering. Making a record of who completes what task by when also serves as a tool for responsibility.

2.6.3. Action

The key to cooperative learning is following through on the steps outlined in the action plan. Teammates can work independently or collaboratively to test presumptions, try out speculations, explore, or collect and evaluate data (Giri, 2019; Hölzle, 2010). The goal of these activities will be to produce knowledge and test preconceptions, not to fulfill a list of chores (Hodgson et al., 2011). As a result, the goal of these activities is to validate or disprove preconceptions and learn solutions to questions that the team doesn't know. Redding contends that what groups do even outside sessions is equally as essential as the sessions themselves because teams can only learn by doing.

2.6.4. Reflect and Learn

After completing the necessary actions outlined in the action-learning strategy, the team must share its results and comment on what each member has gained (Havermans et al., 2019). This contemplation must occur in an atmosphere of openness, sincerity, and trust for it to be successful. Once the team has had an opportunity to convene and comment on the material it has gathered, it can record its findings (Helm & Remington, 2005). Redding offers a format that the teams respond to the following queries.

- What do we know now that we didn't know before?
- Have we faced any revelations? Have we learned any new intuitions? If so, what were they?
- What former suppositions have been maintained or disproved by what we have gained so far?
- How does the team feel the project is continuing at this point?
- How efficient has the team been so far?

If the team follows our lead, they might discover that the underlying reason why stock levels are still so high is that the product being sold by the firm has become out of date or is no longer in fashion. If the group had simply followed the proposal made by the funder, who said that an information system might lower inventory levels through improved productivity, then the team might have achieved only moderate benefits. Keep in mind that how the issue is presented to you is often the root of the issue.

Lessons learned and team learning loops can be recorded and distributed to other workgroups. The conclusion of a group's lessons learned, though, signifies the conclusion of one learning process and the start of another (Liu et al.,2016; Darrell et al., 2010). The team can restart the plan, act, reflect, and learn stages after focusing once again on comprehending and redefining the issue in light of the lessons learned. This idea is demonstrated in Fig 2.10 (Shibani & Sukumar, 2015).

A complete project can be seen as a collection of learning cycles. A first staff meeting can focus on the initial issue or difficulty given to the group. The group can create a first action plan throughout that meeting. The teammates can then do their assigned duties for verifying hypotheses or acquiring data in between meetings (Yang et al., 2021). The group can review its findings, write down its knowledge gained, and then start a new cycle at its following meeting. Redding suggests, however, that three dimensions can be used to assess team learning: speed, depth, and breadth.(Shastri et al., 2021; Kelly et al., 2013).

- *Speed*: To begin, instead of a standard, linear strategy, a team must use a learning cycle method. Second, speed relates to the number of completed learning cycles. As a result, if a team can accomplish more cycles in such a given length of time, the potential to learn increases (Gandomani et al., 2020).
- *Depth*: Increasing the number of learning cycles doesn't ensure that team learning will rise. Consequently, depth of learning relates to a team's ability to get a deeper comprehension of the program from cycle to cycle. This education entails addressing the problem's conceptualization and numerous preconceptions. In brief, depth emphasizes the team's ability to go under the surface to identify the source of the issue (Anantatmula, 2010).
- *Breadth*: The project's effect on the organization is referred to as the breadth of learning. It also concentrates on whether the knowledge gained by the team remains there or is disseminated and applied across the entire company. A team can create a solution that affects the entire corporation if it can unearth complex interactions (Pennypacker & Grant, 2003). For instance, a problem that was initially classified as a marketing issue may in fact span numerous functional or departmental lines.

SUMMARY

Human resources are one of the most important aspects of any IT project. The human resources team is responsible for ensuring that the right people are in place to work on the project and that they have the necessary skills and knowledge to complete the project successfully. Without the right human resources in place, an IT project is likely to fail. The human resources team is also responsible for managing the project budget. They need to ensure that the project has enough money to cover the costs of the people working on the project and the resources they need to complete the project. If the human resources team does not manage the budget properly, the project is likely to overspend and run into financial difficulties. The human resources team also needs to be able to effectively communicate with the other members of the project team. They need to be able to keep everyone on the same page and ensure that everyone is working towards the same goal. Without effective communication, the project is likely to encounter problems and delays. The human resources team also needs to be able to resolve conflicts that may arise during the project. If there are disagreements between team members, it is up to the human resources team to mediate the situation and find a resolution that is acceptable to everyone involved.

REVIEW QUESTIONS

1. What are some common HR problems that can arise during an IT project?
2. What are some best practices for managing HR during an IT project?
3. How can HR be used to effectively manage project risks?
4. What are some tips for recruiting and retaining IT project talent?
5. What are some strategies for managing IT project employees who are located in different geographical areas?
6. How can HR be used to manage cultural differences within an IT project team?
7. What are some tips for managing IT project employees who are from different generations?
8. How can HR be used to effectively manage changes to the project team during an IT project?

MULTIPLE CHOICE QUESTIONS

1. What are the primary responsibilities of a human resources manager in a project management setting?

a. Ensuring the timely completion of the project
b. Managing the project budget
c. Hiring and managing project personnel

d. All of the above

2. **Which of the following is NOT a common task of a human resources manager in a project management setting?**
   a. Hiring and managing project personnel
   b. Ensuring the timely completion of the project
   c. Conducting performance reviews
   d. Creating the project budget
3. **What is the primary difference between a human resources manager and a project manager?**
   a. A human resources manager is responsible for hiring and managing project personnel, whereas a project manager is not.
   b. A human resources manager is responsible for ensuring the timely completion of the project, whereas a project manager is not.
   c. A human resources manager is responsible for overseeing project communications, whereas a project manager is not.
   d. A human resources manager is responsible for managing the project budget, whereas a project manager is not.
4. **Which of the following is NOT a common responsibility of a project manager?**
   a. Hiring and managing project personnel
   b. Ensuring the timely completion of the project
   c. Conducting performance reviews
   d. Creating the project budget
5. **What is the primary difference between a project manager and a human resources manager?**
   a. A project manager is responsible for hiring and managing project personnel, whereas a human resources manager is not.
   b. A project manager is responsible for ensuring the timely completion of the project, whereas a human resources manager is not.
   c. A project manager is responsible for overseeing project communications, whereas a human resources manager is not.
   d. A project manager is responsible for managing the project budget, whereas a human resources manager is not.
6. **Which of the following is NOT a common responsibility of a human resources manager?**
   a. Hiring and managing project personnel
   b. Ensuring the timely completion of the project
   c. Conducting performance reviews

d. Creating the project budget

7. Which of the following is NOT a common responsibility of a project manager?

a. Hiring and managing project personnel
b. Ensuring the timely completion of the project
c. Conducting performance reviews
d. Creating the project budget

Answers to Multiple Choice Questions

1. (d) 2. (d) 3. (c) 4. (d) 5. (a) 6.(d) 7.(d)

REFERENCES

1. Ali, I. M. (2016). Doing the organizational tango: Symbiotic relationship between formal and informal organizational structures for an agile organization. *Interdisciplinary Journal of Information, Knowledge, and Management, 11*(1), 55.
2. Alleman, G. B. (2002, August). Agile project management methods for ERP: how to apply agile processes to complex COTS projects and live to tell about it. In *Conference on Extreme Programming and Agile Methods* (Vol. 1, pp. 70–88). Springer, Berlin, Heidelberg.
3. Allen, T., Katz, R., Grady, J. J., & Slavin, N. (1988). Project team aging and performance: The roles of project and functional managers. *R&D Management, 18*(4), 295–308.
4. Alsène, É. (1999). Internal changes and project management structures within enterprises. *International Journal of Project Management, 17*(6), 367–376.
5. Anantatmula, V. S. (2010). Project manager leadership role in improving project performance. *Engineering Management Journal, 22*(1), 13–22.
6. Atkinson, R., Crawford, L., & Ward, S. (2006). Fundamental uncertainties in projects and the scope of project management. *International Journal of Project Management, 24*(8), 687–698.
7. Behson, S. J. (2005). The relative contribution of formal and informal organizational work–family support. *Journal of Vocational Behavior, 66*(3), 487–500.
8. Besner, C., & Hobbs, B. (2012). Empirical identification of project management toolsets and comparison among project types. *Project Management Journal, 43*(5), 24–46.
9. Betts, M., & Lansley, P. (1995). International Journal of Project Management: a review of the first ten years. *International Journal of Project Management, 13*(4), 207–217.
10. Bredillet, C. N. (2008). Exploring research in project management: Nine schools of project management research (part 4). *Project Management Journal, 39*(1), 2–6.
11. Buckle, P., & Thomas, J. (2003). Deconstructing project management: a gender analysis

of project management guidelines. *International Journal of Project Management, 21*(6), 433–441.

12. Buvik, M. P., & Tvedt, S. D. (2017). The influence of project commitment and team commitment on the relationship between trust and knowledge sharing in project teams. *Project Management Journal, 48*(2), 5–21.
13. Cao, H. (2011, May). Notice of Retraction: On strengthening enterprise informal organization management. In *2011 International Conference on Business Management and Electronic Information* (Vol. 2, pp. 19–22). IEEE.
14. Chan, Y. E. (2008). Why haven't we mastered alignment? The importance of the informal organization structure. *MIS Quarterly Executive, 1*(2), 2.
15. Cheng, M. I., Dainty, A. R., & Moore, D. R. (2005). What makes a good project manager? *Human Resource Management Journal, 15*(1), 25–37.
16. Clarke, N. (2010). The impact of a training program designed to target the emotional intelligence abilities of project managers. *International Journal of Project Management, 28*(5), 461–468.
17. Cooke-Davies, T. J., & Arzymanow, A. (2003). The maturity of project management in different industries: An investigation into variations between project management models. *International Journal of Project Management, 21(*6), 471–478.
18. Crawford, L. (2006). Developing organizational project management capability: Theory and practice. *Project Management Journal, 37*(3), 74–86.
19. Darrell, V., Baccarini, D., & Love, P. E. (2010). Demystifying the folklore of the accidental project manager in the public sector. *Project Management Journal, 41*(5), 56–63.
20. Demchenko, Y. (2004). Virtual organizations in computer grids and identity management. *Information Security Technical Report, 9(*1), 59–76.
21. Dennis, A. R., & Garfield, M. J. (2003). The adoption and use of GSS in project teams: Toward more participative processes and outcomes. *MIS Quarterly, 1*, 289–323.
22. Desouza, K. C., & Evaristo, J. R. (2006). Project management offices: A case of knowledge-based archetypes. *International Journal of Information Management, 26*(5), 414–423.
23. Dewey, J., & Ratner, S. (2008). *The Later Works of John Dewey*, Volume 6, 1925–1953: 1931–1932, Essays, Reviews, and Miscellany, (Vol. 1, pp. 2–8).
24. dos Santos Durão, L. F. C., Grotti, M. V. D. F., Maceta, P. R. M., Zancul, E., Berssaneti, F., & de Carvalho, M. M. (2017). A review of the soft side in project management: concept, trends, and challenges. *Revista Gestão da Produção Operações e Sistemas, 12*(2), 157.
25. Edmondson, A. C., & Nembhard, I. M. (2009). Product development and learning in project teams: The challenges are the benefits. *Journal of Product Innovation Management, 26*(2), 123–138.
26. Egbu, C. O. (2001, June). Knowledge management and human resource management

(HRM): the role of the project manager. In *Proceedings of Fourth European Project Management Conference, London* (Vol. 1, pp. 6–7).

27. Ericksen, J., & Dyer, L. (2004). Right from the start: Exploring the effects of early team events on subsequent project team development and performance. *Administrative Science Quarterly, 49*(3), 438–471.
28. Everett, M. G., & Krackhardt, D. (2012). A second look at Krackhardt's graph theoretical dimensions of informal organizations. *Social Networks, 34*(2), 159–163.
29. Fong, P. S. (2003). Knowledge creation in multidisciplinary project teams: an empirical study of the processes and their dynamic interrelationships. *International Journal of Project Management, 21*(7), 479–486.
30. Ford, C., & Sullivan, D. M. (2004). A time for everything: How the timing of novel contributions influences project team outcomes. *Journal of Organizational Behavior, 25*(2), 279–292.
31. Forgues, D., & Koskela, L. (2009). The influence of a collaborative procurement approach using integrated design in construction on project team performance. *International Journal of Managing Projects in Business,* (Vol. 1, pp. 2–6).
32. Gandomani, T. J., Tavakoli, Z., Zulzalil, H., & Farsani, H. K. (2020). The role of the project manager in agile software teams: A systematic literature review. *IEEE Access, 8,* 117109–117121.
33. Gardner, S. D., Lepak, D. P., & Bartol, K. M. (2003). Virtual HR: The impact of information technology on the human resource professional. *Journal of Vocational Behavior, 63*(2), 159–179.
34. Georg Gemünden, H. (2014). From the editor: Project management as a behavioral discipline and as a driver of productivity and innovations. *Project Management Journal, 45*(6), 2–6.
35. Giri, O. P. (2019). Study the role of the project manager in improving project performance. *Technical Journal, 1*(1), 133–139.
36. Grant, K. P., & Pennypacker, J. S. (2006). Project management maturity: an assessment of project management capabilities among and between selected industries. *IEEE Transactions on engineering management, 53*(1), 59–68.
37. Griffith-Cooper, B., & King, K. (2007). The partnership between project management and organizational change: Integrating change management with change leadership. *Performance Improvement, 46*(1), 14–20.
38. Guide, A. (2001). The project management body of knowledge (pmbok® guide). In *Project Management Institute* (Vol. 11, pp. 7–8).
39. Gulati, R., & Puranam, P. (2009). Renewal through reorganization: The value of inconsistencies between formal and informal organization. *Organization Science, 20*(2), 422–440.
40. Hartman, F., & Ashrafi, R. A. (2002). Project management in the information systems and information technologies industries. *Project Management Journal, 33*(3), 5–15.

41. Havermans, L., Van der Heijden, B. I., Savelsbergh, C., & Storm, P. (2019). Rolling into the profession: Exploring the motivation and experience of becoming a project manager. *Project Management Journal, 50*(3), 346–360.

42. He, J., Butler, B. S., & King, W. R. (2007). Team cognition: Development and evolution in software project teams. *Journal of Management Information Systems, 24*(2), 261–292.

43. Helm, J., & Remington, K. (2005). Effective project sponsorship is an evaluation of the role of the executive sponsor in complex infrastructure projects by senior project managers. *Project Management Journal, 36*(3), 51–61.

44. Henrie, M., & Sousa-Poza, A. (2005). Project management: A cultural literary review. *Project Management Journal, 36*(2), 5–14.

45. Hodgson, D., Paton, S., & Cicmil, S. (2011). Great expectations and hard times: The paradoxical experience of the engineer as project manager. *International Journal of Project Management, 29*(4), 374–382.

46. Hölzle, K. (2010). Designing and implementing a career path for project managers. *International Journal of Project Management, 28*(8), 779–786.

47. Hornstein, H. A. (2015). The integration of project management and organizational change management is now a necessity. *International Journal of Project Management, 33*(2), 291–298.

48. Huffman, B. J., & Kilian, C. M. (2012). The flight of the phoenix: Interpersonal aspects of project management. *Journal of Management Education, 36*(4), 568–600.

49. Hunter, S. (2016). If ever the twain shall meet: graph theoretical dimensions of formal and informal organization structure. *Int'l J. Soc. Sci. Stud., 4,* 79.

50. Jancsics, D. (2015). Imperatives in informal organizational resource exchange in Central Europe. *Journal of Eurasian Studies, 6*(1), 59–68.

51. Jiang, J. J., Klein, G., & Pick, R. A. (2003). The impact of IS department organizational environments upon project team performances. *Information & Management, 40*(3), 213–220.

52. Jones, M. C., & Harrison, A. W. (1996). IS project team performance: An empirical assessment. *Information & Management, 31*(2), 57–65.

53. Jugdev, K., Mathur, G., & Fung, T. S. (2007). Project management assets and their relationship with the project management capability of the firm. *International Journal of Project Management, 25*(6), 560–568.

54. Jurison, J. (2002). Integrating project management and change management in an IS curriculum. *Communications of the Association for Information Systems, 8*(1), 2.

55. Kalogeropoulos, T., Leopoulos, V., Kirytopoulos, K., & Ventoura, Z. (2020). Project-as-practice: Applying Bourdieu's theory of practice on project managers. *Project Management Journal, 51*(6), 599–616.

56. Katzenbach, J. R., & Smith, D. K. (1999). *The Wisdom of Teams: Creating the High-Performance Organization.* Boston: McKinsey & Company, (Vol. 1, pp. 2–8).

57. Keil, M., Lee, H. K., & Deng, T. (2013). Understanding the most critical skills for managing IT projects: A Delphi study of IT project managers. *Information & Management, 50*(7), 398–414.
58. Kelly, N., Edkins, A. J., Smyth, H., & Konstantinou, E. (2013). Reinventing the role of the project manager in mobilizing knowledge in construction. *International Journal of Managing Projects in Business*, (Vol. 1, pp. 4–9).
59. Kolb, D. A., & Yeganeh, B. (2012). Deliberate experiential learning. *Contemporary Organizational Behavior in Action*, (Vol. 1, pp. 4–6).
60. Kolisch, R. (1999). Resource allocation capabilities of commercial project management software packages. *Interfaces, 29*(4), 19–31.
61. Liebowitz, J., & Megbolugbe, I. (2003). A set of frameworks to aid the project manager in conceptualizing and implementing knowledge management initiatives. *International Journal of Project Management, 21*(3), 189–198.
62. Liu, J. Y. C., & Chiu, G. C. T. (2016). Influence of project partnering on stakeholder role ambiguity and project manager risk perception in information system projects. *Project Management Journal, 47*(6), 94–110.
63. Lovell, R. J. (1993). Power and the project manager. *International Journal of Project Management, 11*(2), 73–78.
64. McConkie, M. L., & Boss, R. W. (1986). Organizational stories: One means of moving the informal organization during change efforts. *Public Administration Quarterly, 1,* 189–205.
65. Meares, C. A., & Sargent, J. F. (1999). *The Digital Workforce: Building Infotech Skills at the Speed of Innovation*. DIANE Publishing.
66. Merrow, E. W., & Nandurdikar, N. (2018). *Leading Complex Projects: A Data-Driven Approach to Mastering the Human Side of Project Management*. John Wiley & Sons, (Vol. 1, pp. 5–9).
67. Molina, J. L. (2001). The informal organizational chart in organizations: An approach from the social network analysis. *Connections, 24*(1), 78–91.
68. Moran, L. (2005). Invited reaction: Virtual team culture and the amplification of team boundary permeability on performance. *Human Resource Development Quarterly, 16*(4), 459–463.
69. Mueller, J. (2014). A specific knowledge culture: Cultural antecedents for knowledge sharing between project teams. *European Management Journal, 32*(2), 190–202.
70. Mueller, J. (2015). Formal and informal practices of knowledge sharing between project teams and enacted cultural characteristics. *Project Management Journal, 46*(1), 53–68.
71. Muzio, E., Fisher, D. J., Thomas, E. R., & Peters, V. (2007). Soft skills quantification (SSQ) Foi project manager competencies. *Project Management Journal, 38*(2), 30–38.
72. Navimipour, N. J., & Charband, Y. (2016). Knowledge sharing mechanisms and techniques in project teams: Literature review, classification, and current trends.

Computers in Human Behavior, 62, 730–742.

73. Newell, S., Tansley, C., & Huang, J. (2004). Social capital and knowledge integration in an ERP project team: the importance of bridging and bonding. *British Journal of Management, 15*(S1), 43–57.
74. Nicholas, J. M. (1990). *Managing Business and Engineering Projects: Concepts and Implementation*. Prentice Hall, (Vol. 1, pp. 6–9).
75. Ochieng, E. G., & Price, A. D. (2010). Managing cross-cultural communication in multicultural construction project teams: The case of Kenya and UK. *International Journal of Project Management, 28*(5), 449–460.
76. Olaisen, J., & Revang, O. (2017). The dynamics of intellectual property rights for trust, knowledge sharing, and innovation in project teams. *International Journal of Information Management, 37*(6), 583–589.
77. Olaisen, J., & Revang, O. (2017). Working smarter and greener: Collaborative knowledge sharing in virtual global project teams. *International Journal of Information Management, 37*(1), 1441–1448.
78. Packendorff, J. (1995). Inquiring into the temporary organization: new directions for project management research. *Scandinavian Journal of Management, 11*(4), 319–333.
79. Pant, I., & Baroudi, B. (2008). Project management education: The human skills imperative. *International Journal of Project Management, 26*(2), 124–128.
80. Pennypacker, J. S., & Grant, K. P. (2003). Project management maturity: An industry benchmark. *Project Management Journal, 34*(1), 4–11.
81. Petrič, G., & Roer, K. (2022). The impact of formal and informal organizational norms on susceptibility to phishing: Combining survey and field experiment data. *Telematics and Informatics, 67*(1), 101766.
82. Pheng, L. S., & Chuan, Q. T. (2006). Environmental factors and work performance of project managers in the construction industry. *International Journal of Project Management, 24*(1), 24–37.
83. Pinto, M. B., & Pinto, J. K. (1990). Project team communication and cross-functional cooperation in new program development. *Journal of Product Innovation Management: an International Publication of the Product Development & Management Association, 7*(3), 200–212.
84. Pinto, M. B., Pinto, J. K., & Prescott, J. E. (1993). Antecedents and consequences of project team cross-functional cooperation. *Management Science, 39*(10), 1281–1297.
85. Ramazani, J., & Jergeas, G. (2015). Project managers and the journey from good to great: The benefits of investment in project management training and education. *International Journal of Project Management, 33*(1), 41–52.
86. Redding, J. C. (2000). *The Radical Team Handbook: Harnessing the Power of Team Learning for Breakthrough Results*. Jossey-Bass.
87. Redding, S. (2000). Parents and learning. *International Academy of Education*, Second Edition, 33–36.

88. Reif, W. E., Monczka, R. M., & Newstrom, J. W. (1973). Perceptions of the formal and the informal organizations: Objective measurement through the semantic differential technique. *Academy of Management Journal, 16*(3), 389–403.
89. Robin, V., Rose, B., & Girard, P. (2007). Modeling collaborative knowledge to support engineering design, project manager. *Computers in Industry, 58*(2), 188–198.
90. Ropponen, J., & Lyytinen, K. (2000). Components of software development risk: How to address them? A project manager survey. *IEEE Transactions on Software Engineering, 26*(2), 98–112.
91. Rouse, W. B. (2000). Software Tools for Strategic Management: Special Issue Overview. *Information-Knowledge-Systems Management, 2*(1), 1–5.
92. Sackmann, S. A., & Friesl, M. (2007). Exploring cultural impacts on knowledge sharing behavior in project teams–results from a simulation study. *Journal of Knowledge Management*, (Vol. 1, pp. 1–6).
93. Sarlak, M. A., & Salamzadeh, Y. (2014). Analyzing the impacts of informal organizations on formal routines in a networked organization. *Journal of Asian Scientific Research, 4*(12), 768–783.
94. Scott-Young, C., & Samson, D. (2008). Project success and project team management: Evidence from capital projects in the process industries. *Journal of Operations Management, 26*(6), 749–766.
95. Shastri, Y., Hoda, R., & Amor, R. (2021). The role of the project manager in agile software development projects. *Journal of Systems and Software, 173*, 110871.
96. Shenhar, A. J. (2004). Strategic Project Leadership® Toward a strategic approach to project management. *R&D Management, 34*(5), 569–578.
97. Sherstyuk, O., Olekh, T., & Kolesnikova, K. (2016). The research on role differentiation as a method of forming the project team. *Восточно-Европейский журнал передовых технологий, 2*(3 (80)), 63–68.
98. Shibani, A., & Sukumar, D. (2015). The role of the project manager in construction projects in India. *Chinese Business Review, 14*(6), 298–324.
99. Slevin, D. P., & Pinto, J. K. (2007). An overview of behavioral issues in project management. *The Wiley Guide to Project Organization & Project Management Competencies, Vol.· 1,* 1–19.
100. Soda, G., & Zaheer, A. (2012). A network perspective on organizational architecture: performance effects of the interplay of formal and informal organization. *Strategic Management Journal, 33*(6), 751–771.
101. Swierczek, F. W., & Shrestha, P. K. (2003). Information technology and productivity: a comparison of Japanese and Asia-Pacific banks. *The Journal of High Technology Management Research, 14*(2), 269–288.
102. Thiry, M. (2002). Combining value and project management into an effective program management model. *International Journal of Project Management, 20*(3), 221–227.
103. Thomas, J., & Mengel, T. (2008). Preparing project managers to deal with complexity–

Advanced project management education. *International Journal of Project Management, 26*(3), 304–315.

104. Tohidi, H. (2011). Human Resources Management's main role in Information Technology project management. *Procedia Computer Science, 3*, 925–929.
105. Too, E. G., & Weaver, P. (2014). The management of project management: A conceptual framework for project governance. *International Journal of Project Management, 32*(8), 1382–1394.
106. Tuuli, M. M., Rowlinson, S., Fellows, R., & Liu, A. M. (2012). Empowering the project team: impact of leadership style and team context. *Team Performance Management: An International Journal, 18*(3/4), 149–175.
107. Varajão, J., Dominguez, C., Ribeiro, P., & Paiva, A. (2014). Critical Success Aspects in Project Management: Similarities and Differences Between the Construction and the Software Industry. *Tehnicki Vjesnik/ Technical Gazette, 21*(3).
108. Verma, V. (1995, January). The human aspects of project management: organizing projects for success. *Project Management Institute*, (Vol. 1, pp. 3–6).
109. Verma, V. (1996, January). The human aspects of project management: human resource skills for the project manager, volume two. *Project Management Institute*, (Vol. 1, pp. 11–15).
110. Wagner, S. M., & Hoegl, M. (2006). Involving suppliers in product development: Insights from R&D directors and project managers. *Industrial Marketing Management, 35*(8), 936–943.
111. Weiser, M., & Morrison, J. (1998). Project memory: information management for project teams. *Journal of Management Information Systems, 14*(4), 149–166.
112. White, K. B., & Leifer, R. (1986). Information systems development success: Perspectives from project team participants. *MIS Quarterly*, 215–223.
113. Whitty, S. J., & Schulz, M. F. (2007). The impact of Puritan ideology on aspects of project management. *International Journal of Project Management, 25*(1), 10–20.
114. Wickramasinghe, V., & Widyaratne, R. (2012). Effects of interpersonal trust, team leader support, rewards, and knowledge sharing mechanisms on knowledge sharing in project teams. *Vine,* (Vol. 1, pp. 1–9).
115. Yang, X., He, B., Wang, L., Yu, M., & Zhu, F. (2021). Enabling projects for strategic implementation: Role of the designated project manager in CEO-TMT interface during project front-end investment decisions. *International Journal of Project Management, 39*(6), 620–632.
116. Zhuge, H., Chen, J., Feng, Y., & Shi, X. (2002). A federation–agent–workflow simulation framework for virtual organization development. *Information & Management, 39*(4), 325–336.

117. Ziek, P., & Anderson, J. D. (2015). Communication, dialogue, and project management. *International Journal of Managing Projects in Business,* Fourth Edition, 5–7.

118. Zuofa, T., & Ochieng, E. G. (2017). Working separately but together: appraising virtual project team challenges. *Team Performance Management: An International Journal*, Second Edition, 3–7.

CHAPTER 3

BUDGET MANAGEMENT IN IT PROJECTS

UNIT INTRODUCTION

IT initiatives have a dismal track history of fulfilling budgetary objectives. According to the Standish Group's CHAOS investigations, the estimated cost blowout, defined as the additional percentage or dollar amount by which total expenses exceed forecasts for failed IT projects, went from 180% in 1994 to 43% in 2010. While academic researchers challenge the accuracy of these figures, more thorough, scientifically reviewed studies accept the issue of IT overall project cost increases. For example, three separate surveys of software project cost overruns by Jenkin s, Phan, and Bergeron in 1984, 1988, and 1992, respectively, found that the average cost overrun for all of the projects in their survey samples (not just unsuccessful projects) was 33–34%. Research that appeared in the Harvard Business Review in 2011 assessed IT change initiatives in almost 1,500 projects and found an average price excess of 27%. The analysis of IT programs in this report was thought to be the biggest yet. Enterprise resources planning, company records, and customer relationship management systems were among the initiatives. With an estimated price of 167 million dollars, many initiatives had expensive rates; the most expensive project came in at $33 billion (Bloch et al., 2012). The most important finding in the study, however, was the discovery of a large number of gigantic overages when analyzing the project overrun data. A "black swan" is an elevated occurrence that is uncommon, unanticipated, and not unlikely in hindsight. One in six of all the projects analyzed included "swan black."

It causes the real danger associated with IT reform initiatives: It's not that, contrary to what management experts and scientific work have historically said, they tend to have big cost time overruns in general. The issue is that a disproportionately high percentage of them experience enormous overpayments or black swans. Most managers and consultants have been overlooking the true issue because they have been concentrating on statistics rather than the more harmful exceptions. IT Projects can do better when it comes to achieving financial objectives.

This chapter emphasizes monitoring and maintaining cost estimates across the whole project's lifespan while connecting cost controls with the other success factors (Figure 3.1).

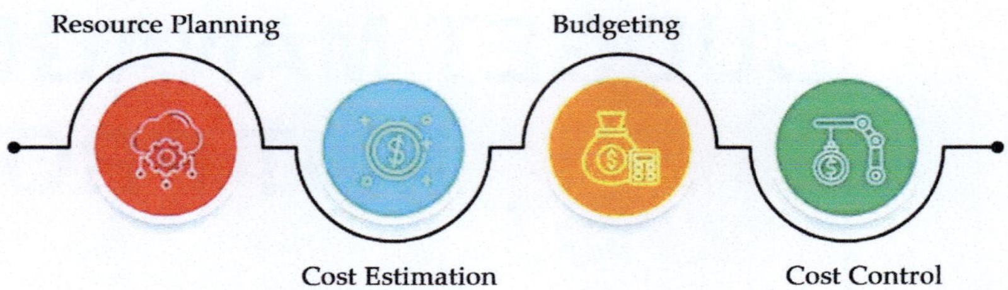

Figure 3.1. Illustration of budget management in project management. (Source: Proprofs, Creative Commons License).

Learning Objectives

At the end of this chapter, the reader will be able to understand:

- The significance of IT project budget management
- The Principles of IT project budget management
- The required resources for IT project budget management
- The problems with IT project cost estimates
- The process of budget development, approval, and execution
- The concept of budget targets

Key Terms

1. Budget Management
2. Tangible Costs
3. Intangible Costs
4. Profit Margin
5. Cash Flow
6. Cost Estimates

7. Financial Revision
8. Work Breakdown Structure
9. Budget Execution
10. Budget Baseline
11. Form of the Accounting Chart (COA)
12. Black Swan
13. Budget Changes

3.1. BUDGET MANAGEMENT

The following procedures and stages make up the sequence of actions in budgetary control, which are designed to assist in controlling the program's expenses (Wysocki et al., 1995):

- Defining the Budget
- Executing the Budget
- Controlling the Budget
- Updating the Budget

3.1.1. Inputs for Budget Management

Papers or other types of data used as input for program budgetary control include those listed below (Bennatan, 1996):

- WBS
- Project contracts or starting expenditure
- Requirements that are needed
- Relevant costs estimation
- Completion time guesstimates
- Historical information
- Current economic conditions
- Sponsor and Organization rules.
- Chart of accounts structure (COA)

Did you Know?

The estimated cost over and timeline excess for these IT black swan initiatives were 200% and nearly 70%, respectively.

3.1.2. Outputs for Budget Management

Using the data provided, the project team will draft three key papers for the program:

- Cost estimates by activity
- The Project Budget
- The Budget Variance Report

Project Budgeting is typically done during the initial phases of the project's design and in tandem with the creation of the program. The planning procedures are heavily reliant on both the projected durations of jobs and the personnel allocated to the project. Budgeting is a management tool that allows real costs to be contrasted to and evaluated against the plan. The cost is frequently a pretty fixed factor in the execution of the project. When a timetable starts to slide, the expense increases accordingly. When project expenses start to rise, the program manager should review the Project Plan to see if the size, price, or deadline must be adjusted.

The applicable cost elements connected with the entire project are determined to build the budget. Expenses for every activity ought to be basic and relevant, consisting of labor, materials, and other actual costs. The cost of finishing a task is proportional to the number of people allocated to the activity, the time of the job, and the price of any non-labor goods needed by the assignment. This chapter focuses on controlling and monitoring the IT project budget plan all through the life cycle of the project, while also connecting budget control to the other desired outcomes.

3.2. BASIC PRINCIPLES OF BUDGET MANAGEMENT

Due to IT employees' lack of understanding of the significance of fundamental accounting and financial concepts, many IT programs never get started. Several projects that are begun never really get completed due to issues with budgetary control. The majority of executive board members are much more engaged in money and possess a better grasp of financial words than IT ones (Roberts, 2011). As a result, IT managers must be able to communicate project documentation in both technical and economic terms. Project managers need to be familiar with some different budgetary control theories, ideas, and terminologies in addition to net current value research, return on investments assessment, and repayment assessment (Aminbakhsh et al., 2013).

TIPS

The proportion of revenues to profits is known as profitability.

This part covers the general subjects including earnings, cash flow forecast, life-cycle assessment, and both intangible and tangible costs and advantages Another important topic is earned value management is one of the key tools and techniques for controlling project costs; it is described in detail in the section on cost control (Wright, 1997).

3.2.1. Profit

Earnings with fewer expenses equal profitability. A business can aim to cut costs, boost sales, or do both to boost profitability. The majority of managers are more focused on their profit than other challenges (Ruiz-Pérez et al., 2021). It's crucial to consider how new content systems and technologies will affect earnings rather than merely revenue or costs while defending expenditures in them. Think up a piece of e-commerce software that you predict will boost a $100 million sales profit by 10%. You cannot measure the potential benefits of the application without knowing the profit margin. (Higdon & Topp, 2004).

3.2.2. Profit Margin

Profit margin is the ratio of revenues to profits. There is a 2% net profit if sales of $100 result in earnings of $2. There is a 2% profit margin if the company fails $2 for every $100 in sales (Sato & Hirao, 2013).

3.2.3. Life Cycle Costing

You may get a comprehensive understanding of the costs associated with a project's life cycle by using service life pricing. This aids in the development of a correct financial benefit and cost prediction for a program. In life cycle pricing, the whole price of possession, which includes both creation and maintenance expenditures, is taken into account.

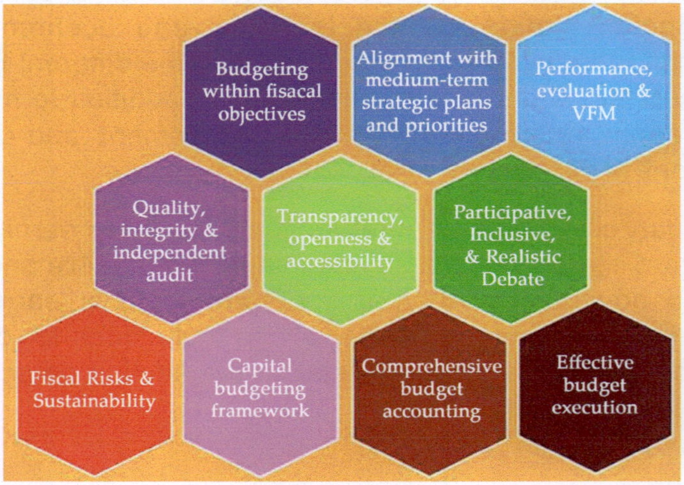

Figure 3.2. Schematic of principles of budgetary governance (Source: OECD Governance, Creative Commons License).

The development and introduction of brand-new customer care technology, for instance, could take a business one or two years to finish, but the proposed program could be in use for ten years. Project leaders should evaluate the costs and advantages of the project throughout its whole life span with the support of money related to their businesses. When dealing with money, top executives and project administrators need to take the project's life cycle costs of initiatives into account (Wateridge, 1998) (Figure 3.2).

In the past, organizations had a history of underfunding the initial stages of IT projects, which has an impact on the total cost of ownership (Weingartner, 1966). For instance, initial trials and user needs definition on IT initiatives are significantly more expensive than waiting for issues to appear after deployment (Wateridge, 1995).

For example, Table 3.1 summarizes the average cost of a minute of downtime for different IT applications. Costs include the cost to bring the system back up, staff cost to make up for the lost work in production during the system downtime, and direct and indirect lost revenue.

Types of IT Applications	Cost/Minute
Security Trading	$73,000
Enterprise Requirements Planning (ERP)	$14,800
Order processing	$13,300
Electronic commerce	$12,600
Supply chain	$11,500
Point of sale (POS)	$ 4,700
Automated teller machine (ATM)	$ 3,600
E-mail	$ 1900

Table 3.1. Tabular Data About the Costs of Downtime for IT Applications (Source: Kathy Schwalbe, Creative Commons License)

3.2.4. Cash Flow Analysis

Cash Flow analysis is a methodology for estimating a project's yearly expenses and benefits, as well as its resulting annual cash flow. Cash flow analysis must be conducted by project leaders to establish net current value (Munns & Bjeirmi, 1996). The majority of people comprehend the fundamental idea of cash flow: if they do not have sufficient funds in their pockets or banking services, they cannot make a transaction. When deciding which initiatives to engage in, top management should take operating cash considerations. If top leadership chooses too several initiatives with significant cash flow requirements during the same fiscal year, the business will be unable to sustain all of its projects and retain profit. Additionally, it is essential to specify the year utilized to assess the dollar amount. For instance, if a corporation bases all of its cost projections on projections for 2012, it must take inflation into account and other considerations when estimating costs and benefits in future dollars (Soares et al., 2020) (Figure 3.3).

Figure 3.3. Diagram of cash flow analysis (Source: Annabelle Amery, Creative Commons License).

3.2.5. Tangible Costs or Benefits

Dollar amounts are a simple way to quantify tangible costs or benefits (Weingartner, 1966). Let's take the Surveyor For example which was discussed in the group's introductory instance and had a pre-feasibility assessment. If a company completed a pro project for $100,000, its tangible cost is $100,000 The measurable benefits of the research for the authorities would be $50,000 if a govt agency determined that it could have completed the study itself for $150,000. In this case, the current regime might have paid Juan's corporation for the research and then reassign the public workers who might have completed it to other tasks.

3.2.6. Intangible Costs or Benefits

It can be challenging to quantify in money units the expenses or advantages of intangibles. Consider Juan and a few others spending their own time exploring study-related topics utilizing govt laptops, textbooks, and other tools. They might be regarded as an indirect cost even if their time and the supplies provided by the government would not be invoiced to the enterprise. Sympathy, reputation, and broad claims of productivity increases are examples of qualitative program advantages that a corporation may find difficult to convert to monetary value. Conceptual costs and advantages are frequently more challenging to explain since they are challenging to measure (Lyneis et al., 2001).

3.3. COMPONENTS OF IT PROJECT BUDGET

The Project Manager can use manual or automated tools to generate the budget estimate. All expenditures must be allocated to implement the project by the Project Manager, and all parts of the project, such as the cost of internal and external people management, technology, transportation, resources, and consumables, must be included. The cost must be significantly more specific than what was presented in the proposed project. If the project leader begins employment with a contractual budget, she/he must analyze the assumptions established during the proposed project phase and ensure that the agreed-upon objective can be fulfilled within the contractual spending plan (Kerzner, 2002).

Remember

How well an organization can describe the projected expenses and benefits for a program is measured in terms of physical and intangible expenses and benefits.

The project manager can create the financial report manually or automatically using the software. Simple worksheets or sophisticated budgetary forecasting software may be used as planning instruments. The Project Manager must always keep notes on how this cost was created for record purposes and to allow the plan to be modified. Bulleted lists for cost estimation aid in trying to make sure that all necessary budgetary data is comprehended and that all areas are touched. The cost of the personnel as well as the tools and supplies required to finish the task must also be accounted for in the plan. The creation of a budget will be directly affected by how personnel and supplies will be obtained for the operation (Bakke & Hellberg, 1991).

How assets like persons, technology, commodities, and material are procured may be governed by a range of organizational, legal, and budgetary limitations. The project manager must be familiar with the current rules, standards, and processes for obtaining finance. Additionally, purchasing choices may be influenced by the tastes of the recipients or the donors' agents. Budget tactics can be understood by studying data from comparable previous similar projects; those that proved effective and appropriate may be taken into account for application to the new work (Jasch, 2008).

New additions could be discovered while the fixed budget is created since the work is now more precisely specified. The WBS and the work plan may need to be updated to reflect the budgetary estimate tasks, such as those provided, supplies, and other non-human assets. The budgetary control plan outlines the process for controlling spending and includes a tentative distribution timetable. For instance, the budgetary control strategy should detail the bookkeeping, spending confirmation, and procurement payroll system. Depending on the requirements of the project stakeholders, the plan may be official or unstructured. The budgetary control plan may include information about sponsor restrictions, spending limits, and degrees of authorization for purchases (Suver & Cooper, 1988) (Figure 3.4).

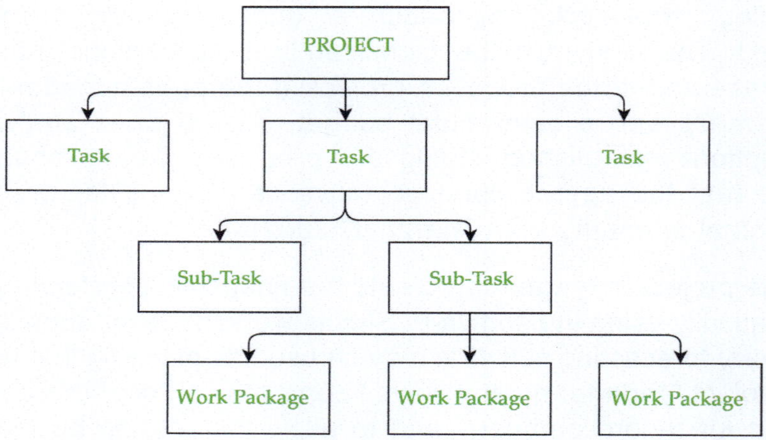

Figure 3.4. Illustration of Work Breakdown Structure (WBS) (Source: Raman, Creative Commons License).

3.3.1. Identification of Budget Resource

Identifying the types and amounts of assets (people, equipment, services, and material) needed to accomplish the task is known as budget allocation (Griffin, 1998).

The WBS, objective definition, based on past, capacity data, and rules are input used to calculate the program's assets. The primary result is a list of resource issues that serve as the foundation for the financial budget and resources evenly and offer crucial details for the project resources management procedure. Every need can be categorized into one of four common kinds of resources (Huntzinger, 2012).

3.3.1.1. Human or Labor resource

It includes technical assistance and is made up of qualified personnel with the knowledge and abilities required to finish the tasks on time for the assignment. People may be recruited for the project's length of time or drawn from within the organization.

Advisers with high-level technical knowledge that is not available within the company or on the local labor market also fall under the category of people skills. The project will create a list of the requirements for human resources that includes the level of competence, regions of experience, training qualifications, and language needs.

3.3.1.2. Equipment and Material Resources

Equipment includes all the specialized tools needed by the project, ranging from water tanks to power energy that will be employed by the venture or provided to the recipients.

It also refers to the requirement for trucks and office items such as computers and printing. The supplies encompass a broader range of necessities such as public utilities such as power, telephone lines, web access, office supplies, office area, and equipment needed by the project. Structural elements that will be utilized to construct buildings, as well as food and medications, may be included in the package.

The project will have a full list of all the needs required for the task as a result of this activity, which can be in the form of a worksheet arranged according to the sequence received from the WBS or by the company's or donor's chart of balances (Agarwal & Rathod, 2006).

3.3.2. IT Project Budget Estimation

Once all project requirements have been documented, the following stage is to establish the expenses of every need, which will lead to the development of the project budget. An estimated cost is the method by which the expenditures that the business will incur in order to obtain or utilize resource requirements (Ivanova et al., 2017).

Budget projections are derived from those in charge of overseeing work efforts. They give the necessary abilities to create the estimates, as well as buy-in and responsibility during the execution of the operations.

As described in planning and scheduling, teammates select the people or labor types required to finish the task and multiply the price of the labor by the amount of time or days required to accomplish the task. Following the documentation of all projects, determining how long the task performance takes is the single most difficult part of deriving a cost estimate. Holiday time, sick leave, meals, conferences, and other day-to-day activities must all be factored into personnel expenditures (Westerveld, 2003). The absence of inclusion of these elements jeopardizes both the timeline and the cost projections. Materials expenditures, transportation, computer systems, and car costs are examples of non-labor costs. Detailing basic assumptions while generating the budget for the project is just as important as developing a project timeline. Monitoring the budget is not only difficult but also unsafe without appropriate documents regarding these expectations (Hall, 2000).

If, for instance, budgeting projected that the materials would be purchased at a certain rate, but weeks after the project began the object's cost increased owing to the market situation, this poses an issue for the plan.

The project manager may unintentionally raise the cost of the project and put the program's chances of succeeding in jeopardy if the presumption is not established. Expenditures for projects are often created by a team of people. It's a good idea to request that the same individuals that looked over the WBS task list and plan also look over the budgets. When a draught budget is finished, speak with the team to confirm that the job titles, schedules, and corresponding expenditures are correct and complete. The project must account for any appropriate taxes, charges, and other charges that are unrelated to materials in addition to the budgeted amount. This will make it easier to see the budget plan in its entirety (Chua et al., 1997).

During a project, three different sorts of annual budget orders estimation, contractual, and definitive—are made. This means changing mainly in terms of when they are made, how they are utilized, and how precise they are (De Bakker et al., 2010).

3.3.2.1. Rough Estimate

The approximate calculation to determine whether an organization or donor would be interested in funding the project, people build the original budget estimates that are used before or throughout the project's beginning phase (Conboy, 2010). Because estimates are based on elevated goals, it gives a rapid overview of the project's outputs, and it gives a rough sense of the budget. Depending upon the project, the majority of rough approximations have a varied range of –25% to +75%. These preliminary estimations should not require a lot of the task manager's job. Considering the number should not be used as a final estimation or as an estimation for an RFP; they should only be utilized to get a solid idea of the initial planning projected expenses (De Bakker et al., 2012) (Figure 3.5).

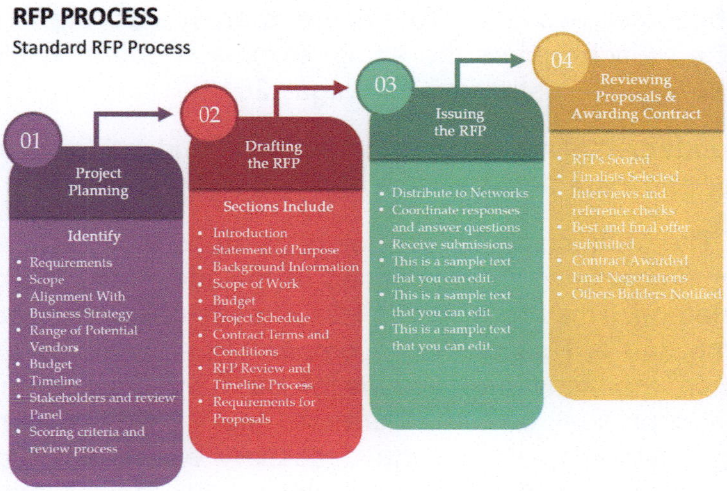

Figure 3.5. The explanation of the RFP process (Source: SketchBubble, Creative Commons License).

3.3.2.2. Contract Estimate

It is more precise, it is established late in the project's initiation phase, and it is based on the donor's RFP criteria, which often include constraints and styles for how to provide a plan - such as bank details. It is founded on comparable estimation, which involves transferring budgetary lessons acquired from a previous project to the latest project. The contractual estimation begins with the problem or opportunity and proceeds to its specifics. Similar to the reasonable approximation, this guesstimate must include circumstances, a region of variation, and any assumptions underlying. The estimation of a deal is swift, but not particularly accurate. The margin of deviation in the budgeted amount is between –10% and +25%. This is the most time-consuming component of a project, and it serves as the foundation for project discussions between the contributor and the organization (Kutsch & Hall, 2005).

3.3.2.3. Definitive Estimate

It represents the most perceiving type, but the most time-consuming to develop. The final estimation utilizes the Work Breakdown Structure (WBS), which is a deliverables-focused description of the budget and schedule. This sort of estimation is typically created during the planning stage to obtain comprehensive information on all contract sums, and it utilizes the organization chart of accounts to track costs in the accounting system (Kutsch & Hall, 2009). The final estimation can be used for calculating the ultimate expenses of the business and for making buying decisions when the exact expenses are necessary payment terms. The final estimation is utilized throughout the project's entire life cycle and is updated whenever new data becomes available. This figure is often accurate to within a range of –5% to +10%, which means the actual expenses could be 5% lower or 10% more than the definite estimates (Didraga, 2013).

There are four fundamental approaches to financial budgeting: analogous, top-down, bottom-up, and parametric estimating (Teller & Kock, 2013).

- *Analogous*: The real costs of a prior, similar scheme are used as the basis for determining the expenses of the presented work in this estimation method. This procedure is less expensive on average, takes a shorter time, but is less precise. Comparable estimations are most accurate when the aims and actions of past work are comparable to those of the present one. Furthermore, the individuals generating the estimations must also have the necessary experience to assess whether certain operations are more or less costly on the big project (Rabechini & Monteiro, 2013).
- *Top-down* estimate: When the overall project cost is established and the project must be aware of the expenses of each effort, it is a budgetary estimation. In this situation, the company decides the number of tasks or outputs it can generate with a certain cost. A fixed budget is broken down using the WBS to calculate the number or amount of tasks that can be completed with the budget. To meet budget constraints, the development team may decide to decrease or expand particular tasks or reduce the amount of WBS levels. Actual costs from similar past projects are used from the top down (Carvalho & Rabechini Junior, 2015).
- *Bottom Up:* In order to calculate the program's total price, it is necessary to determine the costs of each input so each activity separately. To identify all of the identified stakeholders and all resources necessary, including staff, technology, and supplies, a complete WBS is necessary. The minimum rate of the WBS is estimated by employees who are in charge of that operation or who have knowledge of that given place. All figures are then aggregated to provide estimations for each greater level of the WBS, and ultimately for the overall project (Jani, 2011). In this method, the estimation begins with a predetermined number of tasks and determines the overall cost (Figure 3.6).
- *Parametric estimates:* It makes use of predetermined conditions to specify how much an action or task will price at a rate/price or outcome. The annual budget for the action is determined, for instance, by multiplying the expense of training one employee by the necessary amount of people who must be taught. This rate could include expenditures for personnel, materials, and technology. It gives the total budget for the activity. A parametric model is quite popular in such cases. The effectiveness of this project relies on the information available and the model's adaptability to various situations (Thamhain, 2013).

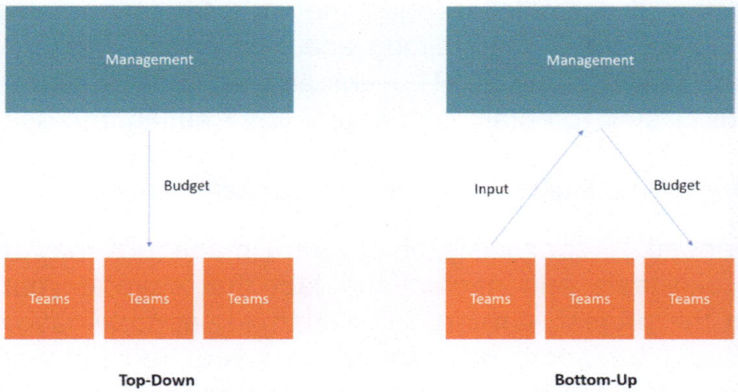

Figure 3.6. Schematic of Top-down and Bottom Estimation (Source: CFI Team, Creative Commons License).

3.3.3. Problems related to IT Project Budget

Even with the help of numerous techniques and methodologies, several IT projects estimated costs are still inaccurate, particularly those for cutting-edge technology or application development. Tom DeMarco, a well-known project management writer, offers four explanations for these errors and possible solutions (DeMarco & Lister, 2013).

3.3.3.1. Estimates Are Done Too Quickly

It takes a lot of work and complexity to create estimates for a substantial given project. Before there are crystal-clear system needs, several estimations should be made fast (Raz & Michael, 2001).

For instance, there is a lot of intricate software design going on with the Surveyors. Someone will need to develop a ROM estimation and budgetary estimations for this work before completely comprehending what data inspectors require in the project. For IT programs, the later, more accurate projected costs are seldom lower than the initial projections. It's crucial to keep in mind that estimations are made at different points throughout the task, and project managers have to justify every forecast (Baccarini et al., 2004).

3.3.3.2. People Lack Estimating Experience

Particularly for large initiatives, cost analysis is generally a skill that is underutilized by those who create computer-estimated costs. Additionally, they may not have access to adequate, trustworthy project information on which to make estimations. A group's estimations can increase if it employs sound methods for managing projects and establishes a track record of maintaining accurate project documentation, particularly estimations (Teller et al., 2014). It will also enhance estimated costs to make it possible for IT staff to obtain cost estimation training and assistance.

3.3.3.3. Human Beings Are Biased Toward Underestimation

For instance, experienced IT specialists or program managers may rely their predictions on their skill sets and neglect the fact that several young folks would be involved in the project. On large IT initiatives, approximations could also overlook to account for additional expenditures required for testing and connectivity. To ensure that the predictions are not biased, it is essential for project leaders and senior management to examine the forecasts and pose pertinent questions (Williams, 1995).

3.3.3.4. Management Desires Accuracy

Administration may request estimation and wants a more precise figure to assist them to develop a bid to secure a huge order or obtain internal funds. It is critical for a project manager to contribute to the development of solid cost and timeline estimations and to employ their management and negotiating abilities to back up those predictions. It is also critical to use caution while estimating the parameters. Upper executives never forget the first forecast and, more often than not, keep forgetting how authorized adjustments impact the forecast (Cagliano et al., 2015). Keeping upper leadership aware is a never-ending and critical activity.

3.3.4. Sample of Budget Estimation

Examining the samples or examples related to estimated costs is one of the greatest ways to understand how the budget estimation system runs. Every cost estimate is unique, just as every project is unique. You should learn more than you can about the program before starting a price estimate, and you should also find out how the company intends to use the cost estimate (Conboy, 2010). The total budget must be a firm approximation and as exact as possible if it will serve as the foundation for contract awards and performance measurement. It's crucial to make the underlying principles and presumptions of the estimation clear (Bode, 1998). For instance, the following suppositions and guidelines are included in the Surveyors Pro program projected cost:

- To demonstrate that it was feasible to create the software and hardware needed by surveyors and connect the new phones to existing data systems, thorough research and proof of idea were conducted before this work. An experimental portable gadget and a large portion of the technology needed to connect to the Global Positioning System (GPS) and other governmental databases used among surveys were built as part of the demonstration of the concept project. There is little published data to anticipate future labor expenses, particularly for application development, as well as the price of portable devices.

- The primary objective of this project is to manufacture 100 handheld devices, continue improving the software (particularly the user interface), test the new system in the field, as well as train 100 surveyors in selected areas to utilize the new system

Depending on the achievement of this project, a follow-up deal for a substantially greater number of gadgets is anticipated.

The program's WBS is as follows:

- Project planning
- Hardware
  a. Portable electronics
  b. Servers
- Software
  c. Legal software
  d. Computer programming
- Testing
- Assistance and instruction
- Reserves
- Expenses should be calculated according to WBS and monthly. The project manager will use generated cost-benefit analyses, which necessitates this kind of assessment, to reflect on the project status.
- The prices will be stated in US dollars. Since the project would last a year, the price will not be taken into account.
- The project director of the administration will oversee it. Four teammates and a part-time project leader are needed for the work. The teammates will contribute their knowledge in the fields of software design, education, and maintenance while helping to oversee different project components. Strategic planning will take up 25% of their total time, product development will consume 25%, training and assistance will take up 25%, and non-project activities will take up 25%.
- Software licenses must be obtained for the project to use the GPS and three other system elements. The creation of the gadgets' user interfaces, an online support system, and a new component for monitoring the surveyor's productivity while using the instrument are all examples of

software design.

- Since the sample work was successful, testing expenses should be minimal. It should be possible to make an approximation by multiplying the sum of the hardware and software estimations by 10%.
- There will be five separate venues for instructional sessions as a part of the training. The development group thinks it will be more efficient to outsource the majority of the training, involving creating the lesson plans, conducting the classes, and providing helpline assistance for three months when the inspectors begin to use their equipment in the fields.
- Include 20% of the approximate total as reserves because this project is subject to several risks.
- You must create a computer model for the estimation so you are able to quickly alter multiple inputs, such as the number of labor hours for different tasks or labor rates.

Thankfully, the project team has easy access to cost estimates as well as actual data from the same projects. . The group can construct the estimates with the help of the demonstration of concept projects, which has a large amount of information, as well as by speaking with the subcontractors who worked on the past work. There are different computer models available, such as a functional point-based software estimate tool (Ahuja et al., 1994). The team first analyses a draft of the project timeline and develops additional estimates as necessary because the estimates must be given by WBS and by the month. Although expenses may be paid at various periods than when the work is executed, the members agree to first calculate the cost of each WBS item before deciding when the work will be conducted. This strategy for the estimation has been authorized by the group's budgeting specialist. For calculating the expenses for each WBS area, the group also has the following message and presumptions (Østergren & Stensaker, 2011):

- The estimation is based on the remuneration of a part-time project manager and 25 % of teammates' time. The budgeting specialist for this project recommended using a labor cost of $100/hour for the project manager and $75/hour for every teammate, assuming an average of 160 full-time hours worked per month. Therefore, the total number of hours for this area for the project director is 960 (160/2 * 12 ¼ 960). Costs are also provided for the four project team members who each contribute 25% of their time, for a total of 160 hours a month for all project staff (160 * 12 ¼ 1920). A supplemental quantity will be added for all contractual labor; it is calculated by multiplying 10% of the overall costings for software creation and testing by the number of contractual labor hours (10% * ($594,000 þ $69,000)).
- Equipment:

- Handheld devices: 100 portable gadgets are projected to cost $600 per unit by the provider.
- Servers: Four computers are anticipated to cost $4,000 each, according to a recent system acquisition.
- *Technology:* Licensed software, the pricing of a license will be discussed with each vendor.

Costs are anticipated to be lower than typical due to the high possibility of future big contracts and widespread exposure if the method is successful (Kivilä et al., 2017). The cost per portable gadget will be $200.

- *Software development:* The estimation for software design will contain two methodologies: labor estimation and discriminant function estimation (Günaydın & Doğan, 2004). A greater estimate will be utilized. If the estimations differ by more than twenty percent, the project will necessitate a third method of estimation. The provider that produced the solid evidence product will supply the labor estimation input, while regional techies will evaluate the validation set (Mohamed et al., 2015).
- *Testing:* Taking into account similar projects, 10% of the total hardware and software cost will be allocated for test results.
- *Training and support*: Depending on comparable projects, training materials will be determined per trainee + travel expenses. The price for each student (100 total) will be $500 and transportation for teachers and project teammates will cost $700 each day for each individual. The crew anticipates that 12 traveling days will be required to complete the job. The labor costs for the people on the project team will be added to this estimation, as they will assist with education and provide support afterward. The estimated labor hours for teammates total 1,920 hours.
- *Reserves:* Following the directive, resources will be calculated at 20% of the entire projection. Using previous information, the project team creates a price structure. The following figure depicts a worksheet that provides a summary of expenditures by WBS component (Figure 3.7).

The WBS components are listed in the first column, and depending on how the expenses are calculated, the elements may occasionally be further subdivided. For instance, the project manager, the project team member, and the subcontractors will participate in some project management techniques, so the project management category involves three elements to estimate expenses for them (Davila et al., 2009).

Pay attention to the columns where you can input the number of units or hours and the price per unit or hour. This method is employed to calculate several objects. Some brief remarks are included in the projection, such as the fact that inventories make up 20% of the overall measure. Additionally, keep in mind that you can simply update the estimates by changing a variety of input parameters, such as the amount of time or the price per hour (Grishunin et al., 2018) (Figure 3.8).

	# Units/Hrs.	Cost/Unit/Hr.	Subtotals	WBS Level 2 Totals	% of Total
WBS Items					
1. Project Management				$306,300	20%
Project manager	960	$100	$96,000		
Project team members	1920	$75	$144,000		
Contractors (10% of software development and testing)			$66,300		
2. Hardware				$76,000	5%
2.1 Handheld devices	100	$600	$60,000		
2.2 Servers	4	$4,000	$16,000		
3. Software				$614,000	40%
3.1 Licensed software	100	$200	$20,000		
3.2 Software development*			$594,000		
4. Testing (10% of total hardware and software costs)			$69,000	$69,000	5%
5. Training and Support				$202,400	13%
Trainee cost	100	$500	$50,000		
Travel cost	12	$700	$8,400		
Project team members	1920	$75	$144,000		
6. Reserves (20% of total estimate)			$253,540	$253,540	17%
Total project cost estimate				$1,521,240	

Figure 3.7. The explanation of the Surveyor Pro Project cost estimate created on October 5 (Source: Jack T. Marchewka, Creative Commons License).

A second source for more data on how this more complex estimation was created is the asterisk next to the software development item. Remember that the greater estimation will be selected as far as both were no more than 20% apart, and that software development should be evaluated utilizing two different methods (Nikias, 2019). The labor estimation was utilized in this instance because it was slightly greater ($594,000 vs. $562,158) than the functional predicted value in Figure 3.8 to explain in detail how the discriminant function estimates were created. As you can see, the mathematically based estimation was produced under many assumptions. Again, you can simply tweak a few variables to modify the estimates by entering the data into a costing system. For more details on discriminant function estimations, consult the cited papers and other resources.

The project budget must be reviewed by various individuals. Analyzing the total dollars in addition to the proportion of the total cost for every significant WBS area is also beneficial. A top executive, for instance, may rapidly assess the Surveyor Pro plan price estimate and determine whether the figures are accurate and the premises are well-supported (Addison & Vallabh, 2002). The estimates in this situation were in line with the $1.5 million contract sum that the administration had established.

1. Labor Estimate	# Units/Hrs.	Cost/Unit/Hr.	Subtotals	Calculations
Contractor labor estimate	3000	$150	$450,000	3000 * 150
Project team member estimate	1920	$75	$144,000	1920 * 75
Total labor estimate			$594,000	Sum above two values
2. Function point estimate**	Quantity	Conversion Factor	Function Points	Calculations
External inputs	10	4	40	10 * 4
External interface files	3	7	21	3 * 7
External outputs	4	5	20	4 * 5
External queries	6	4	24	6 * 4
Logical internal tables	7	10	70	7 * 10
Total function points			175	Sum above function point values
Java 2 languange equivalency value			46	Assumed value from reference
Source lines of code (SLOC) estimate			8,050	175 * 46
Productivity×KSLOC^Penalty (in months)			29.28	3.13 * 8.05^1.072 (see reference)
Total labor hours (160 hours/month)			4,684.65	29.28 * 160
Cost/labor hour ($120/hour)			$120	Assumed value from budget expert
Total function point estimate			$562,158	4684.65 * 120

Figure 3.8. The schematic of Surveyor Pro Software Development Estimate Created October 5 (Source: Jack T. Marchewka, Creative Commons License).

According to comparable past efforts, the WBS Level 2 elements, such as project management, hardware, software, and tests, also appeared to be at suitable proportions of the overall price. In rare circumstances, a committee may also be required to offer a ranging estimation rather than a specific figure for every component (Laslo & Gurevich, 2014). The group could, for instance, predict that the expenses of the assessment will range from $60,000 to $80,000 and record the assumptions they used to arrive at those figures. Cost projections should also be updated, especially if there are any significant changes to a project (Davila, 2000). The group can then assign costs for every month according to the project timeline and when expenditures will be paid after the final estimated cost has been authorized. Additionally, as will be discussed in the following section, many organizations demand that the predicted expenditures be divided up into planned budget areas.

3.3.5. IT Project Budget Development

This process entails assembling everything, particularly data from the organization about cost recovery fees, shared cost pools, taxes, fees, and donor regulations or restrictions (Mishakova et al., 2016). This step also entails the establishment of the project budgetary control strategy, which outlines budgetary authorities and control of the state (Pike, 1988). The budget for the IT project is utilized to explain how much will be spent on certain resources over a specific period. The majority of project budgets are monthly in nature (Raymond & Bergeron, 2008).

3.3.5.1. Chart of Accounts

Two forms are typically used to control the budget: a contributor form that adheres to the overall accounting specifications established by the contributor and the group's overall accounting forms for aggregating accounting data. A chart of accounts is a list of all the accounts tracked by a single accounting system. Its purpose is to collect financial data so that you may make wise financial decisions. A distinctive identification, often bank details, is given to every other institution in the chart. Assets, Liabilities, Equity, Income, and Expenses are the 5 types into which each institution in the chart is divided. The Expense accounts will be used by a contract sum to keep track of project costs. The bookkeeping department of the business is mainly concerned with keeping track of the other accounts, like property, obligations, and revenue. A company has the freedom to modify its accounting chart to best meet its requirements, including establishing entities as necessary (Bogoslavtseva et al., 2019).

3.3.5.2. Budget Reports Requirements

Three parties have reporting obligations: the project, administration, and the sponsor. The donor has some reporting criteria for the project budget, including reporting on the donor's chart of accounts, adhering to the donor's fiscal year, as well as the current reporting standards. (Faleti et al., 2014). Comparable trying to report rules relating to the top operations as well, including the need to use the COA of the organization to gather all project-related accounting transactions; the utilization of a particular budgetary year; and providing information in both the monetary system of the hosting country and the monetary system of the group's head office, for instance, Pesos and Euros. The company must also decide which data it will require to effectively manage the budget and make certain that all operations are making intended use of the budgeted assets. Creating a table that outlines all budgetary reporting obligations, internally and outside of the project, as well as the dates or time frames when these data must be provided, is great training (Rehesaar & Beames, 1998).

3.3.5.3. Budget Management Plan

It is a document that outlines how budgetary variations will be controlled in the program, as well as the amount of responsibility for accepting budget adjustments and the procedure for requesting budgetary modifications. Programs might be as simple as a one-page paper or as complex as extensive procedures and regulations (Rankin et al., 2008; Lappe & Spang, 2014). Every Organization must determine who, when, and how to handle the budget for the project using its internal procedures.

3.3.6. Process of Budget Approval

The final step in the financial budget is receiving approval. The project completion estimate must be evaluated by the development team and a finance department member. Once the project cost is finished, the next step is to obtain authorization for the budgeted cost.

This happens three to four times during the project lifecycle: during project bargaining with the sponsor, who did lead to the interaction spending plan, during the planning phase, when the project cost is established in better detail, following the organization diagram of accounts, and eventually becomes the baseline expenditure (Nguyen et al., 2018).

Talks between the organization and the sponsor may follow the approval of the budget; based on the size of the spending plan, these discussions may take a while before the spending plan is authorized and a contract is concluded.

3.4. PROCESS OF IT PROJECT BUDGET EXECUTION

The cost is determined by assigning the estimated cost of the project to particular material sources or work orders across time. These physical assets or work orders are determined by the project's work package operations. Budgeting input includes the costs management plan, start planning, activities estimated costs, estimation foundation, project timeline, manpower calendar, risk log, contracts, and allocated resources.

The primary objective of the cost planning procedure is to establish an estimated cost for monitoring project outcomes and determining program budget needs (Cozzolino, 1979; Morozov et al., 2017). The procedure may also lead to modifications to plan documentation, such as the addition, deletion, or modification of elements in the statement of work or project timeline.

3.4.1. Project Budget Baseline

Creating a basic budget, which is a moment budget that program management uses and evaluates financial results, is the next stage after the project cost has been examined and approved. The foundation will be compared to the project's true cost as it moves forward; each month, fresh data are generated from people expenditures, procurement of items and services, as well as other construction cost like perks and sharing expenditures (Cools et al., 2017).

The Earned Value estimates will be utilized to manage the budget based on the project's foundation and the amount of work that has been accomplished. The overall project is often multiplied by the number of months or years the program will last. The fact that projects hardly ever proceed linearly is one of the issues with this technique.

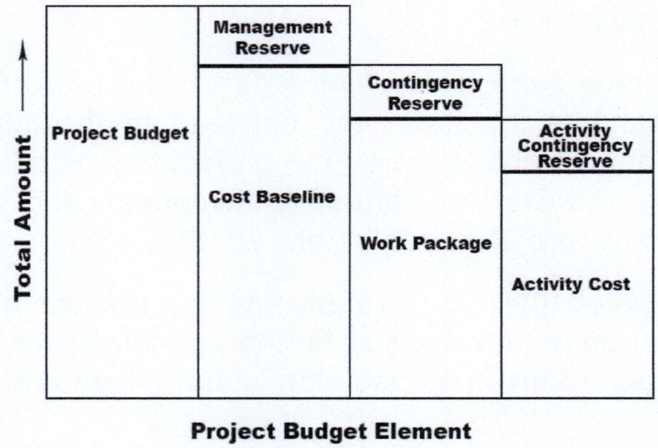

Figure 3.9. Illustration of cost baseline (Source: Fahad Usmani, Creative Commons License).

3.4.2. Announcement of Budget

The authorized plan must be conveyed to those individuals who will oversee, manage, and make choices depending on the information about the budget. The list of people comes from the stakeholder communication needs developed in the project communication management plan (Khadra et al., 2012; Teah et al., 2019). Not all project members are required to obtain a duplicate of the budgeting, and in certain cases, organizations' or sponsors' laws may determine who has access to the financial data, because it could include confidential information such as benefits or salary (Tishler et al., 1996). The donor, leadership, and project team must comprehend the premises that were used to calculate the cost, as they will be altered as the project progresses and, if not managed appropriately, can expose the program to avoidable liabilities. For instance, the sponsor may require the acquisition of a brand image of the police cruiser, and the expenditures are based on the belief that the car can be procured in the home nation at the stated price by a seller. However, if the seller is unable to supply the same car at the price initially cited, due to changes in the conditions, the proposal will incur additional charges to buy foreign the donor-required car. By keeping the please comply, the project will have a greater chance of negotiating options and coming up with solutions (Becker, 2014).

3.4.3. Process of Targets Setting in Budget

Typically, project expenditures are developed following the requirements of the finance team to measure versus predetermined criteria, such as a financial year, but the project may require its own monitoring goals for particular aspects of the operations. One of these categories is the project weekend schedule checkpoints and their related set of tasks (Hale & Douglass, 1977). By establishing financial goals against a timeline, the company will have a greater chance of monitoring and controlling the money. For instance, a stage aim of $60,000 is intended to begin on 1 March and last for three months. On 30 May, the monthly budget survey suggests that $55,000 were expended, which may imply that the project is on schedule. However, a modification of the actions for that step reveals that only 60% have been finished, and with only $5,000 remaining, the proposal will not be able to finish the phase's actions. To evaluate the accomplishment of the project's activity, the project leader must establish financial objectives (Figure 3.10).

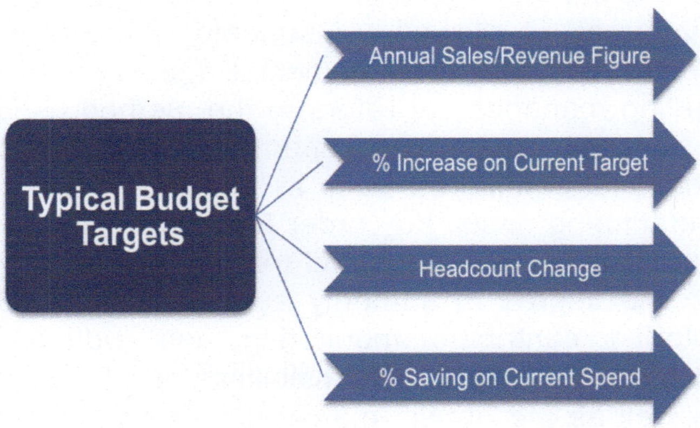

Figure 3.10. Schematic of components of typical budget targets (Source: Free Management Books, Creative Commons License).

3.4.4. Budget Implication

Authorizing expenses according to the organization's policies that decide who can authorize expenses on behalf of the project and the limits of the authorizations. Depending on the amount, some organizations choose to have different levels of authorization; for large amounts, two or three signatures may be required to assure the donor that proper controls are in place to ensure the correct use and application of the funds received from the donor. Following the project timeline plan and the list of resource requirements, the project manager typically approves all purchase orders for materials, equipment, and services. The project would typically rely on the organization's financial and accounting systems for purchasing goods and services, especially when purchasing expensive commodities. The section Resource management examines the procurement plans in greater detail, as well as the processes involved in obtaining bids from vendors and managing vendor contracts.

3.5. PROCESS OF PROJECT BUDGET CONTROL

Checking cost and schedule, guaranteeing that only pertinent project modifications are reflected in an updated budgeted cost, and notifying stakeholders of allowed project status that will influence the budget are all aspects of controlling the project budget (Layer et al., 2002). Cost-controlling elements include the project's management plan, innovative financing needs, information on job performance, and allocated resources. Team effectiveness data, cost projections, modification demands, project plan upgrades, relevant project notifications, and resource upgrades for organizational processes are all products of this procedure. The management of construction costs is aided by many methods and tools. To create processes for modifying the budgetary foundation, you also require a change advisory system as well to software (Huang et al., 2012).

Monitoring and managing the project cost makes ensuring that only the project-related modifications are accounted for in the budgetary foundation, that those in authority are informed of allowed adjustments, and that the required remedial measures are performed. Cost management is a procedure that includes a project budget. Budgeting management refers to the method used to legally identify, authorize, and pay expenses or costs spent on the program. For every group of related operational expenditures, such as consultant fees, equipment and supplies, and manufacturing costs, buy order forms are filled out (Roberts et al., 2004; Erkoyuncu et al., 2011). The project manager approves the goods receipt forms based on the degree of authority and the financial department records them for monitoring, contributor monitoring, and audit reasons. The organization must identify the duties and responsibilities of everybody engaged in budgetary control as well as the project manager's crucial job of managing the cost. As a portion of the regulatory requirements, such as making sure that the correct transactions are utilized and documented, the financial manager is typically responsible for recording, tracking, and monitoring the spending plan from a cost income statement. It also provides reports for the top operations and the sponsor (Roy et al., 2011).

This same financial services component is not in charge of ensuring that the project spending plan adheres to the project goals and objectives; that's the project manager's responsibility, who must use the news stories and supervise the spending plan to ascertain if the finances are being used as planned and also to recognize any variances, modifications, or adjustments to the spending plan. The concentration on operational budgetary control differs significantly from the typical costing system (Kingsman & de Souza, 1997; Laframboise et al., 2007). Cost accounting is involved with the challenges associated with submitting expenditures to the appropriate components of the set cost estimation divisions and accounting codes, and it concentrates on ginning process real cost estimates while paying special attention to the constituents of the system of accounting. This project owner's primary focus is not expense management, but rather expenditures connected to the project's project outcomes. Process costing is typically concerned with past data, however, project budgetary control is concerned with performance enhancement and forecasting the forecast. Smaller initiatives may be handled by the institution's primary financial function's purchasing and accountancy section. As a component of the program's management or documentation operations, the project manager normally keeps basic information on file (Datta & Roy, 2010).

Bigger projects may necessitate their separate business model. To handle with amount of work required on huge, complicated, or collaborative ventures, competent accounting and staff may be required. Certain joint development projects are carried out as completely different entities with their own administrative and organizational structures. The program may even employ accountancy software to keep the project's expenditures independent of the primary bookkeeping of the Organization, although the information would be merged into the mother institution's accounts (Field et al., 2007).

Notifications from the finance division, buy permission requests from the procurement department, and key project reports are utilized to monitor the budget plan and give a perspective on how project expenditure compares to the budget. The structure and substance of the budget summaries required to monitor project spending will be determined by the organization. The standard report comprises a list of all value increases (COA) and sections that detail the budgeted foundation, accumulated expenditures to present, balances to the deadline, and burn ratio, which indicates how the budgeted is consumed concerning the annual proposed budget (Ben-Arieh & Qian, 2003). A simple budgeting report is displayed below:

- *Expense Reports* and Statements detail expenditures by accounts, program identifier, and financing identifier.
- *Variance Reports* indicate the difference between what was spent and what's been authorized, as well as the amount for every account.
- *Burn Ratio Reports,* display the speed at which the business is consuming the money as planned, a fast way to assess if the cost estimate is on schedule.

Control of project expenditures, organizational or overall capital, and human costs, particularly compensation, are all included in scoping report (Busachi et al., 2017).

3.5.1. Budget Performance

Budgeting effectiveness is the operation that determines whether project expenditures are now being carried out following the proposed budget and assists in identifying deviations and developing corrective actions. The approach used to evaluate financial results is determined either by books of accounts that the business uses to manage expenses and spending (Bloch et al., 2012; Lee et al., 2010). If the project only uses the financial reporting system records what cash is available, the picture may be incomplete because the budgeting process only shows total costs and does not login information for connections, customer orders, as well as other money-related responsibilities that have yet to be made accountable for on the accounting records. Financial statements often include information on payments that have been collected to present (Fayaz et al., 2017). The project manager must keep account of real expenditures as well as all economic agreements made to suppliers or contractors in the contract document or customer orders, which will be entered inside the books of accounts unless the expenses are paid. However, simply reviewing the accounting information may give the appearance that the business has more funds than is easily accessible (Smith et al., 1986).

3.5.2. Earned Value Management Model

Earned value management (EVM) is a method for evaluating project outcomes that include scale, schedule, and actual costs. Provided a cost performance benchmark, project team members can compare real statistics to the benchmark to evaluate how the program is achieving dimension, schedule, and budget goals. A foundation is the initial development estimate number minus any allowed adjustments. Real data comprises the degree to which a WBS component was finished, the amount of labor performed, whenever the work commenced and ended, and what the finished product paid (Qian & Xu, 1998; Liu & Wang, 2014).

Previously, generated quality planning was exclusively employed on key government projects. Nowadays, nevertheless, an increasing number of businesses appreciate the significance of employing a such tool to manage expenditures. Indeed, a conversation between many academics specialists in cash flow management and a real-world professional indicated the necessity to define how to compute income statements. Brenda Taylor, a professional project coordinator with P2 Project Management Systems in Johannesburg, South Africa, challenged the reliability of determining income statements by simply multiplying the quantity of the intended value to come by a percentage of the entire worth. Margaret proposed instead that the rate of achievement, as indicated above. Cost-benefit management entails computing three values for every action or summarizing function on a project WBS (Zhang et al., 2011; Xiao et al., 2020) (Figure 3.11).

The planned value (PV) is the percentage of the overall projected cost scheduled to be expended on an operation within a given period, often known as the budget (Zhang et al., 2016). One instance using cost-benefit computations is shown in Table 3.2. Assume a program comprised of the summarized action of buying and deploying a new online server. Assume that, based on the blueprint, this would take one week and cost $10,000 in labor time, equipment, and application.

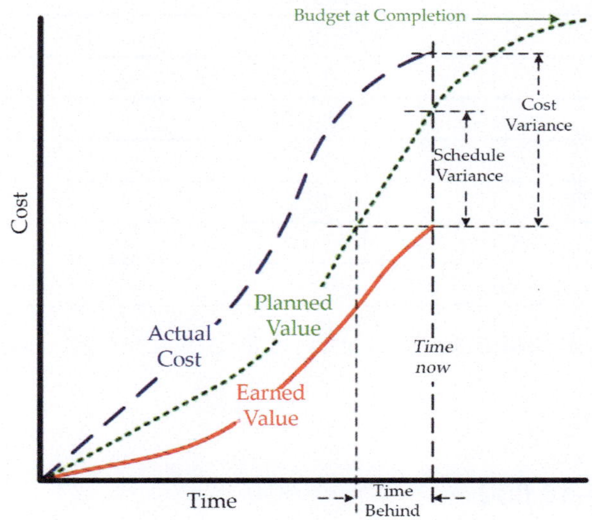

Figure 3.11. The explanation of earned value management (Source: Hany Ismail, Creative Commons License).

Therefore, the PV for the activity that week is $10,000.

The actual cost (AC) is indeed the entire both direct and indirect expenditures involved in completing work on a topic throughout a specific period (Jurison, 1999; Tohidi, 2011). Assume that purchasing and installing the new online servers took two weeks and spent $20,000 in total. Suppose that $15,000 of these real costs were expended in Week 1 and $5,000 in Week 2. These are weekly real costs (AC) for the activities.

The earned value (EV) is an assessment of the real worth of the physical labor accomplished. The originally anticipated expenses for the project or initiative, as well as the rate at that the group has completed the project's work or interaction to date, are used to calculate EV. Its rate of performance (RP) is the ratio of the actual services done to the proportion of scheduled activities to be performed at any particular point in the project or project's life cycle (Lee et al., 2012; Durney & Donnelly, 2015). Assume, for illustration, that the computer deployment was halfway finished at the conclusion of Week 1. The percentage of accomplishment would be 50% since the anticipated timetable indicates that the project should be completed by the conclusion of Week 1, but only 50% of the labor has indeed been accomplished. As shown in Table 3.2 the cost-benefit estimation after one week would be $5,000.

Table 3.2. Earned Value Calculations for One Activity After Week 1 (Source: Kathy Schwalbe, Creative Commons License)

Activity	Week 1
Earned value (EV)	5,000
Planned value (PV)	10,000
Actual cost (AC)	15,000
Cost variance (CV)	10,000
Schedule variance (SV)	5,000
Cost performance index (CPI)	33%
Schedule performance index (SPI)	50%

The earned value calculations in Table 3.2 are carried out as follows (Rodríguez et al., 2017):

EV =10,000 * 50% = 5,000

CV =5,000 *15,000 =-10,000

SV =5,000 –10,000 = –5,000

CPI =5,000/15,000 =-33%

SPI = 5,000/10,000 =-50%

Table 3.3. Outlines the Earned Value Management Method (Source: Kathy Schwalbe, Creative Commons License)

Team	Formula
Earned Value (EV)	EV= PV to date * RP
Cost Variance (CV)	CV =EV - AC
Schedule (SV)	SV =EV - PV
Cost Performance Index (CPI)	CPI = EV/AC
Schedule Performance Index (SPI)	SPI = EV/PV
Estimate at Completion (EAC)	EAC=BAC/CPI
Estimated time to complete	Original time estimate/SPI

Table 3.3 outlines the earned value management methods it is worth noting that the formulae for variations and indices begin with EV or investment appraisal. An index is computed by subtracting the EV from the real price or intended value. Deviations are estimated by subtracting the real price or desired profit from the EV. After totaling the EV, AC, and PV information for all project tasks, you can use the CPI and SPI to forecast how much it will price and how it will take to complete the task based on past performance. Using the budget

at accomplishment and the initial time assessment, reduce by the relevant ratio to compute the guesstimate at accomplishment (EAC) and projected time to finish, maintaining the very same performances. The phrases projected time to finish and preliminary time estimation do not have standardized abbreviations (Keil et al., 1994; Agarwal & Rathod, 2006).

- *Cost variance (CV)*: is indeed the difference between the cash flows and the actual cost. If indeed the variance is negative, it signifies that the operation cost is higher than expected. If indeed the cost variance is favorable, the operation will price less as expected.
- *Schedule variance (SV):* the difference between the achieved and anticipated values. A negative variance indicates that the job was more time-consuming than expected, whereas a positive variance indicates that the job took less time than anticipated.
- *The cost performance index (CPI):* It is the proportion of planned value to real cost; it could be used to determine the project's overall price (Czuchra, 1999; Taylor et al., 2012). If the CPI is one, or 100%, the expected and actual expenses are identical, indicating that the expenses are precise as anticipated (Figure 3.12).

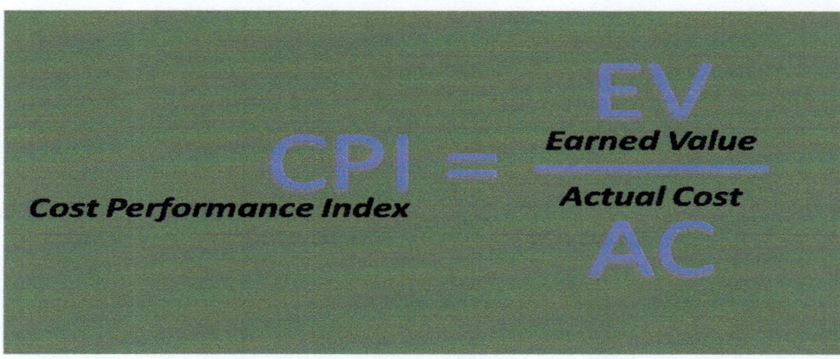

Figure 3.12. Schematic of cost performance index formula (Source: Megan Bell, Created Commons License).

If the CPI is less than one or less than 100%, the project is over budget. If the CPI is greater than one or more than 100%, the project is under budget. It can calculate the estimated duration required to accomplish the assignment (Khatibi, 2020; Hartman & Ashrafi, 2002). An SPI of one, or 100%, indicates that the project is on track comparable to the cost performance measure. If the SPI is higher than one or 100%, then the project is on schedule. If the SPI is much less than one or equal to one hundred percent, the operation is behind budget. It should be noted that negative statistics for cost and time variation generally signal issues in those areas. Negative figures indicate that the operation is spending more than anticipated or consuming longer than anticipated. Similarly, a CPI and SPI of less than or less than 100% suggest issues. The price weighting factor can be utilized to compute the estimated conclusion (EAC), which is the cost of completing the project based on past results. Conversely, the timetable performance can be utilized to predict how long it will take to complete the project (Wysock et al., 1995; Procaccino & Verner, 2006)

Cost-benefit data can be graphed to monitor the performance of the project. Figure 3.13 depicts a five-month cost-benefit graph for just a one-year program. So because data was gathered or approximated at that moment, the real cost and product profitability columns terminate at 5 months. The graph contains three lines and two points, as seen below:

- *Planned value (PV):* The total sum budgeted for all programs monthly. It should be noted that the intended values line continues for the projected duration of the task and terminates at the BAC endpoint (Dos Santos & Sussman, 2000).
- *Actual cost (AC):* The total monthly real expenditures for all operations.
- *Earned value (EV):* The total earning worth for all actions every month.

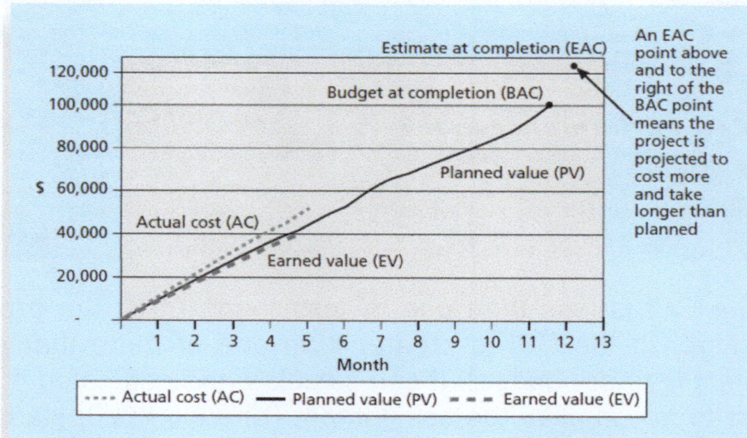

Figure 3.13. Illustration of earned value chart for the project after five months of a certain company (Source: Jack T. Marchewka, Creative Commons License).

- *Budget at completion (BAC):* The initial planning overall budget, or $100,000 in this case. On the graph, the BAC breakpoint is drawn at the approximate project timeline of twelve months.
- *Estimate at completion (EAC):* In this example, the price

is calculated to be $122,308. That figure is determined by taking the BAC, in this example $100,000, and dividing it by the CPI, which was 81.761%. This EAC point is defined on the chart with an expected completion time of 12.74 months. This figure is determined by taking the previous rough guesstimate, which in this case was 12 months, and dividing it by the SPI, which in this case was 94.203%. Displaying earned value data in chart form allows you to see how the status of the project. For example, by glancing at the intended value line, you may see the decision in order. If all goes according to plan, the project will be completed in 12 months and will cost $100,000.

Figure 3.14 shows that the current cost line has always been on and above the cost-benefit lines, indicating that costs are equal to or higher than expected. The projected includes credit is similar to the cost-benefit line and has risen somewhat in the last quarter.

This relationship indicates that now the project was on track until the final quarter when it slipped beyond budget. Great executives in charge of several start operations prefer to examine performance measurements in graph format, including the cost-benefit chart shown in Figure 3.14. In the first scenario, government leaders were analyzing cost-benefit maps and EACs for a range of projects. Cost-benefit charts provide a fast view of how initiatives are progressing (Quinn & Baily, 1994). If major cost and time execution issues arise, top management may opt to cancel initiatives or take alternative corrective measures. The EACs are significant budget decision-making inputs, particularly when overall budgets are low. Whenever utilized properly, generated value engineering is a significant strategy since it assists top and project managers in assessing progress and making informed managerial decisions. For more knowledge and computations regarding cash flows, read the PMBOK® Handbook and other references.

Why doesn't each Organization employ achieved value engineering because it is such an effective cost-cutting weapon? Why do numerous federal programs require it but so few business ventures? The concentration of EVM on measuring true results against intended performances, as well as the relevance of implementing the appropriate data in generating computations, is two explanations. Because many initiatives, especially IT developments, lack solid information, tracking progress against a plan may yield deceptive results. On IT initiatives, several budget plans are typically created, and regular monitoring of both the most recent projected cost and the accompanying real expenses can be difficult. Furthermore, calculating the percentage of tasks completed may yield deceptive results. What exactly does it imply to claim that a task is 75% completed after 3 months? This is not always comparable with declaring the task will be done in one week or after investing an additional 25% of the original expenditure.

Organizations can reduce the amount of information in the management of earned value to make it easier to use while still reaping the advantages of the strategy (Broadbent & Weill, 1997). You can, for instance, use implement the appropriate statistics such as 0% for things not yet commenced, 50% for things in operation, and 100% for finished activities. In this modified implementation the appropriate statistics should include enough summarized data to enable managers to assess how well the program is working overall, as provided as the program is outlined in sufficient depth. Using all these simple percentage full numbers, you may obtain reasonably precise overall project performance metrics. For instance, for a one-year 1% failure rate, use simple percentage correct numbers.

Balanced scorecard information can only be entered and collected at the WBS overview layer. Learned quality planning is frequently discussed by Quentin Fleming, author of the book Cost Benefit Project Management$_{18}$. Several people are expressing expressed dissatisfaction with the difficulty of gathering such comprehensive information.

Remember

It is essential to remember that estimations are at the center of EVM

Fleming & Koppelman (1996) shows that achieved value management does not require information to be collected at the packet level. It is critical to have a WBS that is distributable, and so many WBS elements might summarize numerous sub-deliverables. For illustration, you might just have a work breakdown structure (WBS) for a household that contains aspects for every room. Rather than attempting to gather specific information for each element in the space, such as carpeting, furnishings, and illumination, pay fees earned data and insights for each room will provide valuable information.

The complete EVM process starts with estimation; if the guesstimate is incorrect, all computations will be incorrect (Maizlish & Handler, 2005; Huang et al., 2006). When attempting to employ EVM, a company must first learn to produce precise predictions. The major mechanism for combining productivity, cost, and scheduling information is generated value engineering (Aral & Weill, 2007). It could be a valuable tool for the project's management and top management in assessing the performance of the project (McAfee, 2006; Guo et al., 2014). Columns for gathering cost-benefit and reports that compute deviation statistics are included in project management systems such as Projects 2010. Project 2010 also enables you to create a cost-benefit chart, comparable to the one shown in Figure 3.14, while having to import the information into Microsoft Excel.

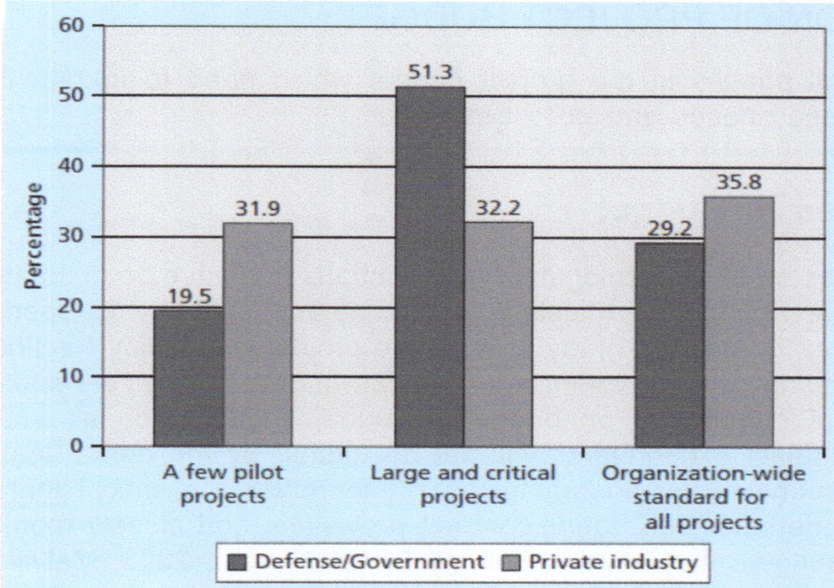

Figure 3.14. Illustration of earned value usage chart of project 2010 (Source: Jack T. Marchewka, Creative Commons License).

3.5.3. Budget Analysis

Determine the reasons for the departures from the strategy. Significant departures from the budgeted baseline must be investigated to identify what produced the discrepancy so that efforts can be made to avoid a repeat of the scenario in the present or with similar works (Yang et al., 2008; Ashrafi & Mueller, 2015).

- *Forecasting:* Earned Value enables the project coordinator to anticipate the final construction cost and timeline results. With Earned, the enterprise does not have to wait until it is nearly finished to discover that there is a cost issue. Generated Value provides a program manager with an "early warning" indication in time to take remedial action and impact the official outcome (Coff, 1997; Rosacker & Rosacker 2010).
- *What if Scenario Analysis:* Scenario planning employs statistical formulas to assist managers in getting the results depending on multiple different possibilities; a project manager can use a worksheet and enter distinct values to calculate the effect on the cost for diverse circumstances ranging from continuing to increase persons to decrease project completion time to the implication for the budget predicated on currency movements.

3.6. UPDATION OF PROJECT BUDGET

There are several phases in the project budget which need to update from time to time. These phases are as follows.

3.6.1. Changes in Budget

Financial upgrades result from budgetary modifications that have been adopted. With most initiatives, budgetary adjustments must be authorized by the sponsor; but, in rare cases, the donation may provide the project with a tiny fraction to cover minor spending cuts (Flyvbjerg et al., 2022). In other cases, the sponsor may impose tight constraints on budgetary modifications, such as stating that any illegal project expenditures will not be funded by the donor, leaving the company responsible for absorbing those expenses. It is critical that the project leader understand the donor contract provisions and closely monitors the account or budgets that have limitations (Jeyaraj et al., 2006; Melville et al., 2004). Failure to do so could result in group and program consequences.

Other forms of adjustments result from external factors which may restrict the project's operations or activities (Jørgensen, 2003). In the instance that a particular project is canceled due to political disturbance or another significant event, your project leader may demand that money previously allotted for that engagement be moved to another activity on which the project can still operate (Hodgson & Drummond, 2009). Other adjustments can result from the donor, which might also decrease the planned budget for the project, either from currency movements, which affect the funds' facilities available (Jørgensen & Moløkken-Østvold, 2006). Annual budgetary modifications must be reported in the organization's monetary system, and the latest project financial statements must reflect this modification (Gammage, 2011; Andrić et al., 2019).

3.6.2. Corrective Action Implication

Some forms of modifications result from external forces that may restrict the project's ability to carry out required operations or tasks (Foote & Halawi, 2018). Civil disturbance or another major event may result in the termination of project tasks; in this instance, the project leader may demand that the money previously allocated for that engagement be moved to some other activity on which the program can still operate. Additional modifications are made by the sponsor, who could cut the planned budget for the project, or by currency movements, that influence the project's available funding (Verhoef & Lemon, 2013). Adjustments to the budgets that have been authorized must be reported in the organization's monetary systems and the latest project financial statements must represent this modification (DiPrete & Buchmann, 2006; Ramos & Mota, 2014). Control measures may be via the use of different scenarios to create the same outcome with input variables. The program manager will apply the corrective measures and evaluate their performance and identify whether they are good at relieving the cost of the project and regaining motivation to exert (Gemino et al., 2007). Corrective measures must be discussed with the development team and those in command of the tasks for modifications to be executed.

3.7. OTHER EXPENDITURES

Resource expenses comprise indirect labor, equipment, consumables, and stockpiles in addition to direct labor (Kinsella 2002). To establish the total project budget, we must incorporate additional expenses. These costs consist of (De Reyck et al., 2005):

- *Indirect costs*: These expenditures comprise rental, electricity, security, and additional administrative costs (Alhawari et al., 2012). For instance, a consulting company may spend $150 per specialist per session. Included in that agreed amount would be the compensation and perks of the advisor plus sufficient headroom to help alleviate the organizational and operational expenses needed to operate the consultancy business.
- *Sunk costs*: Investments that have already been committed before the current undertaking are sunk costs (Stewart, 2008). The latest attempt to construct a software application, for instance, may have failed after 3 months and $200,000 of effort. This $250,000 is a sunk cost, independent of whether any research from the past work can be salvaged or is useful to the construction job.
- *Learning curve*: Frequently, we must "make one and toss it away" to fully comprehend an issue or employ new technology. Furthermore, untrained individuals will make errors, as well as the learning basics curve for new technology, was typically considerable. Consequently, time and effort may be lost. This time should indeed be accounted for in the development's timeline or budgeting (McNish, 2001).
- *Reserves*: Resources give a cushion for unforeseen circumstances. Risk-based contingencies offer the general contractor a range of options. Alternatively, a cost estimate might incorporate some operational alternatives. Resources represent a trade-off. A shrewd project manager will

ACTIVITY 1.1.

Suppose you are starting an IT project in a construction company. Develop a budget plan for the IT project, keeping in view the basic principles of the budget management.

incorporate a reasonable reserve in the development's expenditure, even if top management or the customer considers these items to be unnecessary fat that could be removed from the spending plan. For instance, it would have been unfortunate if the project budget did not enable the project manager to occasionally buy pizza or dinner for the group as a treat for meeting a significant milestone late at night.

SUMMARY

Information technology projects are expensive and complex. They often require a significant investment of time and money. When it comes to budgeting for an IT project, there are a few key things to keep in mind. First, be realistic about the costs. It is important to have a clear understanding of all of the costs associated with the project, both upfront and ongoing. This includes hardware, software, licensing, and support costs. Second, allocate enough money to cover contingencies. No project ever goes exactly as planned, so it is important to have a cushion in the budget to cover unexpected costs. Third, have a clear plan for how the budget will be managed. This includes who will be responsible for tracking costs and approving expenditures. It is also important to have a process in place for managing changes to the budget. Fourth, be flexible. The budget for an IT project is never set in stone. As the project progresses, there may be changes to the scope or the budget. It is important to be flexible and adjust the budget as needed. Fifth, communicate the budget. The budget should be communicated to all stakeholders, including upper management, the project team, and vendors.

REVIEW QUESTIONS

1. What is the role of budget management in information technology projects?
2. What are the key considerations for developing an accurate project budget?
3. How can project managers effectively control project costs?
4. What are the techniques for effective variance analysis and cost control?
5. What are some of the common pitfalls in budget management and how can they be avoided?

MULTIPLE CHOICE QUESTIONS

1. What is the most important factor to consider when creating a budget for an IT project?

a. The cost of the project

b. The resources required

a. The timeline

b. The ROI

2. How can you ensure that your IT project stays within budget?

a. Unforeseen costs

b. By tracking spending and making adjustments as needed

c. The cost of the project

d. All of the above

3. **What is the common cause of IT project budget overruns?**
   a. Unforeseen costs
   b. Set a clear and concise scope
   c. The timeline
   d. All of the above
4. **What can you do to prevent scope creep from happening on your IT project?**
   a. By absorbing the cost into the overall budget
   b. By careful planning
   c. Communicate the scope to all project team members
   d. All of the above
5. **What is the best way to handle unexpected costs on an IT project?**
   a. By absorbing the cost into the overall budget
   b. Cutting costs in other areas to make up for the unexpected cost
   c. Negotiating with vendors to get a lower price
   d. All of the above
6. **What is the best way to stay within budget on an IT project?**
   a. By careful planning
   b. Negotiating with vendors to get a lower price
   c. By absorbing the cost into the overall budget
   d. All of the above
7. **What are some common causes of IT project delays?**
   a. Unforeseen costs
   b. Scope creep
   c. Poor planning
   d. All of the above
8. **What can you do to prevent scope creep from happening on your IT project?**
   a. Set a clear and concise scope
   b. Get sign-off from all stakeholders on the scope

c. Communicate the scope to all project team members

d. All of the above

9. What is the best way to handle unexpected costs on an IT project?

a. By absorbing the cost into the overall budget

b. By using cost-effective resources

c. By careful planning

d. All of the above

10. What is the best way to stay within budget on an IT project?

a. By careful planning

b. By monitoring spending and making adjustments as needed

c. By using cost-effective resources

d. All of the above

Answers to Multiple Choice Questions

1. (a) 2. (b) 3. (a) 4. (c) 5. (a)

6. (a) 7. (d) 8. (d) 9. (a) 10. (d)

REFERENCES

1. Addison, T., & Vallabh, S. (2002, September). Controlling software project risks: an empirical study of methods used by experienced project managers. In *Proceedings of the 2002 Annual Research Conference of the South African Institute of Computer Scientists and Information Technologists on Enablement Through Technology* (Vol. 1, pp. 128–140).
2. Agarwal, N., & Rathod, U. (2006). Defining 'success' for software projects: An exploratory revelation. *International Journal of Project Management, 24*(4), 358–370.
3. Ahuja, H. N., Dozzi, S. P., & Abourizk, S. M. (1994). *Project Management: Techniques in Planning and Controlling Construction Projects*. John Wiley & Sons, Second Edition, pp. 3–9.
4. Alhawari, S., Karadsheh, L., Talet, A. N., & Mansour, E. (2012). Knowledge-based risk management framework for information technology project. *International Journal of Information Management, 32*(1), 50–65.
5. Al-Jibouri, S. H. (2003). Monitoring systems and their effectiveness for project cost control in construction. *International Journal of Project Management, 21*(2), 145–154.

6. Aminbakhsh, S., Gunduz, M., & Sonmez, R. (2013). Safety risk assessment using analytic hierarchy process (AHP) during planning and budgeting of construction projects. *Journal of safety research, 46*, 99–105.
7. Andrić, J. M., Mahamadu, A. M., Wang, J., Zou, P. X., & Zhong, R. (2019). The cost performance and causes of overruns in infrastructure development projects in Asia. *Journal of Civil Engineering and Management, 25*(3), 203–214.
8. Aral, S., & Weill, P. (2007). IT assets, organizational capabilities, and firm performance: How resource allocations and organizational differences explain performance variation. *Organization Science, 18*(5), 763–780.
9. Ashrafi, R., & Mueller, J. (2015). Delineating IT resources and capabilities to obtain competitive advantage and improve firm performance. *Information Systems Management, 32*(1), 15–38.
10. Baccarini, D., Salm, G., & Love, P. E. (2004). Management of risks in information technology projects. *Industrial Management & Data Systems,* Third edition, pp. 3–9.
11. Bakke, N. A., & Hellberg, R. (1991). Relevance lost? A critical discussion of different cost accounting principles in connection with decision-making for both short and long-term production scheduling. *International Journal of Production Economics, 24*(1–2), 1–18.
12. Becker, S. D. (2014). When organizations deinstitutionalise control practices: A multiple-case study of budget abandonment. European Accounting Review, 23(4), 593–623.
13. Ben-Arieh, D., & Qian, L. (2003). Activity-based cost management for the design and development stage. *International Journal of Production Economics, 83*(2), 169–183.
14. Bennatan, E. M. (1996). *On-Time, Within-Budget Software Project Management Practices, and Techniques*. John Wiley & Sons, Inc. (Vol. 1, pp. 3–9).
15. Bloch, M., Blumberg, S., & Laartz, J. (2012). Delivering large-scale IT projects on time, on budget, and value. *Harvard Business Review, 5*(1), 2–7.
16. Bode, J. (1998). Decision support with neural networks in the management of research and development: Concepts and application to cost estimation. *Information & Management, 34*(1), 33–40.
17. Bogoslavtseva, L. V., Karepina, O. I., Bogdanova, O. Y., Takmazyan, A. S., & Terentieva, V. V. (2019, April). Development of the program and project budgeting in the conditions of digitization of the budget process. In *Institute of Scientific Communications Conference* (Vol. 1, pp. 950–959). Springer, Cham.
18. Broadbent, M., & Weill, P. (1997). Management by the maxim: how business and IT managers can create IT infrastructures. *Sloan Management Review, 38*, 77–92.
19. Busachi, A., Erkoyuncu, J., Colegrove, P., Martina, F., Watts, C., & Drake, R. (2017). A review of Additive Manufacturing technology and Cost Estimation techniques for the defense sector. *CIRP Journal of Manufacturing Science and Technology, 19,* 117–128.

20. Cagliano, A. C., Grimaldi, S., & Rafele, C. (2015). Choosing project risk management techniques. A theoretical framework. *Journal of Risk Research, 18*(2), 232–248.
21. Carvalho, M. M. D., & Rabechini Junior, R. (2015). Impact of risk management on project performance: the importance of soft skills. *International Journal of Production Research, 53*(2), 321–340.
22. Chua, D. K. H., Kog, Y. C., Loh, P. K., & Jaselskis, E. J. (1997). Model for construction budget performance—Neural network approach. *Journal of Construction Engineering and Management, 123*(3), 214–222.
23. Coff, R. W. (1997). Human assets and management dilemmas: Coping with hazards on the road to resource-based theory. *Academy of Management Review, 22*(2), 374–402.
24. Conboy, K. (2010). Project failure en masse: a study of loose budgetary control in ISD projects. *European Journal of Information Systems, 19*(3), 273–287.
25. Cools, M., Stouthuysen, K., & Van den Abbeele, A. (2017). Management control for stimulating different types of creativity: The role of budgets. *Journal of Management Accounting Research, 29*(3), 1–21.
26. Cozzolino, J. M. (1979). Controlling risk in capital budgeting: practical use of utility theory for measurement and control of petroleum exploration risk. *The Engineering Economist, 25*(3), 161–186.
27. Czuchra, W. (1999). Optimizing budget spending for software implementation and testing. Computers & operations research, 26(7), 731–747.
28. Datta, P. P., & Roy, R. (2010). Cost modeling techniques for availability type service support contracts: A literature review and empirical study. *CIRP Journal of Manufacturing Science and Technology, 3*(2), 142–157.
29. Davila, A., Foster, G., & Li, M. (2009). Reasons for management control systems adoption: Insights from product development systems choice by early-stage entrepreneurial companies. *Accounting, Organizations and Society, 34*(3–4), 322–347.
30. Davila, T. (2000). An empirical study on the drivers of management control systems design in new product development. *Accounting, Organizations and Society, 25*(4–5), 383–409.
31. De Bakker, K., Boonstra, A., & Wortmann, H. (2010). Does risk management contribute to IT project success? A meta-analysis of empirical evidence. *International Journal of Project Management*, *28*(5), 493–503.
32. de Bakker, K., Boonstra, A., & Wortmann, H. (2012). Risk management's communicative effects influencing IT project success. *International Journal of Project Management, 30*(4), 444–457.
33. De Reyck, B., Grushka-Cockayne, Y., Lockett, M., Calderini, S. R., Moura, M., & Sloper, A. (2005). The impact of project portfolio management on information technology projects. *International Journal of Project Management, 23*(7), 524–537.

34. DeMarco, T., & Lister, T. (2013). *Waltzing with Bears: Managing Risk on Software Projects*. Addison-Wesley (Vol. 1, pp. 1–10).
35. Didraga, O. (2013). The role and the effects of risk management in IT project success. Informatica *Economica, 17*(1).
36. DiPrete, T. A., & Buchmann, C. (2006). Gender-specific trends in the value of education and the emerging gender gap in college completion. *Demography, 43*(1), 1–24.
37. Dos Santos, B., & Sussman, L. (2000). Improving the return on IT investment: the productivity paradox. *International Journal of Information Management, 20*(6), 429–440.
38. Dougherty, M. J., Klase, K. A., & Song, S. G. (2003). Managerial necessity and the art of creating surpluses: The budget-execution process in West Virginia cities. *Public Administration Review, 63*(4), 484–497.
39. Durney, C. P., & Donnelly, R. G. (2015). Managing the effects of rapid technological change on complex information technology projects. *Journal of the Knowledge Economy, 6*(4), 641–664.
40. Dwivedi, Y. K., Venkitachalam, K., Sharif, A. M., Al-Karaghouli, W., & Weerakkody, V. (2011). Research trends in knowledge management: Analyzing the past and predicting the future. Information Systems Management, 28(1), 43–56.
41. Erkoyuncu, J. A., Roy, R., Shehab, E., & Cheruvu, K. (2011). Understanding service uncertainties in industrial product–service system cost estimation. *The International Journal of Advanced Manufacturing Technology, 52*(9), 1223–1238.
42. Faleti, K. O., Faleti, H. O., & Ojeleke, R. O. (2014). Budgetary and management control system for improved efficiency in Public Sector: The implications of "Babariga-Style" Budgeting approach. *Scholary Journal of Business Administration, 4*(2), 44–52.
43. Fayaz, A., Kamal, Y., Amin, S., & Khan, S. (2017). Critical success factors in information technology projects. *Management Science Letters, 7*(2), 73–80.
44. Field, F., Kirchain, R., & Roth, R. (2007). Process cost modeling: Strategic engineering and economic evaluation of materials technologies. *Jom, 59*(10), 21–32.
45. Fleming, Q. W., & Koppelman, J. M. (1996). Integrated project development teams: another fad… or a permanent change. *International Journal of Project Management, 14*(3), 163–168.
46. Flyvbjerg, B., Budzier, A., Lee, J. S., Keil, M., Lunn, D., & Bester, D. W. (2022). The Empirical Reality of IT Project Cost Overruns: Discovering A Power-Law Distribution. *Journal of Management Information Systems, 39*(3), 607–639.
47. Foote, A., & Halawi, L. A. (2018). Knowledge management models within information technology projects. *Journal of Computer Information Systems, 58*(1), 89–97.
48. Gammage, M. (2011). Why your IT project may be riskier than you think. Harvard Business Review, 89(11), 22–22.
49. Gemino, A., Reich, B. H., & Sauer, C. (2007). A temporal model of information technology project performance. *Journal of Management Information Systems, 24*(3), 9–44.

50. Griffin, R. C. (1998). The fundamental principles of cost-benefit analysis. *Water Resources Research, 34*(8), 2063–2071.

51. Grishunin, S., Suloeva, S., & Nekrasova, T. (2018). Development of the mechanism of risk-adjusted scheduling and cost budgeting of R&D projects in telecommunications. In *The Internet of Things, Smart Spaces, and Next Generation Networks and Systems* (Second Edition, pp. 456–470). Springer, Cham.

52. Günaydın, H. M., & Doğan, S. Z. (2004). A neural network approach for early cost estimation of structural systems of buildings. *International Journal of Project Management, 22*(7), 595–602.

53. Guo, T., Sharma, U., Shenoy, P., Wood, T., & Sahu, S. (2014). Cost-aware cloud bursting for enterprise applications. *ACM Transactions on Internet Technology (TOIT), 13*(3), 1–24.

54. Hale, G. E., & Douglass, S. R. (1977). The politics of budget execution: Financial manipulation in state and local government. *Administration & Society, 9*(3), 367–378.

55. Hall, J. H. (2000). Investigating aspects of the capital budgeting process used in the evaluation of investment projects. *South African Journal of Economic and Management Sciences, 3*(3), 353–368.

56. Hartman, F., & Ashrafi, R. A. (2002). Project management in the information systems and information technologies industries. *Project Management Journal, 33*(3), 5–15.

57. Higdon, J., & Topp, R. (2004). How to develop a budget for a research proposal. *Western Journal of Nursing Research, 26*(8), 922–929.

58. Hodgson, J., & Drummond, H. (2009). Learning from fiasco: what causes decision error and how to avoid it. *Journal of General Management, 35*(2), 81–92.

59. Huang, S. M., Ou, C. S., Chen, C. M., & Lin, B. (2006). An empirical study of the relationship between IT investment and firm performance: A resource-based perspective. *European Journal of Operational Research, 173*(3), 984–999.

60. Huang, X. X., Newnes, L. B., & Parry, G. C. (2012). The adaptation of product cost estimation techniques to estimate the cost of service. *International Journal of Computer Integrated Manufacturing, 25*(4–5), 417–431.

61. Huntzinger, J. (2012). Limited Production Principles: Right-Sizing for Effective Lean Operations and Cost Management. *Lean Accounting: Best Practices for Sustainable Integration, 1,* 17–41.

62. Isaac, L., Lawal, M., & Okoli, T. (2015). A systematic review of budgeting and budgetary control in government-owned organizations. *Research Journal of Finance and Accounting, 6*(6), 1–11.

63. Ivanova, O. B., Bogoslavtseva, L. V., Karepina, O. I., & Kostoglodova, E. D. (2017). Providing the budget transparency and state projects efficiency monitoring in Russia, (Vol. 1, pp. 2–9).

64. Jani, A. (2011). Escalation of commitment in troubled IT projects: Influence of project risk factors and self-efficacy on the perception of risk and the commitment to a failing

project. *International Journal of Project Management, 29*(7), 934–945.

65. Jasch, C. M. (2008). *Environmental and Material Flow Cost Accounting: Principles and Procedures* (Vol. 25, pp. 2–9). Springer Science & Business Media.
66. Jeyaraj, A., Rottman, J. W., & Lacity, M. C. (2006). A review of the predictors, linkages, and biases in IT innovation adoption research. *Journal of Information Technology, 21*(1), 1–23.
67. Jørgensen, M. (2003). How much does a vacation cost? Or what is a software cost estimate? *ACM SIGSOFT Software Engineering Notes, 28*(6), 5–5.
68. Jørgensen, M., & Moløkken-Østvold, K. (2006). How large are software cost overruns? A review of the 1994 CHAOS report. *Information and Software Technology, 48*(4), 297–301.
69. Jurison, J. (1999). Software project management: the manager's view. *Communications of the association for Information Systems, 2*(1), pp. 17.
70. Karner, A., Brower Brown, K., Marcantonio, R., & Alcorn, L. G. (2019). The view from the top of Arnstein's ladder: Participatory budgeting and the promise of community control. *Journal of the American Planning Association, 85*(3), 236–254.
71. Keil, M., Mixon, R., Saarinen, T., & Tuunainen, V. (1994). Understanding runaway information technology projects: Results from an international research program based on escalation theory. *Journal of Management Information Systems, 11*(3), 65–85.
72. Kerzner, H. (2002). *Strategic Planning for Project Management Using a Project Management Maturity Model*. John Wiley & Sons (Vol. 1, pp. 4–8).
73. Khadra, H. A., Al-Hayale, T., & Al-Nasir, N. (2012). Contingent effects of system development life cycle critical success factors on accounting information system effectiveness: Using balance scorecard perspectives—Empirical study applied on the Jordanian industrial companies. *International Journal of Information Technology Project Management (IJITPM), 3*(2), 38–61.
74. Khatibi Bardsiri, A. (2020). An intelligent model to predict the development time and budget of software projects. *International Journal of Nonlinear Analysis and Applications, 11*(2), 85–102.
75. Kingsman, B. G., & de Souza, A. A. (1997). A knowledge-based decision support system for cost estimation and pricing decisions in versatile manufacturing companies. *International Journal of Production Economics, 53*(2), 119–139.
76. Kivilä, J., Martinsuo, M., & Vuorinen, L. (2017). Sustainable project management through project control in infrastructure projects. *International Journal of Project Management, 35*(6), 1167–1183.
77. Kutsch, E., & Hall, M. (2005). Intervening conditions on the management of project risk: Dealing with uncertainty in information technology projects. *International Journal of Project Management, 23*(8), 591–599.
78. Kutsch, E., & Hall, M. (2009). The rational choice of not applying project risk management in information technology projects. *Project Management Journal, 40*(3), 72–81.

79. Laframboise, K., Croteau, A. M., Beaudry, A., & Manovas, M. (2007). Interdepartmental knowledge transfer success during information technology projects. *International Journal of Knowledge Management (IJKM), 3*(2), 47–67.
80. Lappe, M., & Spang, K. (2014). Investments in project management are profitable: A case study-based analysis of the relationship between the costs and benefits of project management. *International Journal of Project Management, 32*(4), 603–612.
81. Laslo, Z., & Gurevich, G. (2014). Enhancing project on time within budget performance by implementing proper control routines. *Management: Journal of Sustainable Business and Management Solutions in Emerging Economies, 19*(72), 53–69.
82. Layer, A., Brinke, E. T., Houten, F. V., Kals, H., & Haasis, S. (2002). Recent and future trends in cost estimation. *International Journal of Computer Integrated Manufacturing, 15*(6), 499–510.
83. Lee, J. S., Keil, M., & Kasi, V. (2012). The effect of an initial budget and schedule goal on software project escalation. *Journal of Management Information Systems, 29*(1), 53–78.
84. Lee, L. H., Chen, C. H., Chew, E. P., Li, J., Pujowidianto, N. A., & Zhang, S. (2010). A review of optimal computing budget allocation algorithms for a simulation optimization problem. *International Journal of Operations Research, 7*(2), 19–31.
85. Liu, S., & Deng, Z. (2015). How environment risks moderate the effect of control on performance in information technology projects: Perspectives of project managers and user liaisons. *International Journal of Information Management, 35*(1), 80–97.
86. Liu, S., & Wang, L. (2014). Understanding the impact of risks on performance in internal and outsourced information technology projects: The role of strategic importance. *International Journal of Project Management, 32*(8), 1494–1510.
87. Lyneis, J. M., Cooper, K. G., & Els, S. A. (2001). Strategic management of complex projects: a case study using system dynamics. *System Dynamics Review: The Journal of the System Dynamics Society, 17*(3), 237–260.
88. Maizlish, B., & Handler, R. (2005). *IT (information technology) Portfolio Management Step-By-Step: Unlocking the Business Value of Technology*. John Wiley & Sons, (Vol. 1, pp. 4–7).
89. McAfee, A. (2006). Mastering the three worlds of information technology. *Harvard Business Review, 84*(11), 141.
90. McNish, M. (2001). Guidelines for managing change: A study of their effects on the implementation of new information technology projects in organizations. *Journal of Change Management, 2*(3), 201–211.
91. Melville, N., Kraemer, K., & Gurbaxani, V. (2004). Information technology and organizational performance: An integrative model of IT business value. *MIS Quarterly, 1,* 283–322.
92. Mishakova, A., Vakhrushkina, A., Murgul, V., & Sazonova, T. (2016). Project control based on a mutual application of pert and earned value management methods.

Procedia Engineering, 165, 1812–1817.

93. Mohamed, I. A., Evans, K., & Tirimba, O. I. (2015). Analysis of the effectiveness of budgetary control techniques on organizational performance at Dara-Salaam bank headquarters in Hargeisa Somaliland. *International Journal of Business Management and Economic Research (IJBMER), 6*(6), 327–340.
94. Morozov, V., Kalnichenko, O., Timinsky, A., & Liubyma, I. (2017, September). Projects change management is based on project configuration management for developing complex projects. In *2017 9th IEEE International Conference on Intelligent Data Acquisition and Advanced Computing Systems: Technology and Applications (IDAACS)* (Vol. 2, pp. 939–941). IEEE.
95. Munns, A. K., & Bjeirmi, B. F. (1996). The role of project management in achieving project success. *International Journal of Project Management, 14*(2), 81–87.
96. Nguyen, N. M., Killen, C. P., Kock, A., & Gemünden, H. G. (2018). The use of effectuation in projects: The influence of business case-control, portfolio monitoring intensity, and project innovativeness. *International Journal of Project Management, 36*(8), 1054–1067.
97. Nikias, A. D. (2019). An experimental examination of the effects of information control on budget reporting with relative project evaluation. *Journal of Management Accounting Research, 31*(2), 177–196.
98. Østergren, K., & Stensaker, I. (2011). Management control without budgets: a field study of 'beyond budgeting in practice. *European Accounting Review, 20*(1), 149–181.
99. Perminova, O., Gustafsson, M., & Wikström, K. (2008). Defining uncertainty in projects–a new perspective. *International Journal of Project Management, 26*(1), 73–79.
100. Pike, R. H. (1988). An empirical study of the adoption of sophisticated capital budgeting practices and decision-making effectiveness. *Accounting and Business Research, 18*(72), 341–351.
101. Procaccino, J. D., & Verner, J. M. (2006). Software project managers and project success: An exploratory study. *Journal of Systems and Software, 79*(11), 1541–1551.
102. Qian, Y., & Xu, C. (1998). Innovation and bureaucracy under soft and hard budget constraints. *The Review of Economic Studies, 65*(1), 151–164.
103. Quinn, J. B., & Baily, M. N. (1994). Information technology: Increasing productivity in services. *Academy of Management Perspectives, 8*(3), 28–48.
104. Rabechini Junior, R., & Monteiro de Carvalho, M. (2013). Understanding the impact of project risk management on project performance: An empirical study. *Journal of Technology Management & Innovation, 8,* 6–6.
105. Ramos, P., & Mota, C. (2014). Perceptions of success and failure factors in information technology projects: a study from Brazilian companies. *Procedia-Social and Behavioral Sciences, 119*, 349–357.
106. Rankin, F. W., Schwartz, S. T., & Young, R. A. (2008). The effect of honesty and

superior authority on budget proposals. The *Accounting Review, 83*(4), 1083–1099.

107. Raymond, L., & Bergeron, F. (2008). Project management information systems: An empirical study of their impact on project managers and project success. *International Journal of Project Management*, *26*(2), 213–220.
108. Raz, T., & Michael, E. (2001). Use and benefits of tools for project risk management. *International Journal of Project Management, 19*(1), 9–17.
109. Rehesaar, H., & Beames, E. (1998, January). Project plans and time budgets in information systems projects. In *Proceedings. 1998 International Conference Software Engineering: Education and Practice (Cat. No. 98EX220)* (Vol. 1, pp. 120–124). IEEE.
110. Roberts, P. (2011). *Effective Project Management: Identify and Manage Risks Plan and Budget to Keep Projects Under Control.* Kogan Page Publishers, (Vol. 1, pp. 3–9).
111. Roberts, T. L., Cheney, P. H., Sweeney, P. D., & Hightower, R. T. (2004). The effects of information technology project complexity on group interaction. *Journal of Management Information Systems, 21*(3), 223–247.
112. Rodríguez, A., Ortega, F., & Concepción, R. (2017). An intuitionistic method for the selection of a risk management approach to information technology projects. *Information Sciences, 375*, 202–218.
113. Rosacker, K. M., & Rosacker, R. E. (2010). Information technology project management within public sector organizations. *Journal of Enterprise Information Management*, (Vol. 1, pp. 5–9).
114. Roy, R., Souchoroukov, P., & Shehab, E. (2011). Detailed cost estimating in the automotive industry: Data and information requirements. *International Journal of Production Economics, 133*(2), 694–707.
115. Ruiz-Pérez, M. R., Alba-Rodríguez, M. D., Rivero-Camacho, C., Solís-Guzmán, J., & Marrero, M. (2021). The budget as a basis for ecological management of urbanization projects. A case study in Seville, Spain. *Sustainability, 13*(7), 4078.
116. Sato, T., & Hirao, M. (2013). Optimum budget allocation method for projects with critical risks. *International Journal of Project Management, 31*(1), 126–135.
117. Shenhar, A. J. (2004). Strategic Project Leadership® Toward a strategic approach to project management. *R&D Management, 34*(5), 569–578.
118. Smith, G. L., Green, R. N., Raschke, E., Avis, L. M., Suttles, J. T., Wielicki, B. A., & Davies, R. (1986). Inversion methods for satellite studies of the Earth's radiation budget: Development of algorithms for the ERBE mission. *Reviews of Geophysics, 24*(2), 407–421.
119. Soares, C. A. P., Magalhães, M. A., & Mendes, J. R. (2020). Investment Capital Budget Method Oriented to Project Management. *GSJ, 8*(3), 6–9.
120. Stewart, R. A. (2008). A framework for the life cycle management of information technology projects: project. *International Journal of Project Management, 26*(2), 203–212.

121. Suver, J. D., & Cooper, J. C. (1988). Principles and methods of managerial cost-accounting systems. *American Journal of Hospital Pharmacy, 45*(1), 146–152.
122. Taylor, H., Artman, E., & Woelfer, J. P. (2012). Information technology project risk management: bridging the gap between research and practice. *Journal of Information Technology, 27*(1), 17–34.
123. Taylor, J. (2003). Managing information technology projects: Applying project management strategies to software, hardware, and integration initiatives. *Amacom*, (Vol. 1, pp. 2–9).
124. Teah, T. S., Wong, W. Y., & Beh, H. C. (2019, December). The Practical Implication of Software Quality Assurance of Change Control Management: Why Overall IT Project Activities Matters? In *2019 IEEE 7th Conference on Systems, Process and Control (ICSPC)* (Vol. 1, pp. 131–136). IEEE.
125. Teller, J., & Kock, A. (2013). An empirical investigation on how portfolio risk management influences project portfolio success. *International Journal of Project Management, 31*(6), 817–829.
126. Teller, J., Kock, A., & Gemünden, H. G. (2014). Risk management in project portfolios is more than managing project risks: A contingency perspective on risk management. *Project Management Journal, 45*(4), 67–80.
127. Thamhain, H. (2013). Managing risks in complex projects. *Project Management Journal, 44*(2), 20–35.
128. Tishler, A., Dvir, D., Shenhar, A., & Lipovetsky, S. (1996). Identifying critical success factors in defense development projects: A multivariate analysis. *Technological Forecasting and Social Change, 51*(2), 151–171.
129. Tohidi, H. (2011). Review the benefits of using value engineering in information technology project management. *Procedia Computer Science, 3,* 917–924.
130. Verhoef, P. C., & Lemon, K. N. (2013). Successful customer value management: Key lessons and emerging trends. *European Management Journal, 31*(1), 1–15.
131. Wateridge, J. (1995). IT projects a basis for success. *International Journal of Project Management, 13*(3), 169–172.
132. Wateridge, J. (1998). How can IS/IT projects be measured for success? *International Journal of Project Management, 16*(1), 59–63.
133. Weingartner, H. M. (1966). Capital budgeting of interrelated projects: survey and synthesis. *Management Science, 12*(7), 485–516.
134. Westerveld, E. (2003). The Project Excellence Model®: linking success criteria and critical success factors. *International Journal of Project Management, 21*(6), 411–418.
135. Williams, T. (1995). A classified bibliography of recent research relating to project risk management. *European Journal of Operational Research, 85*(1), 18–38.
136. Wright, J. N. (1997). Time and budget: the twin imperatives of a project sponsor. *International Journal of Project Management, 15*(3), 181–186.
137. Wysocki, R. K., Beck Jr, R., & Crane, D. B. (1995). *Effective project management:*

how to plan, manage, and deliver projects on time and within budget. John Wiley & Sons, Inc. (Vol. 1, pp. 1–15).

138. Xiao, H., Gao, F., & Lee, L. H. (2020). Optimal computing budget allocation for complete ranking with input uncertainty. *IISE Transactions, 52*(5), 489–499.
139. Yang, D., Wang, Q., Li, M., Yang, Y., Ye, K., & Du, J. (2008, October). A survey on software cost estimation in the Chinese software industry. In *Proceedings of the Second ACM-IEEE International Symposium on Empirical Software Engineering and Measurement* (Vol. 1, pp. 253–262).
140. Zhang, S., Chen, P., Lee, L. H., Peng, C. E., & Chen, C. H. (2011, December). Simulation optimization using particle swarm optimization with optimal computing budget allocation. In *Proceedings of the 2011 Winter Simulation Conference (WSC)* (Vol. 1, pp. 4298–4309). IEEE.
141. Zhang, S., Xu, J., Lee, L. H., Chew, E. P., Wong, W. P., & Chen, C. H. (2016). Optimal computing budget allocation for particle swarm optimization in stochastic optimization. *IEEE Transactions on Evolutionary Computation, 21*(2), 206–219.

CHAPTER 4

STAKEHOLDERS IN IT PROJECT MANAGEMENT

UNIT INTRODUCTION

An information technology (IT) system is a collection of individuals, procedures, and materials that work together to receive, save, analyze, and provide knowledge to serve a business. Consumers have a significant effect on project success, particularly in complex projects with a diverse set of stakeholders (Baker & Baker, 2000). As a result, comprehending stakeholder involvement in project impact is critical for the company. As the number of stakeholders involved grows, so does the severity of the issues. Competent stakeholders always understood what they needed and always researched the specifics of the demands ahead of discussions. The participants were managed with much difficulty. Project managers have always been convinced that stakeholder engagement is essential for a successful project. Whenever project leaders discover that the work is just not proceeding according to plan, managers typically convey their expectations. Although if consumers need not grasp underlying technological problems, it's indeed critical that stakeholders comprehend how the technology will perform.

IT Project management is distinct from any other branch of project delivery (Cicmil & Hodgson, 2006). Generally speaking, IT projects are one-of-a-kind since they are specifically designed to satisfy the requirements of a certain intended audience. As a result, IT projects are by definition, creative. So Most initiatives are believed to enhance, advance, or address specific industry challenges, and so they only last a few years (not during the period). Such challenges cause a great deal of ambiguity when building any program since combining the business and objectives of the initiatives demands a lot of experience. As a result of this consideration, every program or deliverable is planned, designed, and estimated continuously.

In a standard IT assignment or project, multiple parties are involved who take part in the development life cycle such as stakeholders, sponsors, the design and implementation team, and the end users. It is found that the more the project managers interact with the different teams the better. On the other hand, traditional project management focuses on project content, technical deliverables, tools and processes, and other approaches that are included as part of the project (Cleland, 2007). Many organizations concentrate on the entire project rather than all of the elements. Many senior managers regard IT as a cost center and frequently fail to demonstrate the necessary passion for supporting IT initiatives (Figure 4.1).

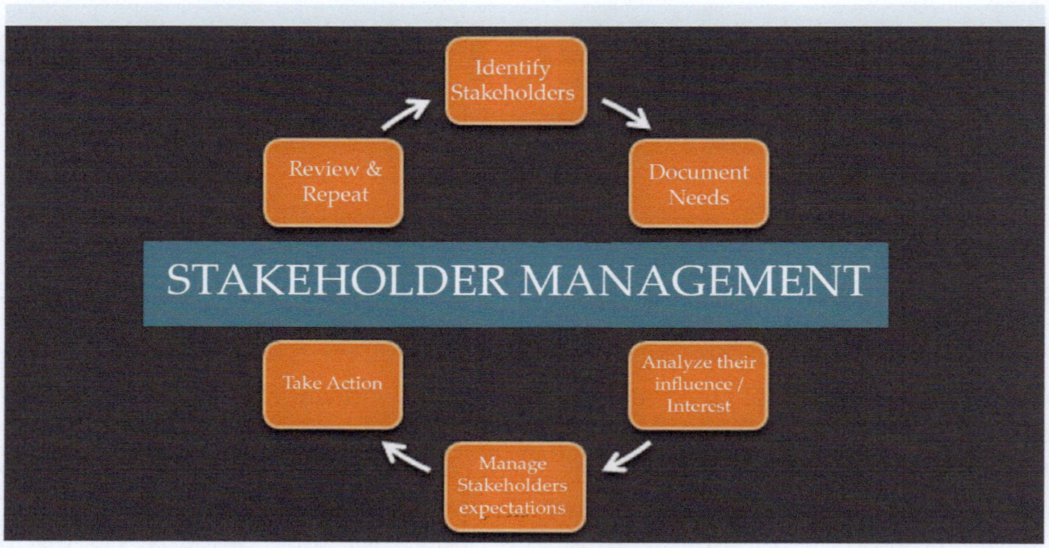

Figure 4.1. Illustration of components of stakeholder management (Source: Simplilearn, Creative Commons License).

Learning Objectives

At the end of this chapter, the reader will be able to understand

- The importance of stakeholders in IT project management
- The concepts of internal stakeholders and external stakeholders
- The process of stakeholders' analysis
- The process of communication management
- The problem in stakeholders' management

Key Terms

1. Stakeholders
2. Project Sponsor
3. Internal Stakeholders
4. External Stakeholders
5. Customer Line Management
6. Communication Management
7. Stakeholder's Analysis

4.1. IMPORTANCE OF STAKEHOLDER

Stakeholder management is integrally a hard task considering the imperceptible nature of the constraints and variables which are engaged. The project's structure and form may also have a significant impact on the quantity and kind of stakeholders involved, and engaged, making decisive project management methods impossible to recommend(Hersey & Blanchard, 1977). For big projects, participants may reverse the SDLC, making the PM's job much more difficult. Furthermore, although PMs may adopt a strategy to influence or succeed consumers, these interested parties may have the ultimate word on whether or not a venture is successful following the conclusion. As just a result, it is advised that every future study must additionally investigate actual engagement and the impact of particular stakeholders or a group of individuals deemed to be especially potent.

Did you Know?

Various parties participate in the development process in a typical IT task or project, including customers, funders, a design, and execution team, and end consumers.

4.2. STAKEHOLDER IDENTIFICATION

The very first stage in successful stakeholder management is to fully identify all participants. According to Cleland (1998), participants are as continues to follow:

Stakeholders are people or organizations who do have, or think they possess, real rights against the project's substantial components. A stake is an involvement, share, or claim in a project; it can range from informal interest in the undertaking, at one extreme, to a legal claim of ownership at the other extreme possession.

Stakeholders are affiliated with both the organization providing the work and the organization receiving the benefits, These are called internal stakeholders. The performance and benefiting organizations might or might not be affiliated with the same corporation, and the contract situation could be official or unofficial. In contrast, there are typically "foreign" investors who do not belong to the aforementioned 2 categories. Historically, the stakeholders involved have been people or groups having close ties to either the benefitting or producing organizations. Long-term shifts in the social, cultural, and economic considerations of initiatives have rendered this no longer always true for a wide range of reasons (Winch, 2004). Currently, there could also be a variety of external parties with major social, geopolitical, or business interests.

4.2.1. Internal Stakeholders

Internal stakeholders related to the *benefiting organization* might include (Kloppenborg et al., 2007):

- Project sponsor
- Shareholders of a company or investors
- Customer line management
- Employees of the client's IT infrastructure
- Clients' accounting department
- Relevant business units of the customer
- Additional consumer representatives
- Consumers of the company
- Suppliers and subcontractors of the consumer
- Client's financiers

Stakeholders associated with the *executing organization* may include (Thoms & Kerwin, 2004):

- Project manager
- Entrepreneurs or shareholders
- Project group
- Line management
- Performing the organization's IT group
- Accountancy division of performing organization
- Performing the organization's other employees
- Clients of the executing organization
- The organization's subcontractors and suppliers
- Financial backers of the performance group

4.2.2. External Stakeholders

External stakeholders might be worried people, businesses, or organizations that represent special interests, or they could be municipal, regional, local, or worldwide government agencies that represent public interests (Winch, 2004). External private interests include interested people, industry groups, environment and conservation associations, community associations, etc. Local authorities, state and local governments, federal government regulators, the federal or international institutions may be open public participants (Tuckman, 1965) (Figure 4.2).

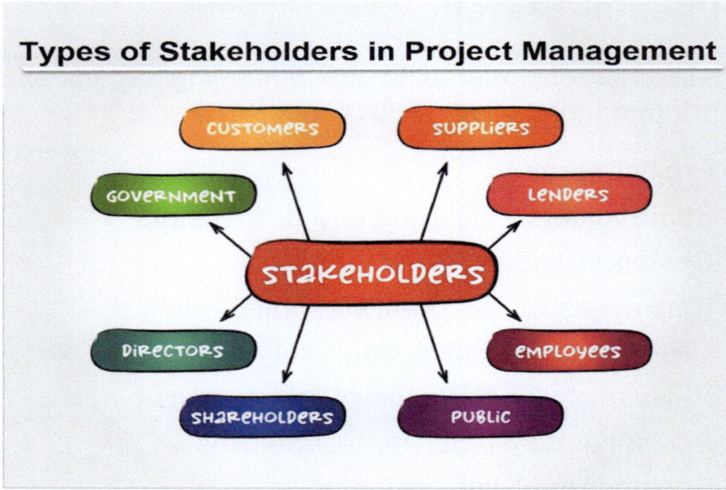

Figure 4.2. Schematic of types of stakeholders (Source: Andrea Steve, Creative Commons License).

4.3. STAKEHOLDERS ANALYSIS

Once the stakeholders are identified, they must be carefully analyzed to establish how that customer will be handled (Aaltonen & Kujala, 2010). Stakeholders who are more worried about just a program will demand separate management than those who are less worried; likewise, that stakeholders who are more powerful will require different management than those who are less strong. Every client or set of stakeholders may have a specific variety of interests in the project, including financial, job security, status, impact, image, or utility interests (time) (Assudani & Kloppenborg, 2010). If the effective completion of projects has the potential to shift the "balance of power" in an organization, the objectives of the group's many members may not coincide. For instance, various stakeholders inside the beneficiary organization are for, against, or indifferent to information about the project, depending on how the final year project materializes or is implemented inside the beneficiary organization. IT ERP in initiatives involving a variety of corporate business components, there is a great deal of social change and social, such as flow of work, guidelines, procedures, organizational structure, etc.; as a result, various stakeholders among the same collective (i.e., the benefiting organization) may well have differing interests in the achievement of such a big project (Winch et al., 2007; Bloch et al., 2012).

Figure 4.3 illustrates a chart of power versus concern that may be used to graphically classify participants into one of these 4 groups. Throughout the duration of the project, it will be necessary to actively supervise influential and highly concerned customers;

these are the individuals who will require their hands bound (Eskerod et al., 2015). For each of these people or groups, the program manager must determine:

1. What is this entire stakeholder's greatest benefit (loss) if the initiative achieves (fails)?
2. What do these stakeholders have to lose most if the initiative failed (succeeds)?

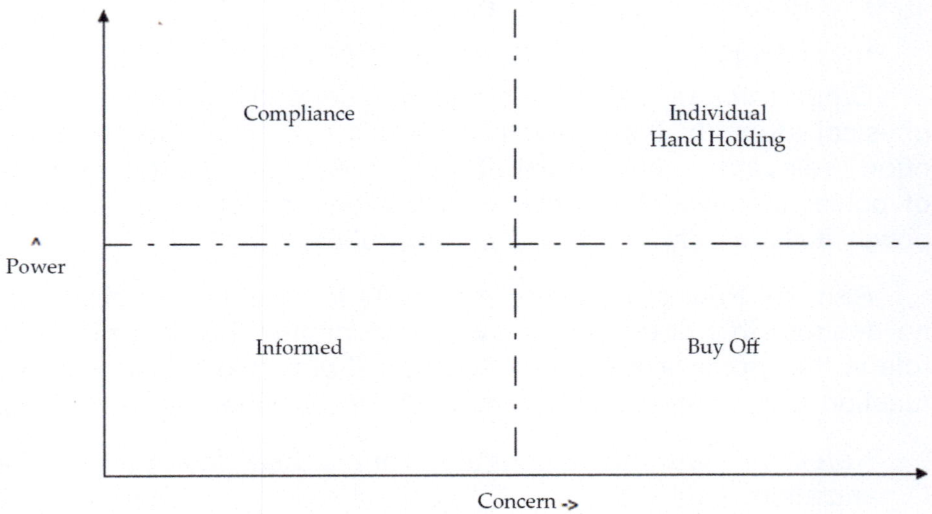

Figure 4.3. Diagram of chart of power verse concern (Source: Dan Brandon, Creative Commons License).

4.3.1. Stakeholders' Engagement in Project

The project leader (or line management) should attempt to connect this individual with the program and obtain provided for free, and then monitor this realignment throughout all of the project's phases. Stakeholders that are powerful but not too concerned, usually have some standards or other manifestation of the principle that they wish to be followed.

An example here is regulatory agencies. This group of individuals is better handled by gaining a thorough understanding of the relevant concepts and norms and then adhering to them. This is the as such buy-off party, which must be associated with the project's objectives for it to be successful.

This is accomplished by first determining why they are so worried, and afterward determining if they are originally linked with the program; they do not require ongoing care like the strong and seriously worried subgroup. Those partners who are neither influential nor seriously bothered must merely be kept updated on a routine basis as a collective (Mok et al., 2015; Uribe et al., 2018).

4.3.2. Influence of Stakeholders

In terms of power and influence over the project affairs most organizations of stakeholders possess four sorts of influence (Doloi, 2011):

- Power due to position (or rank)
- Power due to control over resources (like budget)
- Power due to unique expertise
- Power due to politics and/or charisma

Other authors describe additional sorts of power, such as physical strength, that could be relevant to a sports team but is often irrelevant in the context of project management. Other types of power identified by some as subcategories of the position of power include (Zarghami & Dumrak, 2020):

TIPS

The project manager is not to try to regulate all these multiple variations, but to impact the communication plan for the program's advantage.

Reward: Power is built on the ability to provide a worker what he desires; this does not always mean money, but it might be a role in the group or a favorable appraisal provided by the PM to a function direct supervisor (Brandon, 2006; Voropaev et al., 2016).

Referent: Authority delegated from a high level within the Organization.

Penalty: Power based on being able to penalize someone (may be more than monetary).

A stakeholder activity plan should be created when all stakeholders are identified and reviewed. This strategy will include how another client will be handled and who will be in charge of them (inside the development team, line management, or the project management office) (Derakhshan et al., 2019).

4.4. COMMUNICATION MANAGEMENT

Communications management is the process of controlling the information flow between parties. As noted previously, there are several parties, each with separate roles, interests, priorities, and agendas. There are numerous sorts of data, many of which should be transmitted among diverse participants at various moments and intervals, perhaps through distinct processes. The project manager's role is not to try to control all these differing flows, but to influence project communications to the benefit of the project.

Remember that it is the responsibility of project members to perform their assigned responsibilities and finish their assigned tasks; and that it is the responsibility of general management to develop the project, support the project and defend it from interruptive or unneeded adjustments; even so, the primary role of the project manager is to serve as the integrator and talker for all project participants (Decker et al., 2007). Thus, the project leader acts as the primary interface for the program (Johansen et al., 2014). The PM must attempt to influence communications so that they adhere to the strategy, but he is unable to interact If there are N participants, there will be N*(N-1)/2 viable channels of communication, as shown in Figure 4.4 for five participants.

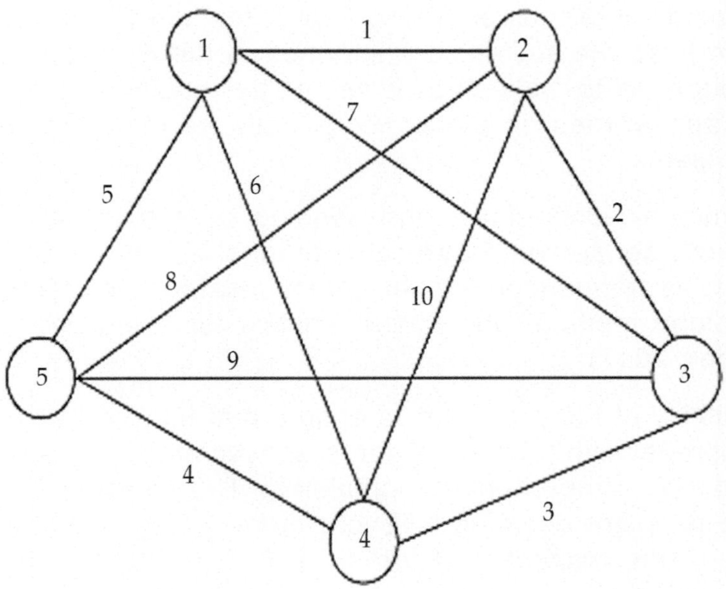

Figure 4.4. Diagram of channels of communication (Source: Dan Brandon, Creative Commons License).

The following are the PMI proper communication procedures (PMI, 2000):

- Communications planning
- Information distribution
- checking up on the success
- Executive shutdown

Poor communication is a leading source of problems, and as a result, project members may lack motivation or be caught up in rumors. Due to a lack of adequate communication, the stakeholder may sometimes become furious. 90% of a normal project owner's time is devoted to talking. This consists of (Hahn, 2008; Saad et al., 2022):

- Approximately two hours a day are spent on meeting
- More than one hour per day is spent inside one mentoring or conversation
- The majority of the remaining time is spent orally and in writing reports

Thus, project managers must possess strong verbal communication skills:

- Upper line management
- The project sponsor
- The task group
- Additional project manager (PM) and project-related groups
- Clients
- Additional parties

As mentioned in the stakeholder engagement, the direct aim of all PM communications is to keep the stakeholder informed to the required level. The direct objective, though, is to "take the pulse" of the stakeholder groups in terms of their view and worries on the project's path, performance, dangers, as well as other problems.

In principle, communication entails the sending of a message between such a receiver and the sender via a particular channel and in a modality with defined criteria (such as frequency). Proper communication requires selecting the appropriate medium, method, and characteristics for a specific message and recipient (Kerzner, 2017).

It is the responsibility of the presenter to ensure that the message is clear, consistent, and comprehensive. The recipient is accountable for ensuring that the message is read and comprehended completely. The sender encodes the information, and the recipient decodes it. Encoding/decoding is performed by each side according to the respective (Hartman & Ashrafi, 2002):

- Languages (and dialects)
- Culture
- Units of measure (currency, size, weight, volume, time, etc.)
- Discipline
- Education and business sector
- Experience

4.5. THE PROBLEM IN STAKEHOLDERS MANAGEMENT

There are several problems in the management of stakeholders, some of which are as follows.

4.5.1. Selection of Stakeholder

It is surprising how so many brainstorms could go away, although almost all protective leaders believe that stakeholders are the easiest step. Too often, the relationships between individuals inside the participating project group are one of the most significant obstacles (Achterkamp & Vos, 2008; Rozanski & Woods, 2011). A few "loud" persons may dominate these meetings, and the project owner's primary responsibility is to guarantee that all participants have an equal say and may participate (Sharp et al., 1999).

Remember

Identifying the players is crucial, and also being loud and dominant is not always correlate to understanding all, therefore enabling the scenario to get the most feedback from your group is essential.

4.5.2. Lack of communication

Clarify the situation. It is challenging to effectively communicate. It is quite difficult. Beginners may believe that producing PowerPoint presentations and sending out daily emails periodically will suffice. Wrong!! Here are a few things to keep in mind (Olander, 2007; Woolridge et al., 2007):

a) Each item of information that the project disseminates must serve a certain function, for example, Are you looking to inform? Are you looking to create influence? Do you wish to generate debate (and therefore action)? Do you wish to strengthen the relationship?

b) Choose appropriate communication channels for every stakeholder (group or individual). You might discover that certain individuals demand specialized approaches. Getting this property may feel like a hassle, but it will eventually be worth it.

c) Examine how two-way communications can be implemented. Several projects have failed in their communication strategy because they believe that communication always comes from the initiative to the users and do not prepare for the opposite direction. How are your partners able to contact you? Would anyone employ the same technique?

4.5.3. Analysis of Stakeholder's Influence

The normal outcome of studying the influence and power of your stakeholder is the definition of how they will be handled throughout the project's duration. Underestimating this will also result in a wrong management strategy. This can result in a misapprehension of the influence of certain stakeholders, considering them of lesser importance, and the discovery that they are the ones that destroy your initiative (Chung & Crawford, 2016).

4.5.4. Inaccurate Grouping of Stakeholders

Frequently, the determining factor is whether an individual is a single person or a part of a group, or whether the organization is a member of some other collective (Damian & Zowghi, 2002; Nguyen et al., 2009). Knowing the influence and strength of each stakeholder at every stage and how effectively to service them throughout the project might be significantly more difficult than it appears (And importantly what their price is (the contribution as a stakeholder in return for deliverables within the project).

This step is time-consuming, and you might desire to sketch out multiple scenarios to determine which one will work much better for your project. Also, keep in mind that identifying stakeholders is not set and unchanging (Ballejos & Montagna, 2008). If you discover throughout the project that the assessment is ineffective or if you obtain new knowledge, you are free to revise it.

4.5.5. Misinterpretation of Stakeholder's Need

Recall that needs are distinct from requirements, which are precise characteristics of your project's deliverables, for example, "I'd like my client interface to be blue." Requirements refer to the continual requirements of your stakeholders throughout the project, for example., a project that delivers machinery to replace shop floor workers could be opposed by trade unions who may need the project to fail. Reviewing organization processes that can be objected to and mapping them using a simple stakeholder's needs assessment box is one technique(Karlsen, 2002); see the sample below. Drawing out these requirements can provide you with useful insights into the desires of your stakeholders, thereby assisting you in managing them.

4.5.6. Ineffective Use of Stakeholder's Resources

In the majority of projects, you manage a variety of stakeholders with diverse requirements and demands. Many projects have a limited quantity of resources, so one of the challenges is to establish how to distribute them among the project team. Spreading your staff too thinly (to actively handle a bigger proportion of stakeholders) may cause you to miss an essential group of influences or to be unable to successfully manage them. If you limit your team to controlling a core group of influences, you risk spreading resources too thinly that they are unable to manage successfully (Manowong & Ogunlana, 2010; Weiss & Anderson Jr, 2004).

4.5.7. Misunderstanding of Stakeholder's Reward

Participants will often want compensation for their participation in the initiative. In other words, he wants results that could benefit his profession in exchange for his time. Workers who embrace a corporate reform initiative may anticipate improved working circumstances, etc.

People and groups may have a huge array (and individuals within groups). When these modifications inside the project or the group misjudge the "price" and, from the perspective of the stakeholders, appear to "underpay," the interested stakeholders may experience enough discomfort (El-Gohary et al., 2006; Olander, 2007). This is sometimes sufficient for them to change sides or alter their objectives, resulting in project modifications.

4.5.8. Ignoring Risks of Stakeholders

Whenever it involves risk management, most working groups neglect stakeholders. Stakeholders can stop a project dead in its tracks (withdrawing funding, influencing controlling stakeholders, etc). Consequently, stakeholder analysis must play an important role in overall identifying risks (Saad et al., 2022).

ACTIVITY 4.1.

As an IT project manager of a food company, identify internal and external stakeholders and analyze their engagements in the project. Also define communication mechanism with all the stakeholders.

4.5.9. Influence of Stakeholders on Each Other

Furthermore, most working groups overlook the fact that stakeholders impact one another. The interaction between stakeholders and the project group is not a simple one-way street between both the development team and the stakeholders; factors that can impact and engage with one another (McVea & Freeman, 2005). Imagine a project that involved the relocation of a company, for instance. Scared of losing employment, the local community might attempt to influence the municipal govt (another stakeholder) to affect the program's result.

While it can be disadvantageous in some cases, perspicacious working groups use it to their benefit where you may have one group/individual that is unaccepting but can be variables influenced by other organizations - trying to establish a strategy on how stakeholders can impact everyone else is a crucial component of stakeholder analysis which should not be neglected (Angelov & Hilliard, 2014).

4.5.10. Inappropriate Management Strategies

A stakeholder management issue is when working groups pick an incorrect approach for dealing with a certain stakeholder. Of course, your plan must be designed to benefit you, your organization, and your stakeholders, but it must also be well-thought-out and outcome-oriented. In so many circumstances, this method is not a one-size-fits-all solution that can be implemented by all stakeholders involved. This is frequently the natural posture of several working groups who, due to time constraints, seek to implement broad plans without taking into account the subtleties inside their stakeholder group (Lopes & Manas, 2013). This is particularly true for varied groups with complicated and varied requirements, resulting in a set of well-thought-out tactics suited to the individual needs of your stakeholders and connecting those requirements with your implementation plan (Figure 4.5).

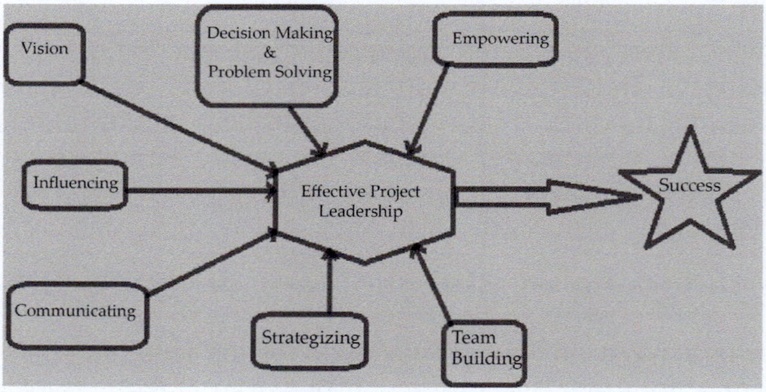

Figure 4.5. Illustration of stakeholder management issues (Source: A. Dekkar & Yang Qing, Creative Commons License).

SUMMARY

When it comes to information technology (IT) project management, stakeholders are individuals or groups who are affected by the project's outcome. They can be internal (e.g., employees of the organization) or external (e.g., shareholders, customers, suppliers, partners, etc.). The successful delivery of an IT project depends on the active involvement and cooperation of all stakeholders. Therefore, it is important to identify and assess them early on in the project planning process. This will allow you to better understand their expectations, needs, and concerns. It will also help you develop strategies for managing and engaging them throughout the project lifecycle.

REVIEW QUESTIONS

1. What is the role of stakeholders in information technology project management?
2. How do stakeholders influence the direction of a project?
3. How can project managers ensure that stakeholders are engaged and informed throughout the project?
4. What are the benefits of involving stakeholders in information technology project management?
5. What challenges can stakeholders pose to information technology project management?

MULTIPLE CHOICE QUESTIONS

1. What is the most important stakeholder in an IT project?

a. The project sponsor
b. The project manager
c. The project team
d. The end users

2. Who is responsible for ensuring that the project stakeholders are kept informed of the project's progress?

a. The project sponsor
b. The project manager
c. The project team
d. The end users

3. Who is responsible for ensuring that the project stakeholders' needs are met?

a. The project sponsor
b. The project manager

c. The project team

d. The end users

4. Which of the following is not a role of the project manager concerning stakeholders?

a. Identifying stakeholders

b. Communicating with stakeholders

c. Managing stakeholder expectations

d. Creating the project schedule

5. Which of the following is not a role of the project sponsor about stakeholders?

a. Identifying stakeholders

b. Communicating with stakeholders

c. Managing stakeholder expectations

d. Providing resources for the project

Answers to Multiple Choice Questions

1. (a) 2. (b) 3. (b) 4. (d) 5. (a)

REFERENCES

1. Aaltonen, K., & Kujala, J. (2010). A project lifecycle perspective on stakeholder influence strategies in global projects. *Scandinavian Journal of Management, 26*(4), 381–397.
2. Achterkamp, M. C., & Vos, J. F. (2008). Investigating the use of the stakeholder notion in project management literature, a meta-analysis. *International Journal of Project Management*, *26*(7), 749–757.
3. Angelov, S., & Hilliard, R. (2014, August). Towards improved stakeholder management for software reference architectures. In *European Conference on Software Architecture* (Vol. 1, pp. 90–97). Springer, Cham.
4. Assudani, R., & Kloppenborg, T. J. (2010). Managing stakeholders for project management success: an emergent model of stakeholders. *Journal of General Management, 35*(3), 67–80.
5. Baker, S., & Baker, K. (2000). *The Complete Idiot's Guide to Project Management* (Vol. 2, pp. 2–8). Indianapolis, IN: Alpha Books.
6. Ballejos, L. C., & Montagna, J. M. (2008). Method for stakeholder identification in inter-organizational environments. *Requirements Engineering, 13*(4), 281–297.
7. Barbalho, S. C., De Toledo, J. C., & Da Silva, I. A. (2019). The effect of stakeholders' satisfaction and project management performance on transitions in a project management office. *IEEE Access, 7*, 169385–169398.

8. Bloch, M., Blumberg, S., & Laartz, J. (2012). Delivering large-scale IT projects on time, on budget, and value. *Harvard Business Review, 5*(1), 2–7.
9. Brandon, D. M. (2006). Developing the Schedule and Cost Plan. In *Project Management for Modern Information Systems* (Vol. 1, pp. 120–156). IGI Global.
10. Brandon, D. M. (2008). Project Management and Web Software Engineering. In *Software Engineering for Modern Web Applications: Methodologies and Technologies* (Vol. 1, pp. 254–291). IGI Global.
11. Chung, K. S. K., & Crawford, L. (2016). The role of social networks theory and methodology for project stakeholder management. *Procedia-Social and Behavioral Sciences, 226*, 372–380.
12. Cicmil, S., & Hodgson, D. (2006). New possibilities for project management theory: A critical engagement. *Project Management Journal, 37*(3), 111–122.
13. Cleland, D. (1998). Stakeholder management. In J. Pinto (Ed.), Project management handbook. New York: Jossey-Bass., Second Edition, pp. 23–25
14. Cleland, D. I. (2007). Strategic management: the project linkages. *The Wiley Guide to Project, Program & Portfolio Management, 1,* 63–79.
15. Damian, D. E., & Zowghi, D. (2002, September). The impact of stakeholders' geographical distribution on managing requirements in a multi-site organization. In *Proceedings IEEE Joint International Conference on Requirements Engineering* (Vol. 1, pp. 319–328). IEEE.
16. Decker, B., Ras, E., Rech, J., Jaubert, P., & Rieth, M. (2007). Wiki-based stakeholder participation in requirements engineering. *IEEE Software, 24*(2), 28–35.
17. Derakhshan, R., Turner, R., & Mancini, M. (2019). Project governance and stakeholders: a literature review. *International Journal of Project Management, 37*(1), 98–116.
18. Doloi, H. K. (2011). Understanding stakeholders' perspective of cost estimation in project management. *International Journal of Project Management, 29*(5), 622–636.
19. El-Gohary, N. M., Osman, H., & El-Diraby, T. E. (2006). Stakeholder management for public-private partnerships. *International Journal of Project Management, 24*(7), 595–604.
20. Eskerod, P., Huemann, M., & Ringhofer, C. (2015). Stakeholder inclusiveness: Enriching project management with general stakeholder theory1. *Project Management Journal, 46*(6), 42–53.
21. Hahn, H. A. (2008). A strategy for stakeholder management on an enterprise-wide software engineering project. In *Proceedings of the 6th Annual Conference on Systems Engineering Research*, (Vol. 1, pp. 3–9).
22. Hartman, F., & Ashrafi, R. A. (2002). Project management in the information systems and information technologies industries. *Project Management Journal, 33*(3), 5–15.
23. Hersey, P. B., & Blanchard, K. KH (1977). *The Management of Organizational Behavior*. Upper Saddle River, NJ: Prentice Hall, (Vol. 1, pp. 4–8).
24. Johansen, A., Eik-Andresen, P., & Ekambaram, A. (2014). Stakeholder benefit

assessment–Project success through management of stakeholders. *Procedia-Social and Behavioral Sciences, 119*, 581–590.

25. Karlsen, J. T. (2002). Project stakeholder management. Engineering management journal, 14(4), 19–24.
26. Kerzner, H. (2017). *Project Management: A Systems Approach to Planning, Scheduling, and Controlling.* John Wiley & Sons, (Vol. 1, pp. 5–9).
27. Kloppenborg, T. J., Tesch, D., Manolis, C., & Heitkamp, M. (2006). An empirical investigation of the sponsor's role in project initiation. *Project Management Journal, 37*(3), 16–25.
28. Lopes, L., & Manas, A. V. (2013). Delays in IT projects due to failures in the stakeholder's management. *Future Studies Research Journal, 5(*2), 158–185.
29. Manowong, E., & Ogunlana, S. (2010). Strategies and tactics for managing construction stakeholders. *Construction Stakeholder Management, 1,* 121–137.
30. McVea, J. F., & Freeman, R. E. (2005). A names-and-faces approach to stakeholder management: How focusing on stakeholders as individuals can bring ethics and entrepreneurial strategy together. *Journal of Management Inquiry, 14*(1), 57–69.
31. Mok, K. Y., Shen, G. Q., & Yang, J. (2015). Stakeholder management studies in mega construction projects: A review and future directions. *International Journal of Project Management, 33*(2), 446–457.
32. Nguyen, N. H., Skitmore, M., & Wong, J. K. W. (2009). Stakeholder impact analysis of infrastructure project management in developing countries: a study of the perception of project managers in state-owned engineering firms in Vietnam. *Construction Management and Economics, 27*(11), 1129–1140.
33. Olander, S. (2007). Stakeholder impact analysis in construction project management. *Construction Management and Economics, 25(*3), 277–287.
34. Rozanski, N., & Woods, E. (2011). *Software Systems Architecture: Working with Stakeholders using Viewpoints and Perspectives.* Addison-Wesley, Second Edition, pp. 2–7.
35. Saad, A., Zahid, S. M., & Muhammad, U. B. (2022). Role of awareness in strengthening the relationship between stakeholder management and project success in the construction industry of Pakistan. *International Journal of Construction Management, 22*(10), 1884–1893.
36. Sharp, H., Finkelstein, A., & Galal, G. (1999, September). Stakeholder identification in the requirements engineering process. In *Proceedings. Tenth International Workshop on Database and Expert Systems Applications.* DEXA 99 (Vol. 1, pp. 387–391). Ieee.
37. Thoms, P., & Kerwin, J. (2004). The leadership of project teams. In *The Wiley guide to managing projects.* J. Pinto & P. Morris, Eds, (Brandon, D. M. (2008ol. 1, pp. 4–6).
38. Tuckman, B. W. (1965). Developmental sequence in small groups. *Psychological Bulletin, 63*(6), 384.

39. Uribe, D. F., Ortiz-Marcos, I., & Uruburu, Á. (2018). What is going on with stakeholder theory in project management literature? A symbiotic relationship for sustainability. *Sustainability, 10*(4), 1300.

40. Voropaev, V., Gelrud, Y., & Klimenko, O. (2016). Who manages what? Project management for different stakeholders. *Procedia-Social and Behavioral Sciences, 226,* 478–485.

41. Weiss, J. W., & Anderson Jr, D. (2004). CIOs and IT professionals as change agents, risk and stakeholder managers: A field study. *Engineering Management Journal, 16*(2), 13–18.

42. Winch, G. M., Morris, P., & Pinto, J. (2007). Managing project stakeholders. *The Wiley Guide to project, Program, and Portfolio Management,* 271–289.

43. Woolridge, R. W., McManus, D. J., & Hale, J. E. (2007). Stakeholder risk assessment: An outcome-based approach. *IEEE Software, 24*(2), 36–45.

44. Zarghami, S. A., & Dumrak, J. (2020). Reimaging stakeholder analysis in project management: network theory and fuzzy logic applications. *Engineering, Construction and Architectural Management*, (Vol. 1, pp. 5–9).

CHAPTER 5

CHANGE MANAGEMENT IN IT PROJECT

UNIT INTRODUCTION

Change management standardizes the process of implementing and introducing changes to information technology in an organization. It offers a crucial set of controls that can minimize financial damage caused by system failures or changes, greatly reduce lost productivity through the change process, and improve overall system reliability. Although steady flow projects cause some interruption to the organization, the IT staff can frequently decrease their impact by operating systems in parallel, doing work during scheduled maintenance windows after hours, and so on (Brandon, 2006). Enabling projects, however, introduce new services and functions to the organization often impacting most users, and by extension introduce greater interruption during both the implementation phase and afterward. Enabling projects to have greater possible rewards: reducing competitive threats (risk), increasing productivity (time and money), or solving a significant problem not addressed by current systems (risk). Given the greater company impact, enabling projects requires greater care (Brown et al., 2005).

- Recognizing and arranging for change,
- Effectively explaining the change to stakeholders,
- In managing change.

Projects necessitate design and planning, integrity and usability, execution, and change management. Technology, planning, execution, and change management are needed for projects. If the change process is not managed, users and management will perceive a failure even with a great plan, technology, and execution. Many IT implementers fail to comprehend the full impact of change on users, set appropriate expectations, and communicate with each stakeholder group at the appropriate level before, during, and after the project. In addition to excellent planning and design, technological components, and execution, successful technology projects must plan for change, communicate change, and manage change. (Brown, 1998).

Learning Objectives

At the end of this chapter, the reader will be able to understand

- The impact of changes on project performance
- The aspects of IT projects
- The process of change management
- Importance of change management
- The importance of communication in change management

Key Terms

1. Project Aspects
2. Management Process
3. Management Plans
4. Management Development
5. Change Management System
6. Communication
7. Budget Adjustments

5.1. ASPECTS OF CHANGE IN IT PROJECTS

Resistance to change is usually rooted in fear of the unknown as PMs and people, in general, prefer stability and predictability. Nevertheless, in order for a project to continue, project leaders must be able to cope with changes efficiently. Many projects fail not because of overall aims and objectives, but due to their plan (or lack of plan) for changing circumstances. The lack of a structured change management system "assures that a project would be afflicted with chaos, mistakes, real harm, reduced performance, and uncontrolled software evolution" (Brown, 2005).

Change can occur for a myriad of purposes; in IT projects, the primary sources or signs of change include (Hallows, 2005):

- The client (benefiting organization) is uncertain of their requirements.
- The consumer is confused about how the needs must be satisfied.
- The performing organization is oblivious to the specifics of the customers' requirements.
- The performing organization is unsure of how to complete the task.
- The installation context has shifted.
- Approaches or algorithms that were supposed to be used turn out to be ineffective.
- Effective methods of creating or implementing the technology have emerged.
- The project's value proposition has evolved.
- Changes in market demographics and/or geography.
- The project's sociopolitical climate has shifted.
- The corporate setting has altered (due to restructurings, mergers, and acquisitions).

Remember

Formal change control is necessary for work requiring an external performance or receiving Organization for one Organization to be adequately reimbursed for the extra efforts.

Changes in a project can occur at any stage of the project, including initial planning until project completion; however, typically modifications in IT projects occur later in the project, like during development, testing, and distribution. Changes coming later in a project are usually much more expensive than if the need for a change were identified earlier (Maull et al., 1992). A change in one aspect of the project deliverables may lead to modifications in many other aspects of the project. It is critical to take efforts early on to wash out customer requirements and potential changes.

Verification of initial product representations with quality stage barriers utilizing techniques such as prototyping, use case walkthroughs with customers, and design reviews with appropriate stakeholders will minimize changes later in a project (Ibbs et al., 2001).

Project change management often focuses on budget adjustments, but other modifications must also be controlled. Often, change control systems are designed to handle just range and deliverables changes; other project changes are typically managed through risk management, In general, scope management refers to the procedures required to ensure that all work is handled and that no extra work is completed. Early stages of the project, scope change control should be planned and methods developed (charter, SOW, contract, overall project plan). Change management is involved with the following points: (Hornstein, 2015):

- Controlling the causes that product development to make sure that the changes are positive.
- Evaluating whether or not a scope change takes place.
- Controlling actual changes whenever they happen.

In the IT environment, the term *change control* can be confusing because those words are often applied to the control of changes to program source code and/or changes to a target hardware/software deployment platform.

(Hwang & Low, 2012).

What about the possibility of change in IT developments? To better grasp the problem, consider the ITIL® description of the change: "the introduction, alteration, and withdrawal of any approved, planned, and authorized system and messaging service that may influence IT services."

Change in an IT project may involve one or more aspects **(**Park & Peña-Mora, 2003**):**

- Architecture
- Processes
- Tools
- Metrics
- Documentation
- IT services area
- Information systems configuration area

Changes in IT projects can be vast, administration can be time-consuming, and the dangers are extremely significant. Moreover, the core of IT projects is high variability resulting from modern technology development dynamics. Add to this, the modifications brought as part of the industry's IT system development, it becomes even more apparent how many employees are impacted by such changes and how severely they impact their everyday job on several levels. Therefore, it is necessary to implement a change management approach (Griffith-Cooper & King, 2007).

We should keep in mind that there is always a large percentage of people who are resistant to change. It is also crucial guidance for those who are responsible for the modifications and determine their deployment. When concentrating on the technological and operational components of IT project modifications, one must never lose sight of a human component; one must consider the convenience and requirements of those impacted by the new (Jaafari, 2003).

5.2. CHANGE MANAGEMENT: PROCESS, PLANS, AND DEVELOPMENT

Here are some guidelines for successful change management. Managing an organizational change will be more effective if such simple ideas are applied. If you apply the very same strategy to achieve personal change, you are more productive. Change management requires careful planning and implementation, as well as engagement with and participation from those impacted by the changes (Hall, 2012). Typically, when change is imposed on individuals, issues develop. Change must be feasible, quantifiable, and realizable. These factors are particularly pertinent to the management of personal change. When initiating organizational change, consider the following: What do we hope to accomplish with this adjustment, why, and how will we recognize it has been successful? Which individuals will be impacted by this development, and how will they respond? How much of this transformation can we do on our own, and where do we need assistance? These factors are also highly relevant to the administration of individual and organizational change (Figure 5.1).

Individuals should not be "sold" on change to expedite "consensus" and deployment. 'Marketing' transformation to individuals is not a permanent success approach, assuming your goal is to be nipped in the behind at a certain unanticipated point in the future. Whenever people are listening to a management high-up' selling' them a change, they often smile and pretend to agree, but they're thinking, "There is no chance, if you think I'm going to stand for that bunch of old bollocks, you've got a big problem..." (And that's just the agreeable ones; more the obstinate kids will be well on their way to transitioning from gamekeepers to poachers.)

Instead, change needs to be understood and managed in a way that people can cope effectively with it. Change can be unsettling, so the manager logically needs to be a settling influence.

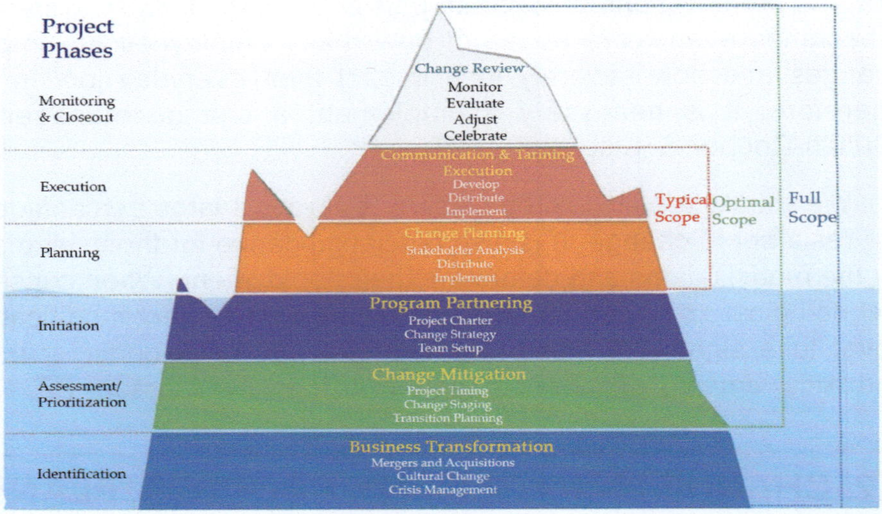

Figure 5.1. Illustration of phases of change management and its scope (Source: Farah McNeel, Creative Commons License).

Verify that those who will be affected concur with, or at least know, the necessity of transition and that they have a chance to choose how the transition will be handled, as well as to participate in its preparation and execution. To tackle sensitive areas of business transformation, use face-to-face interactions (see Mehrabian's studies on transmitting meaning and understanding). Encourage your supervisors to meet with their employees in person if they are assisting you in managing an organizational change. Email and printed notices are particularly ineffective at transmitting information and fostering understanding (Munassar et al., 2013).

If you believe you have to change something immediately, investigate the causes - is the hurry real? Will the consequences of settling on a more reasonable timetable be more damaging than presiding over a disastrous change? Rapid change inhibits application and participation, resulting in problems that require time to address.

Refer to the project management process for complicated adjustments, and be careful to supplement this with collaborative discussions to get agreement and support again for reasons behind the change. Engaging and making people aware also allows them to engage in planning and carrying out the adjustments, which reduces your workload, distributes organizational responsibilities, and fosters a feeling of ownership and awareness among the individuals affected (Love et al., 2002; Alp & Stack, 2012). Check out the wonderful, downloadable judgment template produced by Sharon Drew Morgen with queries that facilitate personal and business creativity and change. Dawn Stanley's RISE Personal Transformation

Model, a simple how-to structure for personal transformation, is also a very valuable reference model for numerous other sorts of transformation (Aubry et al., 2010).

For organizational change involving new activities, goals, and procedures for a team or group of individuals, utilize seminars to create comprehension, participation, planning, performance targets, action, and commitments (Love et al., 2002; Alp & Stack, 2012). If they are assisting you in navigating the change, encourage your team to use seminars with their people.

TIPS

Transition can be stressful; therefore, the manager must remain calm.

You must use these concepts even for the most difficult changes, including layoffs, closures, and the integration of combined or purchased firms. Even more cautious management is necessary for bad news than for regular adjustment (Martinsuo & Hoverfält, 2018). Lying under documents and middle-level management will make issues better. Consultation with others and facilitating their comprehension does not diminish your stance; rather, it enhances it. Leadership who fails to speak with and include their followers in the handling of terrible news is viewed as being feeble and deficient in honesty (Kenny, 2003). People will return compassion and regard if you approach them with these qualities.

Consider that the primary source of anxiety for the majority of employees is changing. Examine the notion of the process of self-development to determine how individuals respond to change. Broadly speaking, experienced executives and directors in charge of overseeing a change in the organization do not fear the future; rather, they live on it. Understand that your people despise and resist change, as it is highly unsettling and scary to them. Your folks share your sense of failure and dread of progress.

5.3. ESTABLISHING A CHANGE MANAGEMENT SYSTEM

Usually, a project scope management system includes paperwork, GPS tracking, and approvals stages to describe the processes through which the scope statement may well be modified. Every change request, either presented internally (by a project team member) or externally (by a third party), must be allocated a code or number (i.e., customer). Typically, this level of formality is applied after an early portion of the process has been finished. Typically, rigorous change of the design phase is established following the completion of the first concept. The advantages and drawbacks of the change must be addressed in light of all project parameters, particularly time and cost implications, and what other adjustments may be required (or desired) as a result of this change (Leybourne, 2006; Pundziene et al., 2007). The proposed change could or might not fall inside the project's cost or the unclaimed money.

Changes can occur at frequent meetings of a change control board, which includes representatives from both the organization and the beneficiary organization. Also recommended is the inclusion of members from other significant stakeholders involved. Delegates must be informed of the procedure they will soon participate in. To maximize the potential benefits of these events and minimize the time spent by attendance, the sessions should not be held too frequently, briefings packets should be distributed to representatives before the meeting, and changes must be categorized and grouped by item functional department (Johansson & Heide, 2008; Aronson et al., 2013). Frequently, numerous minor changes can be studied and discussed as a single change set or release. Errors and noncompliance with requirements and/or standards typically do not undergo formal change control; nevertheless, in some organizations, the change advisory committee may be informed of such concerns throughout the project.

Did you Know?

Occasionally, there is a delicate line between such a shift in scope and violation of the initial standards, and this can inevitably result in disagreements between the entities concerned.

Although the material will not be passed over to the change management board, it is important to capture all such situations and their resolution (Doherty & King, 2005). If the board approves the change, a specific start fresh of authorization may be needed in the level managers of the performance and benefiting organization. If a change falls within the undistributed budget, further authorization is usually not necessary. Following approval, a work breakdown structure (WBS) work package is generated (or an existing packet is amended) to reflect changes, as well as the latest project base cost management plan and timetable; for an outside contractor, a contract transition, known as a "change order," may also be necessary. It is usually preferable to build a new WBS work package that will be a substitute (or addition to) the existing pack; for replacement, the old packet's intended price is set to 0 (or to the amount already spent on it if work on it was already started). Figure 5.2 illustrates a typical overall procedure for dealing with project modifications After a change request is initiated, a decision is taken whether or not the new proposal is included in the original (baseline) range or not. This decision should be made by the CC membership or by project management downstream from the council. (Thiry, 2002; Proctor & Doukakis, 2003).

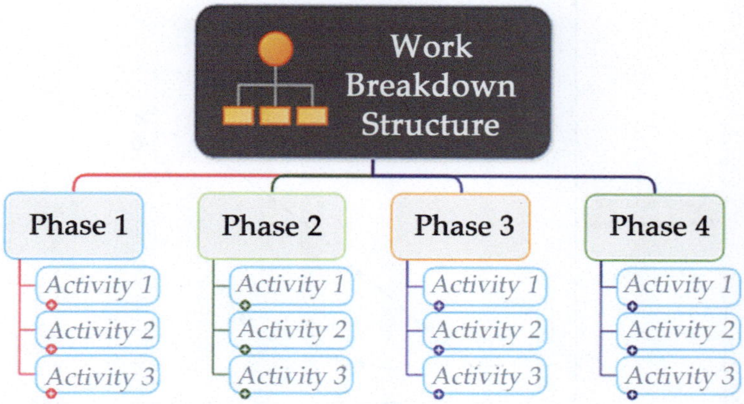

Figure 5.2. Schematic of work breakdown structure (Source: Biggerplate, Creative Commons License).

Those changes hose change requests that are for additional work are sent to the CC board for study (Figure 5.3). Requested changes for further effort are forwarded to the CC board for review. The board studies the request in light of benefit versus project impact and decides whether to implement the change or not Nagarajan et al., 2015). If the decision is taken to go through with the implementation, contract management may be required to estimate future tasks and execute a contractual variation order. If the contractual variation order is accepted (by the benefiting and performing organizations), the modification is transferred to task management. Extent and remedial modifications are often grouped into item versions, which go via version control(Doherty & King, 2005).

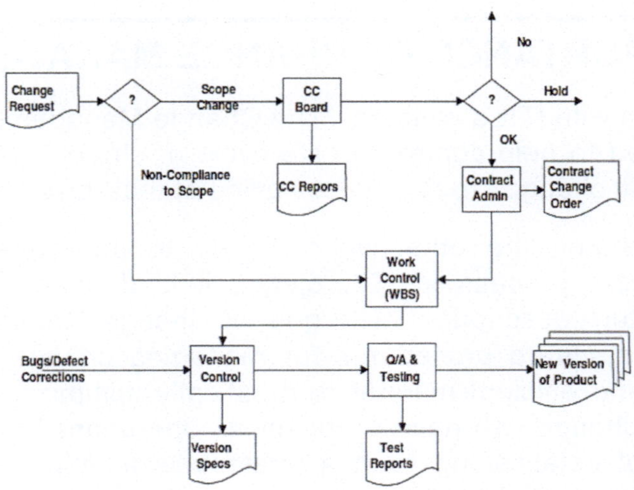

Figure 5.3. Diagram of change control process (Source: Dan Brandon, Creative Commons License).

Figure 5.4 depicts a helpful form of trends chart for cumulative change orders opened and canceled (approved for implementation or rejected).

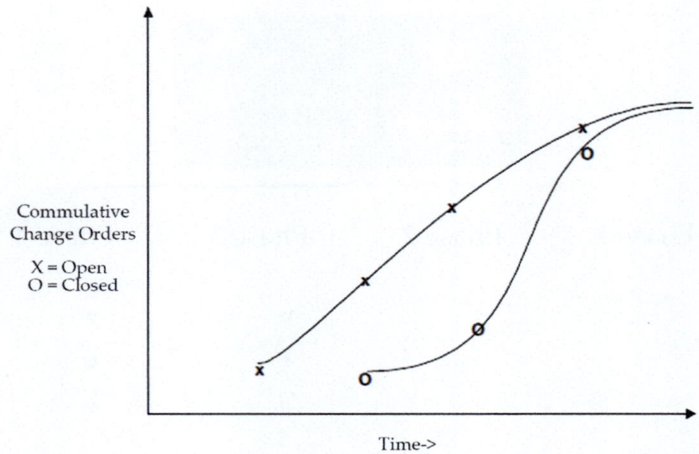

Figure 5.4. Diagram of cumulative change order (Source: Dan Brandon, Creative Commons License).

As the project progresses, one expects to see the difference between open change orders and closed orders closing as the project proceeds. If the distance (between the two curves) widens, there was an error in the scope management declaration.

For IT projects that succeed, 70% of the cost of the product is in the maintenance phase; thus, maintainability is extremely important. A measure of IT product maintainability is the lines of code affected per change order. A comprehensive metric in this area includes both the lines of code affected and the lines of code examined per change order because in implementing a change, programmers spend about half of their time just examining the existing code (Varajão et al., 2014).

5.4. IMPORTANCE OF CHANGE MANAGEMENT

Let's begin with ITIL's concept: "The Change Management" process is designed to help control the life cycle of strategic, tactical, and operational changes to IT services using standardized procedures."

Concerning the objective of trying to introduce a change management process in IT projects, it is desirable to use the ITIL structure description: "The goal of Change Management is to establish standard procedures for managing change requests in an agile and efficient manner to drastically minimize the risk and impact a change can have on business operations." To recap, the purpose of establishing such a strategy is to minimize risk to a group's IT operations and business operations while also ensuring that the advantages of the change itself are maximized (Keller et al., 2004; Simoes & Esposito, 2014).

Implementing changes always involves risk. It is important to note that the goal of well-defined change management in an IT project is not to remove all danger but to effectively manage and control it (Orlikowski & Hofman, 1997; Kellner et al., 1999). The same is true for the impact of the change on the operation of IT systems or business operations. The implementation of change management does not render the company completely unaffected by the change, but it does enable the adverse effect on tests and treatments to be reduced to a level (Bourque et al., 1999; Kitchen & Daly, 2002). Many businesses fail to adopt effective change management, some owing to a lack of understanding of the issue, some because they only partly execute such a procedure, and others because they fail to deal.

Remember

Maintenance is particularly critical for successful IT initiatives because it accounts for 70% of the firm's products and services.

5.5. IMPORTANCE OF COMMUNICATION IN CHANGE MANAGEMENT

It should be emphasized that irrespective of such factors as the technical sophistication of change management tools or the amount of money, the overall effectiveness of the procedure is primarily defined by the organizations /readiness projects for the transition (Herbsleb et al., 2001). Behind such preparation are well-planned and performed communications. Two conditions must be met for communicating effectively during the process of change management. Not just to inform, but also to engage in the changing process (Feiler & Humphrey, 1993).

Good communication can lead the listener throughout 4 phases of transformation (Stelzer & Mellis, 1998; Altamony et al., 2016):

- Awareness
- Understanding
- Acceptance
- Commitment

Even simple messages will fail if they are difficult to comprehend and embrace; the message will not lead to engagement from people who will be immediately impacted by the change. Alternatively, even precisely organized messages will misfire if they are not sent frequently enough. It's not necessarily what you say, but how you say it, as the saying goes.

While it is impossible to exaggerate the necessity of communication, one must keep a single thing in mind. Even the best-planned media campaign cannot compensate for the manager's participation in organizational change. I strongly value their representatives' involvement in such initiatives, particularly upper executives. The reality that all important details on the firm's Covid-19 predicament were frequently provided from the managerial level at Craft ware had a beneficial effect on my feeling of security and comfort throughout this tough time.

Why is this so significant? It's all about power. If the advantages of the change are conveyed from the board or senior leadership levels, the statement is supported by the owner's power. Employees are much more likely to follow the changes if they know it is in keeping with the firm's vision and/or beliefs.

ACTIVITY 5.1.

Suppose you are an IT project manager in a metal production industry. Company has asked manage change in IT project. Keeping in view the concepts of change management presented in this chapter. Devise a change management system including change aspects, processes and plans.

SUMMARY

Change management in information technology projects is the process of identifying, tracking and managing changes to project deliverables. Change management is a critical component of any project, as it helps to ensure that changes are made in a controlled and consistent manner. Change management can be a challenge in projects where there is a lot of change, or where changes are made frequently. In these cases, it is important to have a change management plan in place to ensure that changes are made in a way that is coordinated and approved by the project team.

REVIEW QUESTIONS

1. What is change management in information technology projects?
2. What are the benefits of change management in information technology projects?
3. What are some of the challenges of change management in information technology projects?
4. How can change management be used to effectively manage changes in information technology projects?
5. What should be included in a change management plan for an information technology project?

MULTIPLE CHOICE QUESTIONS

1. What are the three main types of change management in IT projects?

a. Preventative, proactive, and reactive
b. Pre-change, change, and post-change
c. Planning, execution, and monitoring
d. Initiating, controlling, and closing

2. What are the four main stages of change management in IT projects?

a. Initiation, planning, execution, and closure
b. Identification, assessment, planning, and implementation
c. Recognition, diagnosis, response, and monitoring
d. Identification, analysis, planning, and implementation

3. What are the main objectives of change management in IT projects?

a. To ensure changes are made efficiently and effectively
b. To ensure changes are made in line with the project objectives
c. To ensure changes are made in line with the business objectives
d. a and b

4. What are the main benefits of change management in IT projects?

a. It helps to ensure changes are made efficiently and effectively

b. It helps to ensure changes are made in line with the project objectives

c. It helps to ensure changes are made in line with the business objectives

d. It helps to ensure changes are made in line with the organizational objectives

5. What are the main challenges of change management in IT projects?

a. It can be difficult to get all project stakeholders on board with changes

b. It can be difficult to implement changes efficiently and effectively

c. It can be difficult to ensure changes are made in line with the project objectives

d. It can be difficult to ensure changes are made in line with the business objectives

Answers to Multiple Choice Questions

1. (a) 2. (a) 3. (d) 4. (b) 5. (a)

REFERENCES

1. Alp, N., & Stack, B. (2012, July). Scope management and change control process study for project-based companies in the construction and engineering industries. In *2012 Proceedings of PICMET'12: Technology Management for Emerging Technologies* (Vol. 1, pp. 2427–2436). IEEE.
2. Altamony, H., Al-Salti, Z., Gharaibeh, A., & Elyas, T. (2016). The relationship between change management strategy and successful enterprise resource planning (ERP) implementations: A theoretical perspective. *International Journal of Business Management and Economic Research, 7*(4), 690–703.
3. Aronson, Z. H., Shenhar, A. J., & Patanakul, P. (2013). Managing the intangible aspects of a project: The effect of vision, artifacts, and leader values on project spirit and success in technology-driven projects. *Project Management Journal, 44*(1), 35–58.
4. Aubry, M., Müller, R., Hobbs, B., & Blomquist, T. (2010). Project management offices in transition. *International Journal of Project Management, 28*(8), 766–778.
5. Bourque, P., Dupuis, R., Abran, A., Moore, J. W., & Tripp, L. (1999). The guide to the software engineering body of knowledge. *IEEE Software, 16*(6), 35–44.
6. Brandon, D. M. (2006). Change and Closeout Management. In *Project Management for Modern Information Systems* (Vol. 1, pp. 234–247). IGI Global.
7. Brown, A. B., Keller, A., & Hellerstein, J. L. (2005, May). A model of configuration complexity and its application to a change management system. In *2005 9th IFIP/IEEE International Symposium on Integrated Network Management, 2005.* IM 2005. (Vol. 1, pp. 631–644). IEEE.

8. Brown, N. (1998, November). Little book of configuration management. *Software Program Managers Network,* (Vol. 1, pp. 6–9).

9. Butt, A., Naaranoja, M., & Savolainen, J. (2016). Project change stakeholder communication. *International Journal of Project Management, 34*(8), 1579–1595.

10. Doherty, N. F., & King, M. (2005). From technical to socio-technical change: tackling the human and organizational aspects of systems development projects. *European Journal of Information Systems, 14*(1), 1–5.

11. Feiler, P. H., & Humphrey, W. S. (1993, February). Software process development and enactment: Concepts and definitions. In *[1993] Proceedings of the Second International Conference on the Software Process-Continuous Software Process Improvement* (Vol. 1, pp. 28–40). IEEE.

12. Griffith-Cooper, B., & King, K. (2007). The partnership between project management and organizational change: Integrating change management with change leadership. *Performance Improvement, 46*(1), 14–20.

13. Hall, N. G. (2012). Project management: Recent developments and research opportunities. *Journal of Systems Science and Systems Engineering, 21*(2), 129–143.

14. Hallows, J. (2005). Information systems project management: How to deliver function and value in information technology projects. *AMACOM/American Management Association*, (Vol. 1, pp. 4–9).

15. Herbsleb, J. D., Mockus, A., Finholt, T. A., & Grinter, R. E. (2001, May). An empirical study of global software development: distance and speed. In *Proceedings of the 23rd International Conference on Software Engineering. ICSE 2001* (Vol. 1, pp. 81–90). IEEE.

16. Hornstein, H. A. (2015). The integration of project management and organizational change management is now a necessity. *International Journal of Project Management, 33*(2), 291–298.

17. Hwang, B. G., & Low, L. K. (2012). Construction project change management in Singapore: Status, importance, and impact. *International Journal of Project Management, 30*(7), 817–826.

18. Ibbs, C. W., Wong, C. K., & Kwak, Y. H. (2001). Project change management system. *Journal of Management in Engineering, 17*(3), 159–165.

19. Jaafari, A. (2003). Project management in the age of complexity and change. *Project Management Journal, 34*(4), 47–57.

20. Johansson, C., & Heide, M. (2008). Speaking of change: three communication approaches in studies of organizational change. *Corporate Communications: An International Journal, 13*(3), 288–305.

21. Keller, A., Hellerstein, J. L., Wolf, J. L., Wu, K. L., & Krishnan, V. (2004, April). The CHAMPS system: Change management with planning and scheduling. In *2004 IEEE/IFIP Network Operations and Management Symposium (IEEE Cat. No. 04CH37507)* (Vol. 1, pp. 395–408). IEEE.

22. Kellner, M. I., Madachy, R. J., & Raffo, D. M. (1999). Software process simulation modeling: why? what? how?. *Journal of Systems and Software, 46*(2–3), 91–105.
23. Kenny, J. (2003). Effective project management for strategic innovation and change in an organizational context. *Project Management Journal, 34*(1), 43–53.
24. Kitchen, P. J., & Daly, F. (2002). Internal communication during change management. *Corporate Communications: An International Journal, 7*(1), 46–53.
25. Leybourne, S. (2006). Improvisation within the project management of change: some observations from UK financial services. *Journal of Change Management, 6*(4), 365–381.
26. Love, P. E., Holt, G. D., Shen, L. Y., Li, H., & Irani, Z. (2002). Using systems dynamics to better understand change and rework in construction project management systems. *International Journal of Project Management, 20*(6), 425–436.
27. Martinsuo, M., & Hoverfält, P. (2018). Change program management: Toward a capability for managing value-oriented, integrated multi-project change in its context. *International Journal of Project Management, 36*(1), 134–146.
28. Maull, R., Hughes, D., & Bennett, J. (1992). Special feature. The role of the bill-of-materials as a CAD/CAPM interface and the key importance of engineering change control. *Computing & Control Engineering Journal, 3*(2), 63–70.
29. Munassar, F., Ghanim, A., & Dahlan, A. R. A. (2013). Change Management and its contribution to the success of IT project implementation. *International Journal of Information and Communication Technology Research, 3*(4), 4–8.
30. Nagarajan, R., Joseph, A. V., & Sujatha, S. (2015). Behavioral aspects of software project management-in-house software development. *Indian Journal of Science and Technology, 8,* 1–6.
31. Orlikowski, W. J., & Hofman, J. D. (1997). An improvisational model for change management: The case of groupware technologies. *Sloan Management Review, 38*(2), I.
32. Park, M., & Peña-Mora, F. (2003). Dynamic change management for construction: introducing the change cycle into model-based project management. System Dynamics Review: *The Journal of the System Dynamics Society, 19*(3), 213–242.
33. Parker, D., Charlton, J., Ribeiro, A., & Pathak, R. D. (2013). Integration of project-based management and change management: Intervention methodology. *International Journal of Productivity and Performance Management,* (Vol. 1, pp. 2–9).
34. Proctor, T., & Doukakis, I. (2003). Change management: the role of internal communication and employee development. Corporate Communications: An International Journal, (Vol. 1, pp. 3–9).
35. Project Management Institute. (2000). *A Guide to the Project Management Body of Knowledge (PMBOK Guide)* (Vol. 2, pp. 2–3). Project Management Inst.
36. Pundziene, A., Alonderiene, R., & Buoziute-Rafanaviciene, S. (2007). Managers'

change communication competence links with the success of the organizational change. *Engeneering Economics, 4,* 54.

37. Simoes, P. M. M., & Esposito, M. (2014). Improving change management: How communication nature influences resistance to change. *Journal of Management Development*, Second Edition, pp. 2–9.
38. Stelzer, D., & Mellis, W. (1998). Success factors of organizational change in software process improvement. *Software Process: Improvement and Practice, 4*(4), 227–250.
39. Thiry, M. (2002). Combining value and project management into an effective program management model. *International Journal of Project Management, 20*(3), 221–227.
40. Varajão, J., Dominguez, C., Ribeiro, P., & Paiva, A. (2014). Critical Success Aspects in Project Management: Similarities and Differences Between the Construction and the Software Industry. *Tehnicki Vjesnik/Technical Gazette, 21*(3), 2–8.

CHAPTER 6

METHODS AND TOOLS IN IT PROJECT MANAGEMENT

UNIT INTRODUCTION

IT project management tools and methods are used by managers to oversee and coordinate the activities of various IT projects. Its primary goal is to boost productivity (Al-Ahmad et al., 2009). IT project management methods and tools organizations can make by providing users with the resources they have to monitor and track development and effectiveness. This maintains their IT projects on track to meet tight deadlines and budgets. Whatever IT project management system you use, you want it to make your work easier. This should assist you in organization goals and scheduling their completion within a predetermined budget. You also require a solution that links the business team and stakeholders so that everyone is on the same path.

Learning Objectives

At the end of this chapter, the reader will be able to understand:

- The methods of IT project management
- The significance of waterfall methodology
- The process of agile methodology

- The importance of hybrid methodology
- The usage of the Gantt Chart

Key Terms

1. IT Projects
2. Work Breakdown Structure (WBS)
3. Iterative Method
4. Hybrid Methodology
5. Project Management Tools
6. Gantt Chart

6.1. IT PROJECT MANAGEMENT METHODOLOGIES

Project management approaches appear to be as numerous as projects. They are divided into two categories, however: traditional and nontraditional approaches (Barjtya et al., 2017). Let's start with the standard waterfall method, which divides a project's duties into a series of successive project stages, which are all dependent on the completion of the one preceding it.

The business world is evolving swiftly in today's environment. In the recent decade, information technology (IT) had also grown at an accelerating rate (Nakigudde, 2019). For so many businesses, maintaining market position and providing the highest consistent product are among the biggest difficulties. As a result, every year, irrespective of sector, organization size, or geographical country, many IT-related projects are launched to give a competitive advantage to the relevant company. These projects are regarded as effective when they are finished within the agreed-upon budget, on time, and accomplish the company's goals. The leadership of a project is a major influence on its success (or failure) (Berntsson et al., 2006). There are two particularly well-known project management approaches. The first refers to the traditional "waterfall" process, and the other is the "agile" approach. The waterfall methodology is more plan-driven and manuscript and it maintains the chronological implementation of predetermined stages that are not overlapped (Kusters et al., 2017). The agile method, in contrast, hand, emphasizes constant examination and adaption in short and incremental periods, which makes it more flexible, inexpensive, and transition-hospitable (Meyer, 2014). Scrum is the most widely popular agile approach (Schwaber & Sutherland, 2017).

Did you Know?

The Standish Group (1994) produced research, indicating that only 16% of web applications were effective, 31% failed, and 53% were disputed.

At this period, the waterfall method was used to handle practically most operations. In the year 2000, a team comprising 17 technologists developed the agile approach, and in 2001 it was officially introduced as a method for project management with its authorized handbook. By comparing the above statistics to the 2015 Standish Group study, it can be shown that agility projects have a fourfold greater success rate than waterfall projects (Standish Group, 2015). This demonstrates how agile project management techniques may play an important role in a team's achievement. Nevertheless, these methodologies have benefits and drawbacks, and depending on the nature of the project as well as the workplace environment, one may perform much better than another (Batra et al., 2010). The hybrid methods were led by the concept that combining the best aspects of Waterfall with agile methodology. The hybrid strategy allows for the modification of strict procedures based on their usability and requirements. Since there is no "silver bullet" in projects and software production (Brooks & Bullet, 1987), project leaders must devise their solutions or methods. Either conventional or agile techniques are effective in every instance of a business (Standish Group, 2015). This is especially true for complicated tasks, in which several participants are engaged and a variety of special expertise is required to achieve the project's final objective (Lalevée et al., 2020).

6.2. TYPICAL METHODOLOGY

While there are numerous methods for managing IT projects, some things are common. The stages may alter somewhat, but the overall pattern remains the very same (Felderer et al., 2017).

Following are the steps of the typical method, demonstrating how project management software helps you all along the way.

6.2.1. Requirements for Project Management

Documentation is needed before such a project can start. You must identify the project's scope and establish a budget, and establish the stakeholders' needs. All of these papers can be linked to the project using our software, which has infinite file storage space (Küpper et al., 2018; Papadakis & Tsironis, 2020).

6.2.2. Preparation of Team and Gantt Chart

Now that you have gathered the project's needs, you may put together a group with the necessary skills and experience. Make sure to incorporate them into your software for project management so that all communication occurs in one location (Zasa et al., 2020).

To add jobs to a timetable, connect relationships, define deadlines, and visualize critical activities, use a Gantt Chart. However, the entire team is not required to use this typical planning tool because project information is distributed across many project viewpoints: work listings, calendars, and Kanban board (Špundak, 2014; Kusters et al., 2017).

Aspects of a good Gantt Chart: All of the following pieces of data must be included in a Gantt Chart:

- The project start date
- The title or summary of every team project

- Resources assigned to each task
- A beginning and ending date for each work
- The duration of each job
- The connection between jobs
- The project end date

All jobs must be interconnected. A job with no connections or dependents is known as a hanging or orphaned task. Orphaned activities are prohibited by the PMBOK because they hinder planning. However, several sets of concurrent jobs are feasible. There are four distinct types of connections or dependencies available (Lalevée et al., 2020; Wysocki, 2020):

- *Finish to Start (FS):* One duty should be performed before beginning the next. This connection represents the most prevalent option.
- *Start to Start (SS):* In this instance, multiple processes can start concurrently. Consider a construction project: after you started installing sheetrock, someone else will start repainting. It is not necessary to finish drywalling the entire building before painting the very first bedroom.
- *Finish to Finish (FF):* In certain instances, one job cannot conclude till the prior one is finished. For instance, a building could be inspected till its construction is complete.
- *Start to Finish (SF):* This is the least consistent job connection, in which one job cannot conclude till the next begins. Night shifts are a prime illustration of this, as the person on the day shift cannot complete their work till the night shift employee starts.

6.2.3. Usage of Kanban Board

Utilize a kanban board to manage the process of work throughout project implementation. Despite affecting the Gantt Chart, a Project Manager allows you to establish processes, conduct iterations, and operate in an agile method (West et al., 2011; Lei et al., 2017).

Main Principles of Kanban: There are some main principles of Kantan board which are as follow;

a) *Visualization of Work:* As previously indicated, Kanban is a graphical system. That is its main advantage. Kanban's visuals assist teammates in communicating quickly and effectively about all facets of a project (Wells, 2012).
b) *Work-in-Progress Limits*: While multi-tasking has many advantages, it has also been shown to slow down production. If there are too many activities in process at the same time, everything appears to

be completed. Work in progress (WIP) restrictions assist in keeping the process of work so that more gets done in much less period.

c) *Maintaining Flow*: Ideally, work should flow from "to do" to "doing" to "done" in an even and efficient manner. Theoretically, work must flow smoothly and efficiently from "to do" to "doing" to "done." Maintaining adequate flow requires continual observation of this flow to both avoid and fix blockage instances where work can become stalled. Kanban's graphical aspect aids in determining where and why bottlenecks happen.

d) *Continuous Improvement*: A normal and desired secondary effect of Kanban is continued improvement. The more a group uses Kanban to simplify their work, the better they get at fulfilling program goals and deadlines (Figure 6.1).

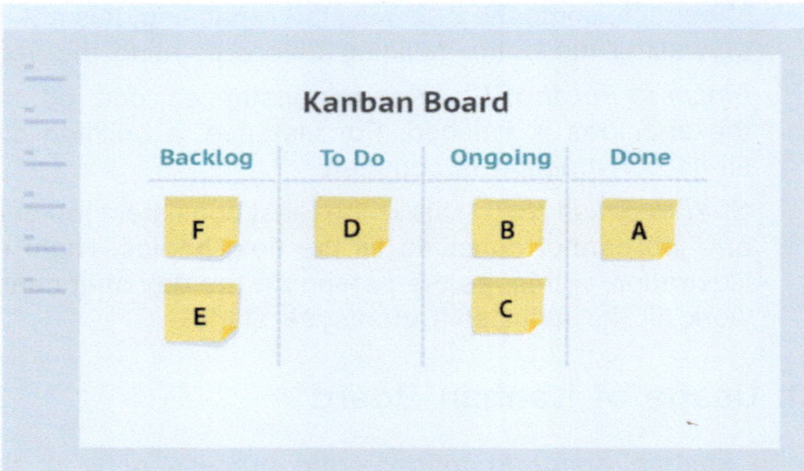

Figure 6.1. Schematic of Kanban Board (Source: Digite, Creative Commons License).

6.2.4. Monitor and Manage Workload

As the project moves forward, the actual progress must match what was planned A true display of software gathers data as it is uploaded. We analyze the figures mechanically and present them in graphs that indicate prices, activities, wellness, and other information. Project management was never simpler (Mahalakshmi & Sundararajan, 2013). IT projects necessitate effective workload control. Are teammates overburdened, or do they have too little coursework? To prevent slow progress, workload space displays who is on vacation and who has enough jobs: you can even redistribute jobs directly from the website (Nakigudde, 2019).

6.2.5. Status Updation

Projects are not fixed. When stakeholders want changes, you must react quickly. The software having WBS or some other methods of project management allow you and your staff to be more flexible with your goals. If a date varies, for example, simply drag & drop the job to the deadline set on the Gantt Chart. This modification is subsequently implemented throughout the program (Webster & Watson, 2002; Meyer, 2014).

The software includes a comprehensive reporting capability for monitoring progress and keeping the stakeholders informed. Many reports are available to assist with IT managing projects. Create an in-depth progress update with a few keystrokes to gather the data you require (Royce, 1970).

TIPS

Kanban is all about progressing to the next production level and effectiveness.

6.3. WATERFALL METHODOLOGY

Waterfall has become the most commonly used approach for IT projects. Although it is a project management style in use for major projects beyond IT, it is equally applicable to IT projects and has been proven effective for formalized and sequential endeavors (Beck et al., 2001). The waterfall method is based on a sequential approach with predetermined deadlines, objectives, and deliverables. Independent implementation groups are not needed to be in continual interaction and, unless particular connections are necessary, are typically self-sufficient when using this strategy. Additionally, teammates tend to work autonomously and are not required to deliver status updates as frequently as in an agile manner. Typically, one phase does not begin till the preceding one concludes.

6.3.1. Stages of Waterfall Methodology

Waterfall has existed since Dr. Winston W. Royce wrote a study on the term in 1970. The waterfall design comprises six stages:

6.3.1.1. Requirement

Initially, the needs are defined, assessed, and documented in a documentation that defines what has been performed and how it is going to be performed. This will be examined by interested parties.

6.3.1.2. Design

The next step is to summarize those decisions made in the first phase in a design specification, which includes a list of all the resources required to accomplish the project.

6.3.1.3. Implementation

The IT project manager and team implement the initial design by requirements, processes, and deadlines.

6.3.1.4. Testing

Screening would be when intended outcomes are compared to the guidelines specified in the design specification and participants do quality control. If it is not met, the procedure is repeated (Marović & Bulatović, 2020).

6.3.1.5. Installation

If the testing passes, the application is ready to be released to the end user. At this stage, every application should be completely operating.

Did you Know?

It is believed that approximately 95% of firms have implemented Agility in some form or another.

6.3.1.6. Maintenance

However, most IT projects do not conclude with delivering: they frequently request help after implementation, such as updates or modifications; however, this is typically the responsibility of a distinct group.

6.3.2. Advantages of the Waterfall Methodology

The Waterfall approach is a basic, well-defined, and time-tested project management technique. Every participant can successfully arrange their schedule for the lifecycle of the building since they are aware of what should be completed and when it must be completed.

Additional welfares of the Waterfall method comprise (Binder et al., 2014):

- During the planning and design phase, developers can detect design problems, preventing them from producing flawed code during the project execution.
- After specifications have been determined, it is possible to

correctly calculate the project's entire cost and duration.

- With an organized method, it is easy to monitor progress using clearly stated benchmarks.
- Developers who join the project in progress can easily get up to speed because everything they need to know should be in the requirements document.
- Consumers do not always add additional project needs, slowing development (Figure 6.2).

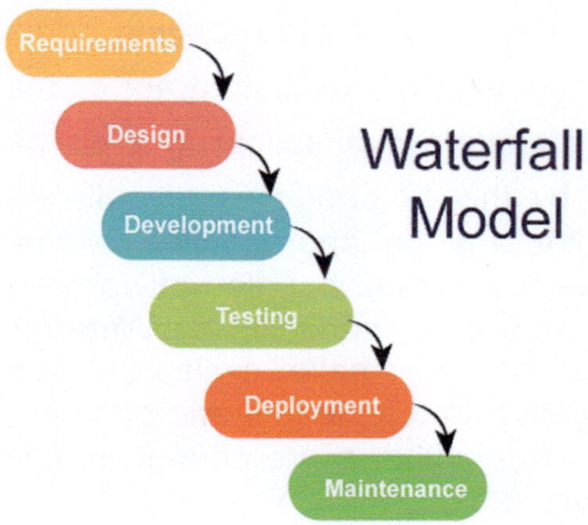

Figure 6.2. Illustration of steps of Waterfall Methodology (Source: Chathmini Jayathilaka, Creative Commons License).

6.4. AGILE METHODOLOGY

Software development has contributed an agile methodology to projects, a much more iterative method that operates in shorter races and is flexible all through the length of the project, as opposed to becoming rigorously plan-driven. Those IT teams have adopted rapid or a portion of its applications for their projects (Cohn, 2009). To make software development increasingly adaptable and more economical, the project management concept was introduced as an alternative to the conventional technique. It has rapidly now become the industry's gold standard for managing projects.

At the same moment, there is still much effort to be done to develop the profession. The history of agile can be traced back to 1957, when Bernie Dimsdale, John von Neumann, Herb Jacobs, and Gerald Weinberg started developing technology for IBM and Motorola utilizing development incremental approaches (which are now recognized as Agile). Despite having no idea how to categorize the methodology they were using, they recognized that it was distinct from Waterfall in so many aspects (Boehm et al., 1987).

The contemporary agile methodology was first presented in 2001 when a committee of 17 software design specialists gathered to examine alternate project approaches. They set out their concept of the adaptable, inexpensive, and collaborative software growth strategy in the agile manifesto. The Declaration, which aims to "locate the ideal ways of producing software," explicitly explains the core concepts of the new strategy (Conforto & Amaral, 2010):

- Through this work, we have come to the assessment
- Personalities and interactions over processes and tools
- Working software over wide-ranging certification
- Customer partnership over contract cooperation
- Answering change over following a plan

Accompanied by the 12 principles of agile development, the idea has evolved into a global and effective new method of project management. Agile techniques handle software engineering in an iteration process. Unlike a simple linear Waterfall method, agile projects are divided up into smaller cycles called Sprints. Each of them is a mini-project with a schedule and phases of development, validation, and delivery within a pre-defined project scope (Dilger et al., 2020) (Figure 6.3).

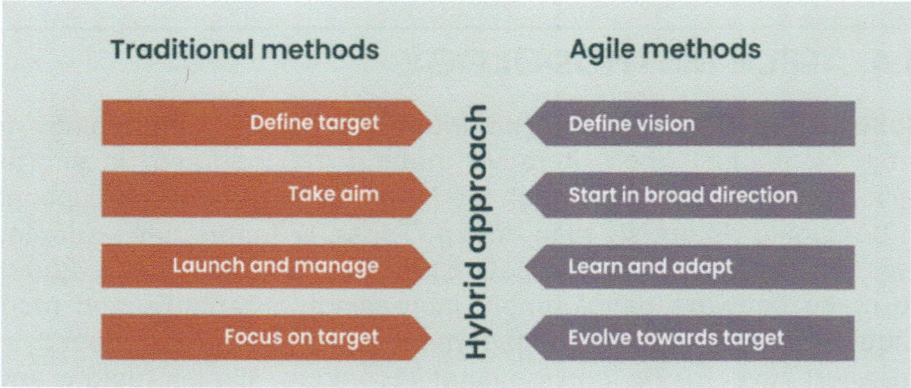

Figure 6.3. Schematic of traditional, agile, and hybrid project management (Source: Association for Project Management, Creative Commons License).

6.4.1. Agile Development Cycle

A possible shippable product incremental is given at the end of every Sprint. Thus, with every iteration new features are added to the product, resulting in gradual project growth, leading to progressive project expansion. With the features being validated early in development, the chances of delivering a potentially failed product are significantly lower. (Hassani et al., 2018) (Figure 6.4).

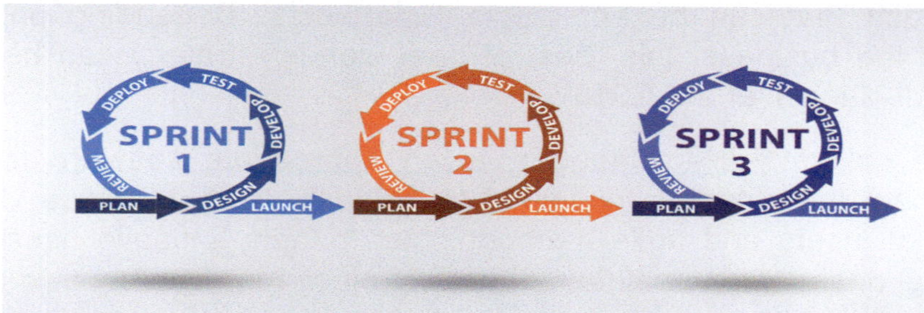

Figure 6.4. Diagram of Agile Development Cycle (Source: John Adam, Creative Commons License).

6.4.2. Aspects of Agile Methodology

There are a few aspects of agile methodology;

- *Flexibility:* The project scope may well be modified according to new requirements.
- *Work breakdown:* The project consists of small cycles (known as Sprints in Scrum).
- *Value of teamwork:* The teammates work collaboratively and have a complete sense of their tasks.
- *Iterative improvements:* There is a constant reevaluation of work performed throughout a loop to enhance the final output (Lalmi et al., 2021).
- *Cooperation with a client:* A consumer is intimately involved in the design process and can alter the criteria or approve the team's suggestions. According to the 14th yearly report on the current state of Agile, participants who have implemented the Agile methodology cite the following advantages:
  - The capacity to handle changing priorities (70%);
  - Increases team effectiveness via daily work assignments (58%); and
  - Improved improving the visual as a result of straightforward strategic planning (65%).

Companies still prioritize flexibility and rapid turnaround as key advantages Agile provides (Hayata & Han, 2011; Bhalerao & Ingle, 2020).

6.5. HYBRID METHODOLOGY

The hybrid method, which mixes waterfalls and agile, is more common among IT groups. It creates a more adaptable and organized approach that can be applied to IT projects. Depending on the circumstances of the business, this "best of both worlds" strategy can be the right path forward (Janjua et al., 2016).

The software called "ProjectManager" is an appropriate software for IT project management for waterfalls or hybrid techniques. It offers online Gantt Charts for waterfall users and agile methodologies panels for agile users. In addition, the true dashboards maintain the IT project manager's up-to-date performance via metrics that may be adjusted to provide the desired data and then distributed (Kitchenham & Charters, 2007).

Combining traditional with agile methods is the trend lately (Batra et al., 2010). A hybrid is a result of mixing or blending diverse qualities to produce the best experience. Project managers are trying to identify new approaches that are more adaptable and can be adapted to the needs of various projects and organizations due to the ever-changing consumer expectations and design specifications (Hassani et al., 2018).

While both agile and waterfall techniques have advantages and drawbacks and are intended for particular situations and need to follow some rules, the hybrid model seeks to blend the best of both methods (Binder et al., 2014). It aims to use the benefit of one approach to offset the disadvantage of others, and conversely. The hybrid approach can be a flexible strategy that can be adapted to the specific demands and expectations of the project (Kuhrmann et al., 2017).

Advantages

- Minor improvements in software/product supply lead to a delighted consumer (Schwaber & Sutherland, 2017)
- More adaptable and open to change (Digital, 2020)
- Interaction is highly valued (Beck et al., 2001)
- A more flexible attitude (Schwaber & Sutherland, 2017)
- Value daily and constant human interaction (Beck et al., 2001)
- Value daily and constant human interaction (Beck et al., 2001)

Disadvantages

- Difficult when dealing with large groups or many groups on a single project (Schwaber & Sutherland, 2017)
- It allows for scope creep (Weisert, 2003)
- It makes establishing a firm cost and program completion date difficult.
- Less predictable (Hassani et al., 2018) (Figure 6.5)

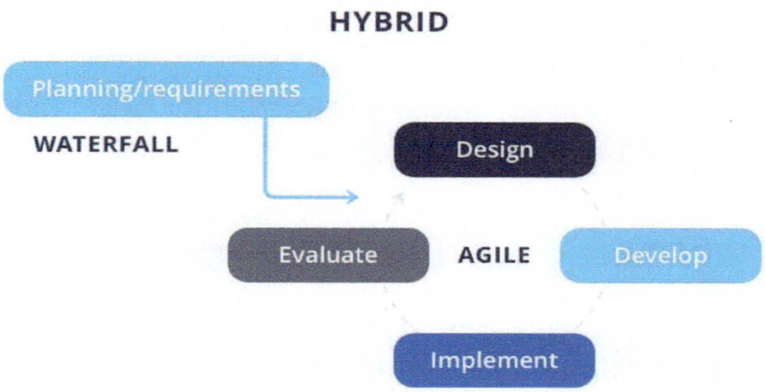

Figure 6.5. Illustration of hybrid methodology (Source: Ivan Ozhiganov, Creative Commons License).

6.6. IT PROJECT MANAGEMENT TOOLS

The correct IT program management tools will help to solve the issues of IT projects by offering managers greater control and employees the resources they have to interact and be more efficient. Luckily, "ProjectManager" is software for managing projects created specifically for IT managing projects (Saleh et al., 2019).

6.6.1. Gantt Charts for Waterfall Plans

"Project Manager's" web Gantt Charts are a tool that suits IT project management like a hand in a glove. The majority of these approaches operate on the timeframe of a Gantt Chart, and ours allows you to link and even allocate dependent jobs (Berntsson-Svensson & Aurum, 2006).

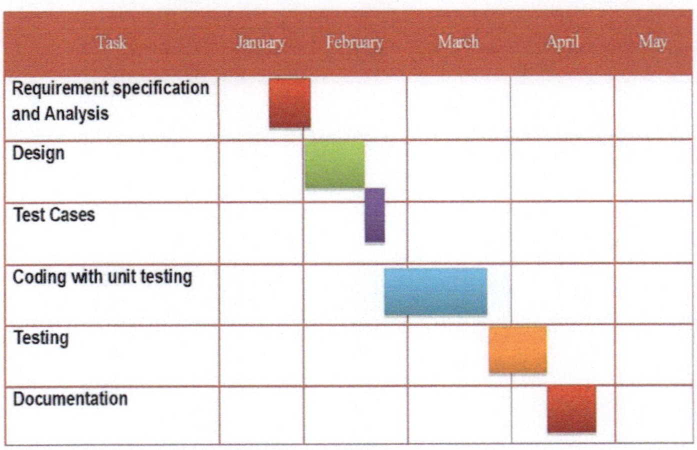

Figure 6.6. Diagram of Gantt Chart (Source: Alam Nawaz, Creative Commons License).

ACTIVITY 6.1.

Enlist some major methods and tools that are used in IT project management. Also describe how these methods and tools can be beneficial for an IT project.

Groups, particularly the IT teamwork work cooperatively and autonomously, like a digital Gantt Chart. This is because they can make comments at the task level. Tasks can also have papers or photographs to add supplementary information, and they can even be signed off again (Berntsson-Svensson et al., 2006) (Figure 6.6).

6.6.2. Dashboards for Live Reporting

Status updates are instantly reflected throughout the program because Project Manager is a cloud-based software for managing projects (Theocharis et al., 2015). That is, your dashboard is providing you with ongoing projects as they occur.

The many indicators monitoring price, effort, time, and other factors can be selected to reveal only the information you require (Watson & Webster, 2020). Then, these colorful, simple graphs can be distributed to team members and stakeholders or printed out for conferences.

SUMMARY

The choice of tools and methods will vary depending on the specific project and the preferences of the project manager. However, all IT project managers should be familiar with the most popular tools and methods so that they can choose the best option for their project. Project management software is an essential tool for IT project managers. It can help them plan, track, and manage their project. Agile project management is a popular method for IT projects. It is a flexible approach that allows project managers to make changes to the project as it progresses. The waterfall is a traditional project management method. It is a linear approach that goes from one stage of the project to the next in a logical order.

REVIEW QUESTIONS

1. What are some methods and tools that can be used in IT project management?
2. How can these methods and tools be used to effectively manage an IT project?
3. What are some benefits of using these methods and tools in IT project management?
4. What are some challenges that can be faced when using these methods and tools in IT project management?
5. How can these challenges be overcome?

MULTIPLE CHOICE QUESTIONS

1. What is the main purpose of using a project management method?

a. To ensure the project is completed on time and within budget

b. To ensure the project team is aware of the tasks they need to complete

c. To ensure communication is clear between the project manager and the project team

d. To ensure the project is completed according to the scope

2. Which of the following is not a tool that can be used in IT project management?

a. Work breakdown structure

b. Gantt Chart

c. Earned value analysis

d. Facebook

3. Which of the following is not a common method used in IT project management?

a. Agile

b. Waterfall

c. Iterative

d. Critical path

4. What are the three main components of the triple constraint in project management?

a. Time, cost, and quality

b. Time, cost, and scope

c. Scope, quality, and risk

d. Schedule, budget, and resources

5. What is the main difference between Agile and Waterfall methods?

a. Agile methods are adaptive and allow for changes to be made throughout the project, while Waterfall methods are more rigid and do not allow for changes to be made once the project has begun

b. Agile methods are more suited for small projects, while Waterfall methods are more suited for large projects

c. Agile methods focus on delivering the project in small increments, while Waterfall methods focus on delivering the project as a whole

d. There is no difference between Agile and Waterfall methods

Answers to Multiple Choice Questions

1. (d) 2. (d) 3. (d) 4. (b) 5. (a)

REFERENCES

1. Al-Ahmad, W., Al-Fagih, K., Khanfar, K., Alsamara, K., Abuleil, S., & Abu-Salem, H. (2009). A taxonomy of an IT project failure: root causes. *International Management Review, 5*(1), 93.
2. Barjtya, S., Sharma, A., & Rani, U. (2017). A detailed study of Software Development Life Cycle (SDLC) models. *International Journal of Engineering And Computer Science, 6*(7), 22097–22100.
3. Batra, D., Xia, W., VanderMeer, D., & Dutta, K. (2010). Balancing agile and structured development approaches to successfully manage large distributed software projects: A case study from the cruise line industry. *Communications of the Association for Information Systems, 27*(1), 21.
4. Beck, K., Beedle, M., Bennekum, A. V., Cockburn, A., Cunningham, W., Fowler, M.,

... & Thomas, D. (2001). Manifesto for agile software development. *Agile Manifesto*, (Vol. 1, pp. 3–9).

5. Berntsson-Svensson, R., & Aurum, A. (2006, September). Successful software project and products: An empirical investigation. In *Proceedings of the 2006 ACM/IEEE International Symposium on Empirical Software Engineering* (Vol. 1, pp. 144–153).
6. Berntsson-Svensson, R., Aurum, A., Wohlin, C., & Hu, G. (2006). Successful Software Project and Products: An Empirical Investigation Comparing Australia and Sweden. *ACIS 2006 Proceedings,* Vol. 1, pp. 97.
7. Bhalerao, S., & Ingle, M. (2020). Hybrid agile project management practices: Novel approach for improving project management. *IJRAR-International Journal of Research and Analytical Reviews (IJRAR), 7*(1), 723–727.
8. Binder, J., Aillaud, L. I., & Schilli, L. (2014). The project management cocktail model: An approach for balancing agile and ISO 21500. *Procedia-Social and Behavioral Sciences, 119,* 182–191.
9. Boehm, B. W., Boehm, B., & Turner, R. (2004). Balancing agility and discipline: A guide for the perplexed. *Addison-Wesley Professional,* (Vol. 1, pp. 2–8).
10. Brooks, F. P., & Bullet, N. S. (1987). Essence and accidents of software engineering. *IEEE Computer, 20*(4), 10–19.
11. Cohn, M. (2009). *Succeeding with Agile: Software Development Using Scrum.* Addison-Wesley, (Vol. 1, pp. 2–9).
12. Conforto, E. C., & Amaral, D. C. (2010). Evaluating an agile method for planning and controlling innovative projects. *Project Management Journal, 41*(2), 73–80.
13. Dilger, T., Ploder, C., Haas, W., Schöttle, P., & Bernsteiner, R. (2020, October). Continuous Planning and Forecasting Framework (CPFF) for Agile Project Management: Overcoming the. In *Proceedings of the 21st Annual Conference on Information Technology Education* (Vol. 1, pp. 371–377).
14. Felderer, M., Winkler, D., & Biffl, S. (2017, November). Hybrid software and system development in practice: initial results from Austria. In *International Conference on Product-Focused Software Process Improvement* (Vol. 1, pp. 435–442). Springer, Cham.
15. Hassani, R., El Bouzekri El Idrissi, Y., & Abouabdellah, A. (2018, January). Digital project management in the era of digital transformation: Hybrid method. In *Proceedings of the 2018 International Conference on Software Engineering and Information Management* (Vol. 1, pp. 98–103).
16. Hayata, T., & Han, J. (2011, July). A hybrid model for IT projects with Scrum. In *Proceedings of 2011 IEEE International Conference on Service Operations, Logistics and Informatics* (Vol. 1, pp. 285–290). IEEE.
17. Janjua, J. I., Ali, A., & Chaudhry, M. U. (2016, July). OPENTCQ: Towards Change Management in Hybrid Agile Model. In *Proceedings of the 7th International Conference on Computing Communication and Networking Technologies* (Vol. 1, pp. 1–8).

18. Kitchenham, B., & Charters, S. (2007). *Guidelines for Performing Systematic Literature Reviews in Software Engineering,* (Vol. 1, pp. 5–8).
19. Kuhrmann, M., Diebold, P., Münch, J., Tell, P., Garousi, V., Felderer, M., ... & Prause, C. R. (2017, July). Hybrid software and system development in practice: waterfall, scrum, and beyond. In *Proceedings of the 2017 International Conference on Software and System Process* (Vol. 1, pp. 30–39).
20. Küpper, S., Rausch, A., & Andelfinger, U. (2018, May). Towards the systematic development of hybrid software development processes. In *Proceedings of the 2018 International Conference on Software and System Process (*Vol. 1, pp. 157–161).
21. Kusters, R. J., van de Leur, Y., Rutten, W. G., & Trienekens, J. J. (2017, April). When agile meets waterfall-investigating risks and problems on the interface between agile and traditional software development in a hybrid development organization. In *International Conference on Enterprise Information Systems* (Vol. 2, pp. 271–278). SCITEPRESS.
22. Lalevée, A., Troussier, N., Blanco, É., & Berlioz, M. (2020). The interest in an evolution of Value Management methodology in Complex Technical Projects for improving Project Management. *Procedia CIRP, 90*, 411–415.
23. Lalmi, A., Fernandes, G., & Souad, S. B. (2021). A conceptual hybrid project management model for construction projects. *Procedia Computer Science, 181*, 921–930.
24. Lei, H., Ganjeizadeh, F., Jayachandran, P. K., & Ozcan, P. (2017). A statistical analysis of the effects of Scrum and Kanban on software development projects. *Robotics and Computer-Integrated Manufacturing, 43,* 59–67.
25. Mahalakshmi, M., & Sundararajan, M. (2013). Traditional SDLC vs scrum methodology–a comparative study. *International Journal of Emerging Technology and Advanced Engineering, 3*(6), 192–196.
26. Marović, I., & Bulatović, G. (2020). Development of a Hybrid Agile Management Model in Local Self-Government Units. *Tehnički vjesnik, 27*(5), 1418–1426.
27. Meyer, B. (2014). *Agile! Bertrand Meyer Good, the Hype, and the Ugl.* Springer-Verlag Berlin Heidelberg, (Vol. 1, pp. 2–9).
28. Nakigudde, S. (2019). Project Management Models and Software Development Project Success, (Vol. 1, pp. 5–7).
29. Papadakis, E., & Tsironis, L. (2020). Towards a hybrid project management framework: A systematic literature review on traditional, agile and hybrid techniques. *The Journal of Modern Project Management, 8*(2), 3–7.
30. Royce, W. W. (1970). Managing the development of large software systems. *Proceedings of IEEE WESCON.* Los Angeles, Vol. 1, 328–388.
31. Saleh, S. M., Huq, S. M., & Rahman, M. A. (2019, February). Comparative studies within Scrum, Kanban, XP focused on their practices. In *2019 International Conference on Electrical, Computer and Communication Engineering (ECCE)* (Vol. 1, pp. 1–6). IEEE.

32. Špundak, M. (2014). Mixed agile/traditional project management methodology–reality or illusion? *Procedia-Social and Behavioral Sciences, 119*, 939–948.
33. Theocharis, G., Kuhrmann, M., Münch, J., & Diebold, P. (2015, December). Is water-scrum-fall reality? on the use of agile and traditional development practices. In *International Conference on Product-Focused Software Process Improvement* (Vol. 1, pp. 149–166). Springer, Cham.
34. Watson, R. T., & Webster, J. (2020). Analyzing the past to prepare for the future: Writing a literature review and a roadmap for release 2.0. *Journal of Decision Systems, 29*(3), 129–147.
35. Webster, J., & Watson, R. T. (2002). Analyzing the past to prepare for the future: Writing a literature review. *MIS Quarterly,* Vol. 1, xiii–xxiii.
36. Wells, H. (2012). How effective are project management methodologies? An explorative evaluation of their benefits in practice. *Project Management Journal, 43*(6), 43–58.
37. West, D., Gilpin, M., Grant, T., & Anderson, A. (2011). Water-scrum-fall is the reality of agile for most organizations today. *Forrester Research, 26*(2011), 1–17.
38. Wysocki, W. (2020). A hybrid software processes management support model. *Procedia Computer Science, 176,* 2312–2321.
39. Zasa, F. P., Patrucco, A., & Pellizzoni, E. (2020). Managing the hybrid organization: How can agile and traditional project management coexist? *Research-Technology Management, 64*(1), 54–63.

CHAPTER 7

CHALLENGES IN IT PROJECT MANAGEMENT

UNIT INTRODUCTION

A project manager is responsible for the program either success or failure. Discussed in this chapter the issues that project managers managed in the IT project are highlighted. Solutions are offered for the problems of collecting information, delegating tasks, interacting with the group, resolving conflicts, related measures, managing deadlines, and budgets, firing employees, evaluating the product, and system integration. Project Management is the major emphasis region for the achievement of organizational goals. The project manager's responsibilities are comparable to the role of the captain of a ship. He is accountable for the achievement of the project's objectives as well as its regulatory compliance (da Silva et al., 2010). In this chapter, we will examine a few of the difficulties project leaders in the Information Technology (IT) project face. Dealing with a varied group of individuals from a variety of departments presents several inherent difficulties in IT project planning. A good manager must balance the requirements and desires of all associates, keep their organization on track, and improve communication with their personnel and customers (Hoda & Murugesan, 2016). To say the very least, it is a large task, and it is no surprise that most decision-makers encounter problems along the road.

Project managers, often known as PMs in the IT industry, are assigned to fulfill set requirements or problems within a set time frame or within the project's timeline. Do you believe is it easy to be a project manager? Certainly, it is not an easy process, as we believe. As a result, it is understandable that they will face numerous problems in effectively completing the project. A few problems are the primary concerns of the project manager in the IT industry. It may involve breaking down the complex elements of managing the project. So, to be an excellent project manager, you should be aware of the major difficulties that will be encountered when managing the project.

The project manager's major responsibility is to handle certain complexities, and avoiding those obstacles will result in a successful project deliverable (Ojiako et al., 2011). As a result, it is critical for the project manager to anticipate the obstacles that will arise when managing the project. In this chapter, you will learn about the most prevalent issues that project managers confront in the IT industry.

Learning Objectives

At the end of this chapter, the reader will be able to understand:

- The challenges in IT project management
- The issue related to the work delegation during project management
- The problem caused by lack of communication in teams
- The challenge of cost and schedule maintenance
- The problem caused by hiring and firing the employees

Key Terms

1. IT Project Challenges
2. Knowledge-Based Industries
3. Java Language
4. Budget Planning
5. Budget Forecasting
6. Change Control Board (CCB)
7. Schedule Maintenance
8. Product Testing

7.1. ISSUE OF DATA GATHERING

The issues that are faced by the project manager begin with acquiring the project's or product's needs (Singh et al., 2009). The project manager typically has little opportunity to interact with the project's consumers. If that happens, there will be less chance for the requirement to be unclear. A conference between the project manager and the end user must be arranged by the consumer. Typically, the customer sends the high-level requirement to the offshore staff. These needs will be discussed in detail by the offshore staff as they create the required functionality. In the situation of the product, the project leader develops the business needs for the item with assistance from the advertising team and business analyst. Once the functional specifications are ready, the designed discussions can take place. (Shenhar & Dvir, 2007). Once the project manager gets the requirements from the customer, it is desirable to get a sign-off from all the stakeholders, to make the subsequent stakeholder management easier.

The biggest problem that is faced by the project manager today is obtaining the stakeholder's early approval for the documentation (Hwang & Ng, 2013). We all know that requirement gathering is the first stage of any IT project, and the project manager wants to be well aware of the customer's desires throughout this stage. This makes it easier to oversee the project and find remedies. For requirements management, there are readily available tools on the market, such as Caliber RM (Figure 7.1).

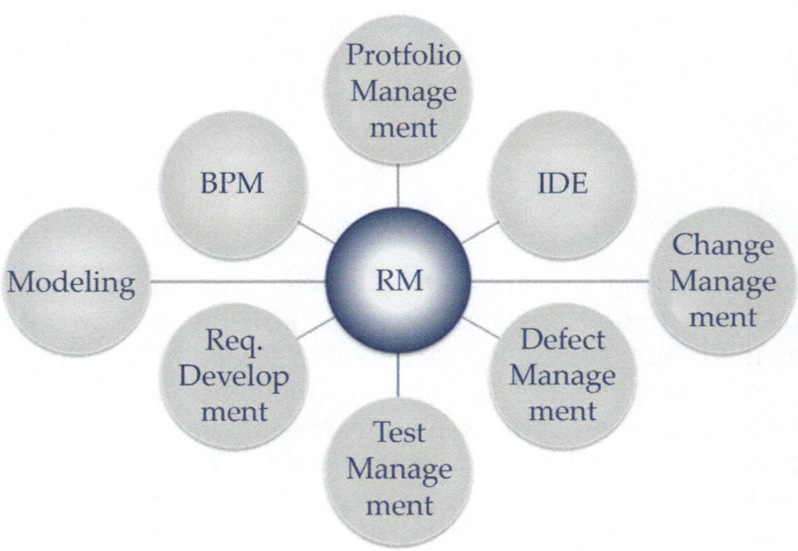

Figure 7.1. Illustration of tools of RM Caliber software (Source: Gerald Heller, Creative Commons License).

The following challenges are encountered during the stage of requirement gathering (Engwall & Jerbrant, 2003):

- Poorly defined project objectives confuse project objectives and make planning difficult.
- Customers ' expectations may be inappropriate during this point. For example, an unrealistic deadline, increased quality, and a low project budget.

7.2. THE PROBLEM IS WORK DELEGATION

Work delegation is another difficulty for the project manager because, in knowledge-based industries, colleagues compete to take on the more legitimate task. When the task of work delegation is performed, the project manager should take into account the group members' capabilities and interests. This is beneficial in finishing the project on schedule and with excellent quality (Niazi et al., 2016). Otherwise, a significant amount of effort would have been invested in bug fixes. The Duties Assignment Matrix (RAM) can be useful in this situation. This matrix shows the activities and the materials allotted to those activities in a columnar style. Another problem that the project manager encounters throughout work delegation is leveling the project's capabilities (Ogunde et al., 2017). In this case, Microsoft Project', can be used to level resources (Figure 7.2).

RESPONSIBILITY ASSIGNMENT MATRIX

	PERSON 1	PERSON 2	PERSON 3	PERSON 4	PERSON 5	PERSON 6	PERSON 7	PERSON 8
Work package 1	R		C		A	I		
Work package 2		A	I				A	R
Work package 3		C		R		A	I	
Work package 4	I		A		C	R		

Figure 7.2. Diagram of Responsibilities Assignment Matrix (RAM) Template (Source: Stakeholder map, Creative Commons License).

When working on long-term projects, your project team can change, with people leaving for other projects or new jobs. It's aggravating, but you must recalibrate. Examine the unfinished tasks and assignments that leaving employees were given (this is simple if you use online project management software) and search for new personnel to replace them. Do not be enticed to jump in immediately if you are a supervisor with the required skills. Your responsibility is to oversee the project rather than to carry it out. Consider looking outside of your organization to address the unexpected need. Changes have several interconnected shapes, and it is not always illogical. No magic ball could inform you or your decision makers of how unforeseen developments will affect the project at the beginning of it. You simply must be prepared for something.

7.3. ISSUES IN COMMUNICATION

The project leader must communicate with the group on a regular or as-needed basis. In several demanding scenarios, the availability of meeting rooms or a location for group sessions is also one of the manager's concerns. The project manager must arrange a suitable meeting location for the group. A project manager's responsibility is to provide a supportive atmosphere for group interaction. The project manager can control the atmosphere (Masood & Farooq, 2017). Executives need to plan presentations. How he interacts with his teammates, including the spacing, pitch, speech, and terminology, is crucial. He must be capable of expressing his concepts simply and straightforwardly. The team members must be capable of receiving and comprehending the information (Dolfi & Andrews, 2007).

Developing an IT task involves a large team of individuals from many corporate areas. To be effective, you must ensure that your technicians communicate with your architects. You also want to be sure that everyone keeps your marketing team updated on their progress so that marketing can roll out an appropriate public campaign. Regrettably, this is frequently simpler stated than accomplished. Your company's various departments act autonomously of one another and do not know how to communicate with each other (Söderlund & Maylor, 2012). To track the development of their work, they could make use of various records, statistics, and technologies. Because your employees do not speak the same language, interaction becomes even more difficult.

Untimely requests for details from parties beyond the project present additional difficulty for the project manager. This occurs because of incomplete stakeholder identification and inadequate communication management plan. The project manager must determine the project's key stakeholders at the outset. Stakeholder identification is an ongoing process that should remain all across the project, which is both true and correct. The project manager must develop a communication strategy based on the stakeholders who have been recognized (Sommer et al., 2014). The content that stakeholders are engaged in, at the appropriate frequency, is included in this plan. Unforeseen enquiries can be decreased if the stakeholders are identified, and a continuous improvement plan is created with clarity and thoroughness.

Like a project manager, you may enhance communication by arranging activities in a variety of styles. Arrange meetings and conferences, small group and whole-team events, as well as video and telephone calls. It's also a great suggestion to motivate your team to foster confidence by becoming friends with one another informally. The more varied the methods you can connect, the better off you will be when it comes time to speak regarding your joint achievements (Hwang & Ng, 2013).

7.4. THE ISSUE IN CONFLICT RESOLUTION

In highly technological businesses, the task of a project manager is to settle teammates' disputes. There is a chance of disputes amongst teammates in every department. Scheduling, challenges, project priorities, resources, costs, and personalities are a few factors that can lead to disputes. The project manager is not accountable for dispute resolution. The group of individuals who are in conflict is responsible for addressing their issues independently. The project manager is the sole individual who can organize meetings where teammates can address and settle their concerns. It is possible to employ techniques for resolving conflicts such as soothing, confronting, negotiation, disengagement, and force can be used. The most successful dispute-resolution strategy is confronting (Wen et al., 2017). It results in a win-win scenario for all parties involved. It clarifies all the data and facts and concludes the dispute. In most technical talks, teammates engage in disagreement. For example, one group member may like to develop using C++ while another prefers Java. This leads to a dispute, and the project leader must arrange sessions to assist them to settle it. Managers have also resourced people who manage the resources with a unique perspective, particular purpose, and personalities that can become inflated under specific conditions (Hoda & Murugesan, 2016).

TIPS

It is the responsibility of the project manager to guarantee that these disagreements are dealt with and resolved peacefully so that they do not affect the final product.

The following are the challenges a project manager faces while dealing with disagreement:

- Developing positive interactions with team members throughout time-restricted tasks.
- A lack of understanding of the situation results in misinterpretation among teammates.
- Establishing a mutual view to prevent additional overreaction.

7.5. CHALLENGE OF QUALITY MANAGEMENT

An additional issue for the project manager is keeping the products of top standard. Even after having significant rounds of reviews of the deliverables, the item does not always fulfill the quality standards. Product development relies heavily on evaluation effectiveness and efficacy (Isern, 2015). For example, the number of pages of programming language inspected each hour illustrates the reviewing effectiveness. The success of the evaluation is visible in the decrease of bugs in the products and the code's extensibility soon.

To ensure high performance in deliverables, it is excellent practice to perform external as well as internal inspections on the project under consideration. The audits result in Non-Conformance (NC) reports for the project. The project manager's key challenge is to concentrate on and solve the NC identified (Meissonier & Houzé, 2010). These NCs are typically reported in top meetings with management. These NCs are used by top leadership to judge the quality of the steps involved in the design. The project manager or a representative of the relevant team is in charge of closing the relevant NCs. The standard audit instruments will track the both open and closed state of these NCs (Eberlein, 2008).

Remember

The program manager's task is to maintain the NC count as low as possible so that the program does not receive special attention from upper executives.

7.6. MAINTENANCE OF PROJECT SCHEDULES AND RESOURCES

The three restrictions for each project are size, duration, and price (Bevilacqua et al., 2009). In a project, the postponement of one item might lead to the entire project being delayed, which can have a financial effect on the firm. As a result, the project manager strives to complete the task within the time specified. The delay in the schedule may result in cost overruns. Maintaining deadlines is another issue for the consultant.

If the triple limitations alter, other additional limitations like client satisfaction, cost, and quality influence the project's progress. The task of the project leader is to increase customer satisfaction with his work. He must strive hard to achieve a high level of client satisfaction. This is feasible if the work is accomplished under cost and with great quality within the time frame specified (Lappe & Spang, 2014).

You can be asked to increase your production times if changing the company situation makes your task more strategic. Analyze and debate resource allocation (both financial and human) before coming to any conclusion to ensure that you can meet the shortened deadline. An unanticipated circumstance could also cause your job to be downgraded, giving you more time. The problem then becomes motivating your team to work on a task that is no longer as strategically important as it once was.

You have to reorganize your task to stretch most of the vital resources when the allotted supplies begin to decrease (Stark & Oman, 1997; Liu et al., 2011). Discuss the project's objectives, capabilities, and deadlines with your senior leadership to account for such modifications. You may be able to do more with fewer resources, but even before making any changes to your project plan, acquire your company's approval on how you will do it (Rodrigues & Bowers, 1996).

Once the requirements have been correctly gathered, the next difficulty for a project manager is to ensure the stages for the project's well-defined goals (Ali & Kidd, 2014). Here, the project leader must assign responsibilities associated with each milestone.

The following challenges are encountered when establishing work progress (Liu et al., 2009; Whyte et al., 2016).

- An unorganized plan or objectives can undermine the ultimate delivery of a project. It will interfere with the project's timetable or timeline.
- Lack of the required skills within the organization to complete the project. It may be necessary for project leaders to determine the appropriate resources needed for the project.

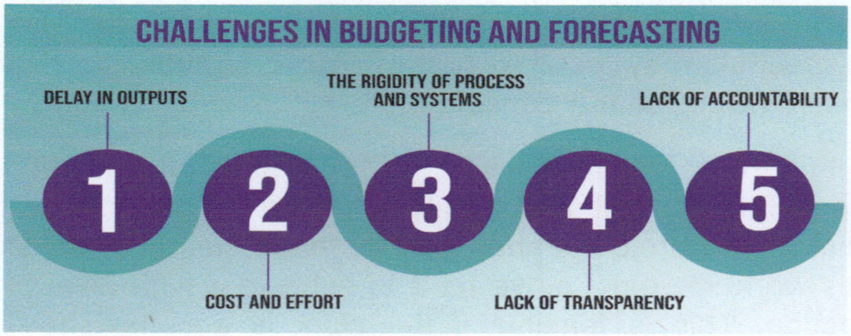

Figure 7.3. Illustration of challenges in budget forecasting (Source: SattvaCFO, Creative Commons License).

Can you imagine delivering a product without generating a profit? If so, would this be regarded as an effective delivery? It cannot be termed a successful project. To guarantee the success of a project, the program's price and net profit must be assessed. This will assist us to plan resources accordingly. The following are a few of the challenges that budgetary planning will bring up (Estublier et al., 2002).

- Vague terms of service among clients and IT organizations run the risk of causing unintended problems with project budgetary allocations.
- Controlling the labor of the project and non-labor costs.
- Mismatch of project estimates concerning the real-time cost of the project (Figure 7.3)

7.7. HIRING AND FIRING

Typically, the teammates who meet the requirement must be hired by the project leader. When the project is at its busiest, the team size will be at its highest. When the group has completed the deliveries, the project leader must release them. The teammates will not have a home department to return to when the project is finished in project-oriented organizations. They must move to some other job after the current one is completed. A project manager's duties also include issuing awards, relocation, and new tasks as well as conducting performance evaluations (De & Vijayakumaran, 2020). His difficulty is to match his team's expectations for salary increases and benefits. The project manager must maintain expenditures within the budget allocation from the perspective of the executing company (Morozov et al., 2017).

Nowadays, the project manager's biggest issue is finding an experienced team. In large corporations, important teammates are acquired via negotiations. As a result, to secure the teammates, the project leader must bargain with decision-makers and his colleagues. Once the acquisition is over, the manager has to train team members with the latest technologies. Finding the team members' skill level and gaps to meet the required level are responsibilities of the project manager. The project manager must train the teammates to fill any holes found to increase productivity (Ko et al., 2009). For example, in the Indian IT sector, teammates quitting their employment is a hurdle for project leaders as well. In other words, teammates could quit the project or the company before it is finished, not having finished the task that was given to them. The project manager must take care of this because it could cause delays in schedules, expense overruns, and poor product quality.

Project managers must control the abilities of the assets to complete the work at the cheapest price possible. The talents must correspond to the duties of the task at hand. The proper resource allocation of the project is involved in skill management. (Al-Tabtabai et al., 2001).

The following are the challenges that the project manager encountered in skill management (Jiang et al., 2014).

- Insufficient funds to complete the objectives of the project.
- Insufficient professional skills in comparison to existing resources of the organization or among the group.

- Handling the unexpected attrition rate involved in the project.

7.8. TESTING THE PRODUCT

The additional difficulty the project manager faces is the lack of a software application to evaluate the product throughout the testing phase. As a result, "user acceptability testing" may include a variety of surprises User acceptance testing is generally done by the customer. Getting customer acceptability for the products or outcome is difficult for the project leader. Only criteria that have been set and primary outputs that have been approved at each stage of the product's development process can accomplish this (Cheung & Chuah, 1999). A Change Control Board (CCB) should be in place within the execution organization to manage requests for revisions to the requirements.

ACTIVITY 7.1.

Enlist some major challenges that an IT project manager can encounter during the planning, execution and closing of an IT project.

7.9. CONFIGURATION MANAGEMENT

When an item is involved, one should be concerned about the various product iterations that are released. Keeping software configuration simple is a problem for the project manager. He ought to have no trouble getting the relevant product version from the version management system. Another challenge that he faces is to release patches for specific product releases based on customer requests. (Parolia et al., 2015; Parolia et al., 2020).

Indian Scenario: Numerous IT companies in India offer Offshore Development Centers (ODC) to their clients in the US and Europe. Here, the main areas of focus are communicating and managing teams. Top management in the Indian IT sector occasionally finds it difficult to match the requirements of their clients regarding human resources. Several businesses are investing millions of dollars in worker technological training courses due to the lack of competent labor Young engineers want to get global exposure quickly at a very early stage of their career. Another problem facing project managers nowadays is achieving their on-site goals and visions. The attrition in the Indian IT industry is not decreasing as a result of the economic boom. For the interest of both professionals and the Indian IT industry, they must work to keep this number as low as possible.

SUMMARY

Over the past few years, the number of IT projects has increased significantly. This means that the demand for IT project managers has also increased. However, there are several challenges that IT project managers face. Lastly, one of the challenges that IT project managers face is dealing with changes. Changes are inevitable in any project. However, in an IT project, changes can be especially difficult to manage. This is because changes can often have a ripple effect, causing other parts of the project to be impacted. The project manager needs to have a good change management plan in place to deal with changes.

REVIEW QUESTIONS

1. What are some common challenges faced during IT project management?
2. How can these challenges be effectively addressed?
3. What are some best practices for successful IT project management?

MULTIPLE CHOICE QUESTIONS

1. **What are some of the challenges in IT project management?**
   a. Ensuring timely completion of tasks
   b. Managing costs
   c. Dealing with scope creep
   d. All of the above
2. **What is scope creep?**
   a. When the project manager does not properly manage the project's budget
   b. When the project's scope expands beyond its original parameters
   c. When the project team is not properly coordinated
   d. When the project manager does not properly communicate with stakeholders
3. **The project manager must take care of this because it could cause delays in schedules, expense overruns, and poor product quality.**
   a. True
   b. False
4. **What is the main goal of IT project management?**
   a. To ensure the timely completion of tasks
   b. To ensure the project is completed within budget
   c. To ensure the project is completed according to its original scope
   d. All of the above

5. **Work delegation is another difficulty for the project manager because, in knowledge-based industries, colleagues compete to take on the more legitimate task.**
   a. True
   b. False

Answers to Multiple Choice Questions

1. (d) 2. (b) 3. (a) 4. (c) 5. (a)

REFERENCES

1. Ali, U., & Kidd, C. (2014). Barriers to an effective configuration management application in a project context: An empirical investigation. *International Journal of Project Management, 32*(3), 508–518.
2. Al-Tabtabai, H., Alex, A. P., & Abou-alfotouh, A. (2001). Conflict resolution using cognitive analysis approach. *Project Management Journal, 32*(2), 4–16.
3. Bevilacqua, M., Ciarapica, F. E., & Giacchetta, G. (2009). Critical chain and risk analysis applied to high-risk industry maintenance: A case study. *International Journal of Project Management, 27*(4), 419–432.
4. Cheung, C. C., & Chuah, K. B. (1999). Conflict management styles in Hong Kong industries. *International Journal of Project Management, 17*(6), 393–399.
5. da Silva, F. Q., Costa, C., Franca, A. C. C., & Prikladinicki, R. (2010, August). Challenges and *solutions in distributed software development project management: A systematic literature review. In 2010 5th IEEE International Conference on Global Software Engineering* (Vol. 1, pp. 87–96). IEEE.
6. De, S., & Vijayakumaran, V. (2020, November). An Efficient Algorithm in Project Management for Resource Scheduling and Conflict Management using Graph Coloring Technique. In *2020 IEEE International Conference for Innovation in Technology (INOCON*) (Vol. 1, pp. 1–6). IEEE.
7. Dolfi, J., & Andrews, E. J. (2007). The subliminal characteristics of project managers: An exploratory study of optimism overcoming challenges in the project management work environment. *International Journal of Project Management, 25*(7), 674–682.
8. Eberlein, M. (2008). Culture as a critical success factor for successful global project management in multi-national IT service projects. *Journal of Information Technology Management, 19*(3), 27–42.
9. Engwall, M., & Jerbrant, A. (2003). The resource allocation syndrome: the prime challenge of multi-project management. *International Journal of Project Management, 21*(6), 403–409.
10. Estublier, J., Leblang, D., Clemm, G., Conradi, R., Tichy, W., van der Hoek, A., &

Wiborg-Weber, D. (2002). Impact of the research community on the field of software configuration management: summary of an impact project report. *ACM SIGSOFT Software Engineering Notes, 27*(5), 31–39.

11. Hoda, R., & Murugesan, L. K. (2016). Multi-level agile project management challenges: A self-organizing team perspective. *Journal of Systems and Software, 117*, 245–257.
12. Hwang, B. G., & Ng, W. J. (2013). Project management knowledge and skills for green construction: Overcoming challenges. *International Journal of Project Management, 31*(2), 272–284.
13. Isern, G. (2015). Intercultural project management for IT: issues and challenges. Journal of Intercultural Management, 7(3), 53–67.
14. Jiang, J. J., Chang, J. Y., Chen, H. G., Wang, E. T., & Klein, G. (2014). Achieving IT program goals with integrative conflict management. *Journal of Management Information Systems, 31*(1), 79–106.
15. Ko, H. U., & Park, H. K. (2009). A Study of Development of Change Process for Configuration Management in Construction Project Management. *KSCE Journal of Civil and Environmental Engineering Research, 29*(1D), 81–89.
16. Lappe, M., & Spang, K. (2014). Investments in project management are profitable: A case study-based analysis of the relationship between the costs and benefits of project management. *International Journal of Project Management, 32*(4), 603–612.
17. Liu, J. Y., Chiang, J. C., Yang, M. H., & Klein, G. (2011). Partnering effects on the user–developer conflict and role ambiguity in information system projects. *Information and Software Technology, 53*(7), 722–729.
18. Liu, J. Y., Klein, G., Chen, J. V., & Jiang, J. J. (2009). The negative impact of conflict on the information system development process, product, and project. *Journal of Computer Information Systems, 49*(4), 98–104.
19. Masood, Z., & Farooq, S. (2017). The benefits and key challenges of agile project management under recent research opportunities. *International Research Journal of Management Sciences, 5*(1), 20–28.
20. Meissonier, R., & Houzé, E. (2010). Toward an 'IT Conflict-Resistance Theory': action research during IT pre-implementation. *European Journal of Information Systems, 19*(5), 540–561.
21. Morozov, V., Kalnichenko, O., Timinsky, A., & Liubyma, I. (2017, September). Projects change management is based on project configuration management for developing complex projects. In *2017 9th IEEE International Conference on Intelligent Data Acquisition and Advanced Computing Systems: Technology and Applications (IDAACS)* (Vol. 2, pp. 939–941). IEEE.
22. Niazi, M., Mahmood, S., Alshayeb, M., Riaz, M. R., Faisal, K., Cerpa, N., ... & Richardson, I. (2016). Challenges of project management in global software development: A client-vendor analysis. *Information and Software Technology, 80*, 1–19.
23. Ogunde, A. O., Olaolu, O., Afolabi, A., Owolabi, J., & Ojelabi, R. (2017). Challenges

confronting construction project management system for sustainable construction in developing countries: Professionals perspectives (a case study of Nigeria). *Journal of Building Performance ISSN, 8*(1), 2017.

24. Ojiako, U., Ashleigh, M., Chipulu, M., & Maguire, S. (2011). Learning and teaching challenges in project management. *International Journal of Project Management, 29*(3), 268–278.
25. Parolia, N., Chen, J. V., Jiang, J. J., & Klein, G. (2015). Conflict resolution effectiveness on the implementation efficiency and achievement of business objectives in IT programs: A study of IT vendors. *Information and Software Technology, 66*, 30–39.
26. Rodrigues, A., & Bowers, J. (1996). The role of system dynamics in project management. *International Journal of Project Management, 14*(4), 213–220.
27. Shenhar, A. J., & Dvir, D. (2007). Project management research—The challenge and opportunity. *Project √, 38*(2), 93–99.
28. Silva, M. M., Poleto, T., de Gusmao, A. P. H., & Costa, A. P. C. S. (2020). A strategic conflict analysis in IT outsourcing using the graph model for conflict resolution. *Journal of Enterprise Information Management, 33*(6), 1581–1598.
29. Singh, R., Keil, M., & Kasi, V. (2009). Identifying and overcoming the challenges of implementing a project management office. *European Journal of Information Systems, 18*(5), 409–427.
30. Söderlund, J., & Maylor, H. (2012). Project management scholarship: Relevance, impact and five integrative challenges for business and management schools. *International Journal of Project Management, 30*(6), 686–696.
31. Sommer, A. F., Dukovska-Popovska, I., & Steger-Jensen, K. (2014). Barriers towards integrated product development—Challenges from a holistic project management perspective. *International Journal of Project Management, 32(*6), 970–982.
32. Stark, G. E., & Oman, P. W. (1997). Software maintenance management strategies: observations from the field. *Journal of Software Maintenance: Research and Practice, 9*(6), 365–378.
33. Wen, Q., Qiang, M., & An, N. (2017). Collaborating with construction management consultants in project execution: Responsibility delegation and capability integration. *Journal of Construction Engineering and Management,* 143(7), 04017021.
34. Whyte, J., Stasis, A., & Lindkvist, C. (2016). Managing change in the delivery of complex projects: Configuration management, asset information, and 'big data'. *International Journal of Project Management, 34(*2), 339–351.

CHAPTER 8

PROSPECTS IN IT PROJECT MANAGEMENT

UNIT INTRODUCTION

Globally, more money has been spent on information technology (IT). So according to Gartner, the global IT investment will reach $3.9 trillion in 2020, implying that the requirement for improved IT project management is much more urgent than before. Opportunities for IT project management reveal that working remotely and security are major priorities for numerous of these professions. With the global move to remote work caused by the COVID-19 crisis in 2020, IT project managers will have a greater responsibility than ever to handle increasingly unpredictable personnel, assets, and circumstances. Project managers have substantial problems due to the increasing complexity of IT projects, rapidly evolving technology, business services market dynamics, and the increased price of failure of the project (Webster & Knutson, 2006; Mishra & Mishra, 2013).

Intelligent IT project leaders maintain their expenses within their budgets while maintaining an eye out for the greatest industry developments to meet consumer needs and keep their organizations on the sharp end. Establishing objectives to preserve organizational agility, select appropriate technologies, and acquire new skills keeps these project managers agile and effective. They also form a strong foundation for their employers and companies to thrive.

Learning Objectives

At the end of this chapter, the reader will be able to understand

- The Prospects in change management
- The trend of remote work and its advantages and disadvantages
- The importance of cybersecurity
- The significance of customer satisfaction
- The role of artificial intelligence in IT project management

Key Terms

1. Remote Work
2. Covid-19
3. Customer Satisfaction
4. Artificial Intelligence
5. Customer Relations Management (CRM)
6. Robotics Process Automation

8.1. REMOTE WORK

A near-universal shift to working remotely is the strongest impact on the concept of IT professionals in the next century. And there is no sign that this tendency will reverse. Business executives believe that several organizations will remain to have a portion of their workforce, roughly two-fifths, working from home after the pandemic has been contained. This evolution in working remotely has caused major shifts in the project management industry and business as a whole. Virtual workers face obstacles that their coworkers do not usually face (Ika et al., 2020). Ineffective communication, asynchronous workflows and time regions, decreased insight into one another's work, and a group's inability to keep a higher speed are examples of such issues. These issues necessitate the use of technology solutions such as Wrike, which assist groups in organizing communication and cooperation, delegating work, and coordinating large and small projects. Working remotely also puts a larger premium on the leadership and interpersonal abilities of IT project managers. Such managers are frequently required to collaborate with stakeholders and groups from various time zones, nations, and languages. To maintain operational effectiveness, any IT project manager must have great leadership and interpersonal abilities (McGrath & Whitty, 2020).

TIPS

When you combine a good number of project management software with a remote workplace environment, the outcome is a resounding hit on all dimensions.

The trends in project management go beyond technology or new methodologies and more. As technology advances, numerous organizations worldwide do not sit back and wait for it to pass by (Hofmann et al., 2020). Consider the case of the COVID-19 pandemic. No one could have predicted what a pandemic will shortly besiege the entire globe in 2019. As a result, activities like remote work stayed stable, only gradually increasing. Then the pandemic struck, and remote work took off. 59% of recent remote employees in the United States would opt to continue to work remotely after the pandemic.

With remote work, the benefits are numerous including:(MacDonell & Shepperd, 2003; Bhavsar et al., 2019):

- Adaptability and production since employees are much more inclined to complete tasks on their turf
- Personnel costs are lowered.
- Workforce heterogeneity will increase as geographical barriers become less important.
- Virtual employment improves teamwork inside an organization.

- Let us not overlook how much better telecommuting is for the surroundings due to its lower carbon footprint.

This trend in project management has also altered over time. There are multiple sorts of telecommuting options accessible today (Dwivedula, 2019).

Working remotely was previously popular, but in recent years, its popularity has been boosted to unprecedented levels. Whereas the pandemic caused firms to allow employees to telecommute because of security concerns, remote employment is expected to continue. This presents some intriguing problems to project managers (Auth et al., 2019). According to data, up to 97% of professionals are unwilling to return to their workplaces comprehensively.

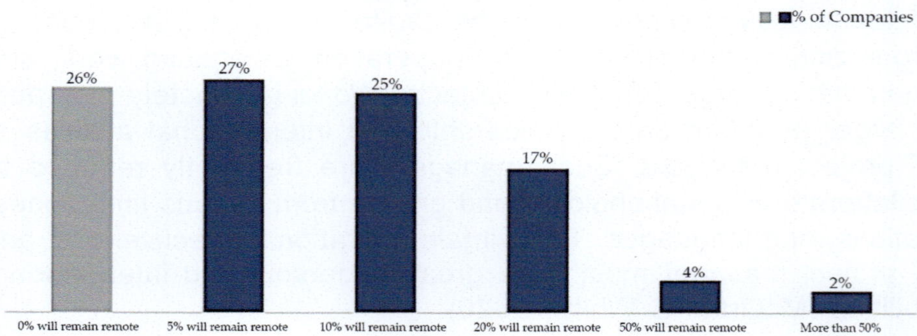

Figure 8.1. Illustration of the percentage of workplaces that will remain permanently remote after COVID, who were not remote before COVID (Source: Arpan Patra, Creative Commons License).

Cloud-based project management software can be extremely useful in such situations. Such technologies are independently deployable worldwide in hybrid or remote workforces, enabling them to effortlessly keep on top of their respective duties and projects (Dacre et al., 2019; Uzoamaka et al., 2015). Regardless of the work schedule or location, The software could collect all important data that has to be monitored, checked, and utilized by project executives to make more informed decisions in real time.

8.2. TALENT RETENTION AND CYBER SECURITY

Information technology is a highly competitive profession. A shortage of experienced project managers makes it challenging for smaller businesses to hire competent IT managers. If such organizations are not able to recruit personnel with the necessary qualifications and expertise, they must train and hire professional project directors inside. Worker training and workshops are becoming common as a way to deliver organized training, and as a result, PMOs become more widely used for delivering consistent training. The

Project Management Institute (PMI) provides Project Management Professional (PMP) credentials that are beneficial (Fridgeirsson et al., 2021).

Gaining skills IT professionals with project managerial skills has emerged as a significant thing affecting IT project management (Dunne & Martin, 2006; Laurson et al., 2009). In far too many organizations, It has proven to be a valuable way of attracting and retaining top project management talent in many companies. A well-established route for advancement inside the firm is an additional motivation to retain experienced project managers. Include every PM inside the conversation if you are unsure what training courses or rewards will fit them. Inquire about what they require to advance and succeed in the organization. The most efficient professional growth occurs not through formal programs, but in little encounters work. Project managers must be provided adequate leeway and liberty to manage their groups and make timely choices (Shakeri & Khalilzadeh, 2020).

With the development of big data and digital phones, Information Technology projects are becoming more complex and larger. Alongside greater complexity comes more staff to manage, more agencies to collaborate with, and much more customers to satisfy. Large tasks may also imply that an entire group of project managers is directing overall operations rather than a single manager. This implies that teamwork is more important than ever (Cha & Maytorena-Sanchez, 2019). Having your distant team operate better collectively is now a question of project success or failure. In addition to these concerns, hackers are not a hypothetical danger. Several businesses have lost valuable information and thousands of dollars as a result of cyber-attack in recent times. As a result, increased focus on cyber security is yet another significant issue impacting IT project management nowadays. Security features like two-factor identification, improved encryption protocols, and more frequent security upgrades are standard features of the finest IT project management software, services, and platforms (Reja & Varghese, 2019; Rothenberg et al., 2022).

Remember

The World Economic Forum's Future of Employment research backs up businesses' increased demand for interpersonal skills as well as other interpersonal skills.

8.3. DEMAND FOR EMOTIONAL INTELLIGENCE (EI)

While organizational and analytical skills are required for project managers, emotional intelligence (EI) has grown in popularity in recent years.

This is important for project managers because their employment entails a thorough knowledge of individuals (Sher, 2022). To conduct successful projects, they should manage their human resources more effectively, and to do so, they must first understand these individuals. The ability to connect and empathize with others has become a lot more important due to one of the other project management trends: the rise in remote working.

Dave Birdsall, senior manager at The Parker Avery Group, is an excellent example of using emotional intelligence for the greater good (Parker et al., 2002). He has observed a captivating project management tendency of arranging daily touchpoint sessions for purposes other than work. "...the objectives for such routine checks are no longer just focused on work." These sessions not only serve to keep track of business matters, but also provide an opportunity for members to socialize. I've discovered that by doing so.

8.4. ARTIFICIAL INTELLIGENCE AND AUTOMATION

Keeping all of a project's components on schedule is indeed an ongoing struggle for employees in organizations. Nevertheless, with artificial intelligence and automation, these activities have become progressively simple and clear (Kerzner, 2022).

Als contribution is important in project management in numerous ways (Balaji & Murugaiyan, 2012):

- AI makes it simpler for team members to manage areas of a project that consume valuable human skills, such as scheduling or follow-ups. AI technology may very well manage these tasks.
- AI might offer assistance other than completely taking over a project. This might take the shape of analyzing several studies will be based on the project's success.
- AI not just to saves time for the team, but it also reduces costs and maximizes revenues or deliverables in general.
- It is also essential for a company to employ AI to figure out the exact length of a project. Alternatively, they risk underestimation, which, combined with some environmental factors, could put them off budget and cause the timeframe to be extended.

The Project Management Institute, PMI, selected three AI technologies that have a significant impact on enterprises, as well as three that will gain traction in the next years (Eberle et al., 2011). Experience and understanding Systems, Deep Learning, Effective Transition, Intelligent Agents, Learning Techniques, and Robotics Process Automation are examples of these (Kumar et al., 2014). Manufacturers, ranging from software development to healthcare, have developed creative methods to employ these for maximum efficiency. According to the Project Management Institute, 81% of experts believe AI is affecting their organizations. This figure is expected to rise more in the future years. According to Thilo Huellmann, Chief Technology Officer at Levity.ai, robotics offers enormous promise. “By automating low-value-add tasks, project managers can direct their energy and attention onto duties that will most drastically help respective organizations, enabling them to effect bigger change and improving the likelihood of each project meeting its strategic objectives.”

In recent years, corporations have adopted AI on a broader scale to guarantee effective entire projects in a wide range of ways, including (Andrei et al., 2019):

- Producing behavioral insight
- Supporting the decision-making processes
- Estimating and forecasting
- Improving resource allocation
- Making data visualization possible
- Conducting vulnerability assessment

Technology is constantly changing, and if you want to compete, you must know what’s going on with the tools you employ. Finally, AI, bots, and RPA exist to make project team members’ lives easier, simplify work, and allow us more time to do the things that machines cannot (Rao et al., 2011). “If you can have your project management application provide for you with having to lift a finger, you can save cash and increase productivity,” explains Lindsey Allard, CEO, and Co-Founder of PlaybookUX. “Use robotics to assist you to accomplish simple activities, arrange certain items, and sometimes even generate valuable information.”

“I have seen just how useful automated can be in project management, and I am looking towards seeing how technology can enhance my procedures in the future year,” she says. Xebrio’s Managing Director, Varada Patwardhan, agrees. “Within business, project managers are turning into project leaders,” she explains. “They will be expected to incorporate AI technologies into their methods of project management as well as place a greater premium on emotional intelligence and people skills such as creativity, communications, and problem-solving ability.” Applying AI Capabilities may assist project companies and managers achieve openness. By data analysis from several projects at the same time, AI can effectively spot possible dangers inside the development and supplement a project leader’s decision-making ability.”

What you can do

i. Examine how you can leverage most of the AI capabilities of the technologies you have already.

ii. Consider how you could use new technologies with automation and artificial intelligence features to accelerate routine tasks and data processing.

8.5. ADVANCED RESOURCE AND SOFTWARE

This demonstrates how project management software can no longer be overlooked. When integrated with AI-based advanced features, project management tools can affect beneficial modifications to the way organizations manage their projects, regardless of how difficult they are (Aroral, 2021).

> **Did you Know?**
>
> Based on a Wellington 2020 analysis, 54% of businesses lack access to current KPIs for business initiatives, and more than a third of them waste more than a day gathering data.

Here are some examples of how using the correct technology may make a substantial difference (yaw Koi-Akrofi et al., 2019):

- Use prior project data to improve proposals and strategies for future projects.
- View resources, abilities, and other information to make the allocation of resources easier.
- AI can automatically record all affected time on activities and projects.
- To remain on top of finances, easily assign and monitor expenditures.
- Capture all expenses with invoices for all projects in real-time.
- Monitor all projects with customizable widgets to make better choices on the fly.
- Keeping all customers and team members up to date on the project's status, performance, and modifications in real-time.

8.6. CHANGE IN TECHNOLOGIES

It is frequently stated as change is unavoidable. Do you know what else is continuous? Technical advancement. The reality that this subject is even included in the project management themes attests to how innovation continues at almost every level in the industry. It's not unexpected that innovations and adjustments are being made to stay up with tremendous demands. Almost every organization with an active project management strategy relies on cutting-edge technologies to make effective attempts (Love et al., 2002; Huskins et al., 2013).

With these modifications, several factors have been brought into play, such as (Wiewiora et al., 2020):

- Distribution and utilization of centralized data.
- Before UCaaS, there were only Integrated Telecommunications; later tech advances to UCaaS. Now, it is possible to merge all communications technology into a unified system.
- The Customer Relations Management (CRM) platform is another option. With this, all customer data may be saved in a centralized spot available to all teammates. Imagine merging UCaaS and CRM solutions!
- Improves risk mitigation. With the rapidly evolving face of technologies affecting virtually every choice or stage in managing projects, you can be certain of a significantly smaller range.
- Enhancements in the management of assets. What would a project be without the resources necessary? With automation, a resource from allocation to utilization is significantly more effective and economical.
- Precise monitoring is available, including both conventional timesheets and monitoring with less quantitative information (Auth et al., 2019).

No matter what component of the group's project is at issue, the most recent technology developments allow them to keep track of it.

ACTIVITY 8.1.

Enlist some major prospects of the IT project management.

8.7. RESILIENCE AS A PRIORITY

We are aware that undertaking a task is demanding. Protecting our mental and emotional well-being as well as that of our employees must be a top priority for the innovative leadership team. Personal resiliency, project adaptability, and corporate adaptability are important for the organization(Ika et al., 2020; Zaman et al., 2020).

Companies were fast to implement the tools necessary for employees to work online. However, the corresponding support systems for remote and hybrid work have not emerged as rapidly. And with the constant disruption, regular downs, ups, and current economic consequences, resilience is at the top of the list for every organization (Galanti et al., 2021). "At the time, companies had the time or awareness to provide their employees with the psychological support they required to adapt to this change," says Karine O'Donnell, Director, of projects training and mentor at the Australian consulting firm Projecting With People.

"More and more, projects are being influenced by emotional and cultural aspects brought about by changes in how people work," she adds. "I've already seen numerous organizations create projects to address the emotional demands of the hybrid model of working, in which some members of the team work from home and others from the office." It has been expected that more organizations will launch projects for well-being at work, such as:

- New HR legislation for those who work from home part-time or full-time
- Timesheet projects to assist firms in addressing productivity concerns
- Electronic tools to help with online communication work tasks, planning, and scheduling, and administration
- Online mindfulness training to help with employee worry, tension, and fatigue.

Why is it significant?

- People are our most valuable asset. It is not sufficient to merely execute the work. We must complete the assignment in a way that does not damage us.
- The Great Resignation, silent departing, job strain, and needing to keep the pressure on while coworkers are away have all had an impact on organizations.

Figure 8.2. Schematic of components of Resilience (Source: Graham Millward, Creative Commons License).

Taking care of one another must be a major concern.

- What are your options?

- Utilize resource monitoring to verify that no one is overburdened. If you do not have resources management software, check in with the group verbally at most weekly.
- Create psychological safety at work so people feel it's OK to tell you they are struggling.
- Live it. Don't be the kind of boss that says everyone should have a work/life integration and yet send emails at 2 am while you're still working. Model the environment you want to create (Figure 8.2).

SUMMARY

There has been a shift in recent years from reactive to proactive IT change management. This means that instead of waiting for something to break and then fixing it, companies are now taking a proactive approach to managing changes. They are doing this by implementing processes and tools that help them to identify potential problems before they occur. This allows them to avoid or resolve issues before they cause disruptions. There has also been an increase in the use of automation in IT change management. This is because it can help to speed up the process of identifying and implementing changes. It can also help to reduce the chances of human error. Another trend that is becoming more common is the use of data to drive changes. This means that instead of making changes based on guesswork or intuition, companies are now using data to determine what needs to be changed and how those changes should be made. This helps to ensure that changes are made in a way that is effective and efficient.

REVIEW QUESTIONS

1. What are some common trends in IT change management?
2. What are some common challenges associated with IT change management?
3. What are some common best practices for IT change management?

MULTIPLE CHOICE QUESTIONS

1. What is the primary purpose of change management?
   a. To ensure that changes are made smoothly and efficiently
   b. To control and coordinate all aspects of the change process
   c. To minimize the impact of change on employees and other stakeholders
   d. To ensure that changes are made in line with the company's strategic objectives

2. What is the first step in the change management process?
   a. Defining the problem or opportunity that necessitates a change
   b. Assessing the current state of the organization
   c. Planning the change
   d. Implementing the change

3. What are the three key components of successful change management?
   a. Communication, training, and support
   b. Coordination, control, and communication

c. Commitment, capability, and capacity

d. Change agents, champions, and stakeholders

4. What are some common reasons why change initiatives fail?

a. Lack of commitment from senior management

b. Lack of communication and training

c. Lack of resources

d. All of the above

5. What are some common signs that a change initiative is in trouble?

a. Employees are resistant to the change

b. Implementation is behind schedule

c. Costs are spiraling out of control

d. All of the above

Answers to Multiple Choice Questions

1. (a) 2. (a) 3. (a) 4. (d) 5. (d)

REFERENCES

1. Andrei, B. A., Casu-Pop, A. C., Gheorghe, S. C., & Boiangiu, C. A. (2019). A study on using a waterfall and agile methods in software project management. *Journal of Information Systems & Operations Management, 1*, 125–135.
2. Aroral, H. K. (2021). Waterfall Process Operations in the Fast-paced World: Project Management Exploratory Analysis. *International Journal of Applied Business and Management Studies, 6*(1), 91–99.
3. Auth, G., JokischPavel, O., & Dürk, C. (2019). Revisiting automated project management in the digital age–a survey of AI approaches. *Online Journal of Applied Knowledge Management (OJAKM), 7*(1), 27–39.
4. Balaji, S., & Murugaiyan, M. S. (2012). Waterfall vs. V-Model vs. Agile: A comparative study on SDLC. *International Journal of Information Technology and Business Management, 2*(1), 26–30.
5. Bhavsar, K., Shah, V., & Gopalan, S. (2019). Business Process Reengineering: A Scope of Automation in Software Project Management Using Artificial Intelligence. *International Journal of Engineering and Advanced Technology (IJEAT), 9*(2), 3589–3595.

6. Cha, J., & Maytorena-Sanchez, E. (2019). Prioritizing project management competencies across the software project life cycle. *International Journal of Managing Projects in Business, 1,* 3–9.
7. Dacre, N., Senyo, P. K., & Reynolds, D. (2019). Is an Engineering Project Management Degree Worth it? Developing Agile Digital Skills for Future Practice. *Engineering Education Research Network, 1*, 2–8.
8. Dunne, D., & Martin, R. (2006). Design thinking and how it will change management education: An interview and discussion. *Academy of Management Learning & Education, 5*(4), 512–523.
9. Dwivedula, R. (2019). Human resource management in project management: ideas at the cusp. *European Project Management Journal, 9*(1), 34–41.
10. Eberle, A., Meyer, H., & Rosen, D. (2011). A comparison of PMI and IPMA approaches. Analysis to support the project management standard and certification system selection, (Vol. 1, pp. 5–9).
11. Fridgeirsson, T. V., Ingason, H. T., Jonasson, H. I., & Jonsdottir, H. (2021). An authoritative study on the near future effect of artificial intelligence on project management knowledge areas. *Sustainability, 13*(4), 2345.
12. Galanti, T., Guidetti, G., Mazzei, E., Zappalà, S., & Toscano, F. (2021). Work from home during the COVID-19 outbreak: The impact on employees' remote work productivity, engagement, and stress. *Journal of Occupational and Environmental Medicine, 63*(7), e426.
13. Hofmann, P., Jöhnk, J., Protschky, D., & Urbach, N. (2020, March). Developing Purposeful AI Use Cases-A Structured Method and Its Application in Project Management. In *Wirtschaftsinformatik (Zentrale Tracks)*, *1*, 33–49.
14. Huskins, M., Kaplan, J., & Krishnakanthan, K. (2013). Enhancing the efficiency and effectiveness of application development. *An Article, Mckinsey, 1*, 1–5.
15. Ika, L. A., Söderlund, J., Munro, L. T., & Landoni, P. (2020). Cross-learning between project management and international development: Analysis and research agenda. *International Journal of Project Management, 38*(8), 548–558.
16. Ika, L. A., Söderlund, J., Munro, L. T., & Landoni, P. (2020). When project management meets international development, what can we learn? *International Journal of Project Management, 38*(8), 469–473.
17. Kumar, R., Gupta, A., & Singh, H. (2014). Agile methodologies: Working mechanism with pros and cons. *Gian Jyoti E-Journal, 4*(2), 18–27.
18. Laurson, M., Kuuskankare, M., & Norilo, V. (2009). An overview of PWGL, a visual programming environment for music. *Computer Music Journal, 33*(1), 19–31.
19. Love, P. E., Holt, G. D., Shen, L. Y., Li, H., & Irani, Z. (2002). Using systems dynamics to better understand change and rework in construction project management systems. *International journal of Project Management, 20*(6), 425–436.
20. MacDonell, S. G., & Shepperd, M. J. (2003). Combining techniques to optimize

effort predictions in software project management. *Journal of Systems and Software, 66*(2), 91–98.

21. McGrath, S. K., & Whitty, S. J. (2020). What do project management practitioners think governance is? A study on perceptions in Queensland, Australia. *International Journal of Managing Projects in Business, 13*(5), 961–980.
22. Mishra, A., & Mishra, D. (2013). Software project management tools: a brief comparative view. *ACM SIGSOFT Software Engineering Notes, 38(*3), 1–4.
23. Paiva, D. C., & Rabechini Jr, R. (2022). Project capabilities in industry 4.0: future research opportunities in project management. *Future Studies Research Journal: Trends and Strategies, 14*(1), e0581–e0581.
24. Parker, P., Letcher, R., Jakeman, A., Beck, M. B., Harris, G., Argent, R. M., ... & Bin, S. (2002). Progress in integrated assessment and modeling. *Environmental Modelling & Software, 17*(3), 209–217.
25. Rao, K. N., Naidu, G. K., & Chakka, P. (2011). A study of the Agile software development methods, applicability, and implications in industry. *International Journal of Software Engineering and Its Applications, 5*(2), 35–45.
26. Reja, V. K., & Varghese, K. (2019, May). Impact of 5G technology on IoT applications in construction project management. In ISARC. *Proc. Int. Symp. Autom. Robot. Constr., 36*, 209–217.
27. Rothenberg, W. A., Lansford, J. E., Godwin, J. W., Dodge, K. A., Copeland, W. E., Odgers, C. L., ... & Conduct Problems Prevention Research Group. (2022). Intergenerational effects of the Fast Track intervention on the home environment: A randomized control trial. *Journal of Child Psychology and Psychiatry*, *1*, 7–9.
28. Shakeri, H., & Khalilzadeh, M. (2020). Analysis of factors affecting project communications with a hybrid DEMATEL-ISM approach (A case study in Iran). *Heliyon, 6*(8), e04430.
29. Sher, B. (2022). Challenges to Project Management in Distributed Software Development: A Systematic Literature Review. *Evolving Software Processes: Trends and Future Directions, 1*, 241–251.
30. Uzoamaka, O. E., Ngozi, E., & Okey, E. T. (2015). Team-spirited approach for innovation and success in change management in Nigerian manufacturing organizations: strategies, challenges, and prospects. *International Journal of Asian Social Science, 5*(8), 446–460.
31. Webster, F. M., & Knutson, J. (2006). What is project management? *Project Management Concepts and Methodologies*, *1*, 2–7.
32. Wiewiora, A., Chang, A., & Smidt, M. (2020). Individual, project, and organizational learning flows within a global project-based organization: exploring what, how, and who. *International Journal of Project Management, 38*(4), 201–214.
33. yaw Koi-Akrofi, G., Koi-Akrofi, J., & Matey, H. A. (2019). Understanding the characteristics, benefits, and challenges of agile project management: A literature-

based perspective. *International Journal of Software Engineering & Applications (IJSEA), 10*(5), 25–44.

34. Zaman, U., Nawaz, S., & Nadeem, R. D. (2020). Navigating Innovation Success through Projects. Role of CEO Transformational Leadership, Project Management Best Practices, and Project Management Technology Quotient. *Journal of Open Innovation: Technology, Market, and Complexity, 6*(4), 168.

INDEX

D

J

K

L

M

N

O

R

S

T

U

V

W